LITERACY
for Visual Learners

by the same author

Colour Coding for Learners with Autism
A Resource Book for Creating Meaning
through Colour at Home and School
ISBN 978 1 84905 441 6
eISBN 978 0 85700 812 1

of related interest

Sensory Stories for Children and Teens
with Special Educational Needs
A Practical Guide
Joanna Grace
ISBN 978 1 84905 484 3
eISBN 978 0 85700 874 9

Once Upon a Touch...
Story Massage for Children
Mary Atkinson and Sandra Hooper
ISBN 978 1 84819 287 4
eISBN 978 0 85701 234 0

Music for Special Kids
Musical Activities, Songs,
Instruments and Resources
Pamela Ott
ISBN 978 1 84905 858 2
eISBN 978 0 85700 426 0

LITERACY
for Visual Learners

Teaching Children with Learning Differences
to Read, Write, Communicate and Create

ADELE DEVINE

Illustrated by Quentin Devine

Jessica Kingsley *Publishers*
London and Philadelphia

Makaton line drawings of signs (on page 75) are reproduced with permission
from The Makaton Charity (www.makaton.org) © 2015.

First published in 2016
by Jessica Kingsley Publishers
73 Collier Street
London N1 9BE, UK
and
400 Market Street, Suite 400
Philadelphia, PA 19106, USA

www.jkp.com

Copyright © Adele Devine 2016
Illustrations copyright © Quentin Devine 2016

Front cover image source: © Quentin Devine.

Library of Congress Cataloging in Publication Data
Devine, Adele.
  Literacy for visual learners : teaching children with learning difficulties to read, write, communicate and
create / Adele Devine.
     pages cm
  Includes bibliographical references and index.
  ISBN 978-1-84905-598-7 (alk. paper)
 1. Learning disabled children--Education--Language arts. 2. Autistic children--Education--Language arts.
3. Language disorders in children. 4. Visual learning. 5. Communication--Study and teaching. I. Title.
  LC4704.85.D48 2016
  371.9--dc23
                     2015016681

British Library Cataloguing in Publication Data
A CIP catalogue record for this book is available from the British Library

ISBN 978 1 84905 598 7
eISBN 978 1 78450 054 2

Printed and bound in the United States

For the children, who have been my best teachers.

Acknowledgements

My first thank you will always be to my husband Quentin, who finds the time between his million other creative projects to make my teacher ideas a reality. He is also the most involved, amazing Daddy to our three pickles.

Thanks to Malachy, Donovan and Darcy for sharing 'Mummy' with the children at school and for occasionally allowing me time to add a few words or even sentences to this book. Thank you to Annabel Stocchetti for inspiring and 'getting' our boys when they were in her class.

I thank my parents for the never-ending abundance of unconditional love and for listening to and encouraging our many ideas. There are simply not enough words to express how grateful we are for their constant support.

My life would be so very different if it were not for my uncle Philip. He fought so that my cousin Louise, who has severe Cerebral Palsy could communicate and be included. He introduced me to Augmentative and Alternative Communication and inspired me to want to fight for every child to achieve their potential. He was also our family rock, loved and missed by us all.

Behind every good special needs teacher there is always a very, very good team of teaching assistants, who somehow manage to organize, prioritize and make things work. They keep us on track with recording, remind us what we are actually supposed to be doing and amidst it all know exactly where to locate that nameless missing pair of shorts. I am forever grateful to have had and to continue to have the support of such fantastic staff.

Alongside our wonderful teaching assistants I've been lucky enough to job share and bounce ideas off some incredibly creative, dedicated teachers. Special thanks must go to my brilliant friend and fellow communication enthusiast Clare Walker.

Thank you to the special children who provide the inspiration and motivation to keep me writing, creating and believing. I love how they make each day so unpredictable, rewarding and full of 'wows'.

Thank you to the parents and young people who have allowed me to share the case studies and photographs which are in this book.

And finally thank you to everyone at Jessica Kingsley Publishers. I love the books they publish and I am incredibly proud to be a 'Jessica Kingsley author'.

Contents

List of Downloadable Resources

The resources listed here can be downloaded from the following link to be used in conjunction with the text: www.jkp.com/catalogue/book/9781849055987.

Motivators

SEN Assist characters – vehicles, animals, fantasy, people
SEN Assist tokens – fantasy, vehicles, people and animals

Writing

Pre-writing worksheets
Overwriting Alphabet – Large uppercase
Overwriting Alphabet – Medium uppercase
Overwriting Alphabet – Small uppercase
Overwriting Alphabet – Large lowercase
Overwriting Alphabet – Medium lowercase
Overwriting Alphabet – Small lowercase

Reading

High Frequency Words – Reading (the learner masters a new word set at each level building a bank of words that they can read)
First 100 High Frequency Words – Levels 1–8
High Frequency Words Recording Sheet
Fish Resource
Read, build, write – Level 1, Yellow (I, up, on, go, we, off)
Read, build, write – Level 2, Orange (in, can, see, a, mum, want)
Read, build, write – Level 3, Red (get, it, for, me, she, said)
Read, build, write – Level 4, Pink (look, went, at, day, no, yes)
Read, build, write – Level 5, Purple (and, cat, dog, dad, the, big)
Read, build, write – Level 6, Blue (am, he, is, to, play, all)
Read, build, write – Level 7, Green (was, of, like, they, you, are)
Read, build, write – Level 8, Grey (going, away, this, my, help, come)

Speaking and Listening

Volume control

Red Riding Hood Resources – Matching, spelling, sequencing, pronouns, prepositions, comprehension and masks

The Three Pigs Resources – Matching, spelling, sequencing, pronouns, prepositions, comprehension and masks

Jack and the Beanstalk Resources – Matching, spelling, sequencing, pronouns, prepositions, comprehension and masks

The Billy Goats Gruff Resources – Matching, spelling, sequencing, pronouns, prepositions, comprehension and masks

The Gingerbread Man Resources – Matching, spelling, sequencing, pronouns, prepositions, comprehension and masks

The Three Bears Resources – Matching, spelling, sequencing, pronouns, prepositions, comprehension and masks

Hot seating resources

Rules for Listening poster

Introduction

A Fairy Tale

Everything in creation has its appointed painter or poet and remains in bondage like the princess in the fairy tale 'til its appropriate liberator comes to set it free.

Ralph Waldo Emerson (1803–1882)

Background
1999 – Fireflies

A door opened to Fairy Land and there they were, all dancing before our eyes. We were silent watchers, breathing in the detail. Millions of Tinkerbells lighting up the field and us – so close, almost touching…

That was the start of the summer of '99 at Camp Eagle Springs in Pennsylvania, USA. Set amidst magical forest, Camp Eagle Springs offers holidays for adults with learning difficulties. They recruit their counsellors and tutors from all over the world.

The first 'vacationers' (adults with learning difficulties), as they were referred to on our camp, were due to arrive the next day. I was on the way to find the washing machine with a friend. Quentin was walking down to see the barn with his new room mate. Our paths crossed, but instead of walking by, muttering the typical 'hellos', we stopped to see the fireflies. The friends we were with faded into the background, not sure how to react, probably covering embarrassment up with 'small talk'. I don't know…they were no longer on our radar.

Quentin and I were together, seeing Fairy Land, forgetting where we were originally headed. It felt as though we had known each other forever. This Irish 'Heathcliff' with dark, curly hair and laughter lines I'd dreamed about was suddenly real. He was standing with me and looking out in the same direction. He has been ever since.

The following night Quentin called his mother in Ireland and told her he had met the girl he was going to marry…

2010 – The kitchen table

I could linger in that magic time longer, but sticking to the purpose of *this* book I must fast-forward ten years.

So, a wedding and two mischief makers later...

We were living in a tiny village called Gortin in Northern Ireland, having decided to bring up our boys in the country. We were renting our dream home by a trickling stream with panoramic views of the greenest fields. In the evenings, once our boys were in bed, Quentin and I would sit at the kitchen table. Talking to each other and sharing ideas and dreams has always been more interesting than watching TV. We would light the candles, put on some music and reflect on the antics of our quirky boys.

Those kitchen table talks led us to an idea. What if we combined all of my knowledge about teaching children with special educational needs (SEN) with Quentin's talents for creative design and animation? Could we make new software to motivate children with SEN?

2012 – Two's a company

We were completely buzzing with our new idea and spent the evenings brainstorming. We came up with the name 'SEN Assist' believing that it would represent the ideal special educational needs assistant. We wanted to offer a way for parents and teachers without training in special education to have an immediate way to see what a child *can* achieve with the right support. I will go into greater detail about this later, but for now I will say that we were thrilled when in 2012 we heard we'd been shortlisted for the biggest UK award for educational resources. Our Fairy Tales software won the Education Resources Award for 'Best Special Educational Needs Resource or Equipment with ICT'. It was an incredible moment and felt like a real turning point. Suddenly people were noticing our work. One of the judges was Sean Stockdale (editor of the magazine *Special*), and after we collected the award he stood up to congratulate us. I found out who he was when I submitted an article to *Special* about using ICT to help children with autism. He printed the entire article as a four-page ICT feature!

2013 – Shakespeare

The following year we were back at the awards. This time we were shortlisted for the same award, but for our Early Shakespeare software. We had the same gate-crashing a wedding feeling. 'We won't win,' we told the people on our table.

We were a husband and wife team and the competition were huge companies with tables full of people representing the team. But once again we won! This time Lorraine Peterson (then Chair of NASEN) stood up and gave me a hug. Amazing!

Later in 2013 we were nominated for an International Naturally Autistic award for 'Excellence in Technology'. We couldn't go to the awards as they were held in Canada, but were absolutely blown away to win this too. Scott James, an inspirational singer who found fame through *X Factor* and was another UK winner for Performing Arts, delivered our award.

2014 – A book

At this time I was teaching at an autism-specific school in Surrey and another idea was forming. Teaching is so much about empathy and seeing how children see, so that you can learn together and explore hand in hand. As I became more in tune with these children I started to examine the visuals we were using to support them. I found that they were not perfect. Another mammoth task began. Could we make things better? Could we work together and create fresh visuals? There were so many. Was it possible? A little voice echoed in my head, 'The visuals are not right. There's more we can do. Children deserve better.'

We believed in this so much, but knew we would need a publisher to get this right. I sent a proposal to Jessica Kingsley and two weeks later I got one of the best emails of my life. They wanted to publish our book *Colour Coding for Learners with Autism*.

2015 – This book

So many children with special educational needs are visual learners. This can be linked to physical disabilities affecting communication, or to their perception, processing or learning style. Special needs teachers adapt resources according to the needs of each individual child. We spend hours laminating matching activities, creating specially adapted books with less language and symbols to go with the words. What about the child in mainstream education, who does not have access to these resources based on specialist knowledge? These are not only children with autism. There are so many other children who benefit from a visual approach – children with dyslexia, Down's Syndrome, Cerebral Palsy, Global Delay, English as a second language; the list goes on...

And what about the teachers? Teachers are on the front line, being told what to do from above, teaching children who learn differently without specific training, and the parents often know this. Parents will have done the research and know their child needs a more individual approach. There is no worse feeling for a dedicated teacher than knowing that they are not getting it right for a child, but every year there are new pressures… I *know* the 'to do' list is exhausting. Teachers may not physically have time in the day to develop strategies or create a host of individual resources.

Too many children in mainstream schools are being let down. They are being knocked aside and their self esteem is getting shattered in the process. This has to change.

Why literacy?

Literacy is not just another school subject to pass or fail. Literacy skills are vital for living independently.

To quote Janice Light, Director of the Literacy Program at Penn State University:

> Literacy skills are critical to all of our lives. They are fundamental to education, employment, social networking, access to technology, and the activities of daily living. (Quoted in LaJeunesse 2014)

Books

I love books – seeing them, touching them, handling them, turning pages, sharing them… After university I even spent a year working in a book shop. I worked in the children's department and enjoyed sharing stories with children, seeing their eyes light up with excitement.

'Excellent PR, excellent PR…,' said the store manager. I thought he would frown upon this non-typical behaviour, but he was at the till seeing delighted parents buying whichever children's book I'd been reading. He also knew those parents would be back. I'd been creating new custom – children who could get excited by books. I had not given a thought to the sales figures that motivated my manager. The feeling of transferring my love of books to children was my motivation.

I love old books – that musty crunchiness, those old leather covers with gold embossed letters, the thin paper and the curiosity. Who else has read them? Finding exciting little clues about past readers inside…

I love reading books to our children, seeing them completely involved. I love it that when we visit a store like TK Maxx our three busy children will each find a book and sit so quietly and contentedly. In a good book they find their calm.

My heart sings when I see children in my class go and sit in our book corner, pick up a book and start turning the pages. No one has told them to go and look at a book. They look at books because they want to.

I love libraries, book shops, charity shops, other people's book shelves. I love writing books. The process, the polishing, the anticipation, the waiting… Many authors compare their new books to having children. I get that.

When a child notices their parents and teachers enjoying books this sparks *their* curiosity. Children may not always be listening, but they are watching. See how they collect our mannerisms and copy routines in play. If we want to create future readers and writers the starting point is to immerse them in seeing adults and other children loving books.

Writing

I have always loved creative writing. I love putting words together, jiggling and perfecting them. I love editors, who jiggle words even more and then add the missing bits (like punctuation).

I love teaching children to write, seeing them form that first letter of their name, seeing them learn to write their name, teaching letter formation, getting past anxieties, finding new techniques and resources.

I prefer typing a letter on the computer to handwriting. There is spell check and grammar check, and you can proof-read, tweak, delete and start all over... I feel well placed supporting children who find writing challenging. I love encouraging them, setting them up to succeed and using my teacher's instinct. I know when to guide and when to leave mistakes be. Children need to feel brilliant about what they *can* do because this will inspire them to keep trying.

When writing is difficult, when it causes anxiety, it must be taught in an intuitive and purposeful way. Maybe they could type their work, but always write their name on it? We have computers, laptops and tablets which are great tools for children who find writing difficult, but if a child could potentially learn to handwrite it is important that honing the skill required to hold a pencil and write is not neglected.

Handwriting is impossible to perfect immediately. There is a process to go through, and some children do not see that there are stages to learning. If they cannot do perfect writing like their peers, they think they will *never* be able to. This can make them angry, upset and frustrated. This may appear as challenging behaviour or opting out. It is not always understood. Teachers often feel they have to adhere to the whole school approach. The rule from above might be: 'Every child will learn a cursive font'. But when a child cannot form a recognizable letter shape at all and is far behind their peer group, a cursive font is too complex. It is not the starting point. There must always be exceptions and exemptions.

What about the children in special needs schools? Are they making the progress that they should? Are they getting the practice or the 1:1 guidance to learn to form letters correctly? Do they have the pencil grips, the sloped surfaces, the supports to aid correct positioning?

Testing children, testing teachers...

Instinctive teachers constantly assess children and know when a child needs additional practice or a little push to move on. Children develop differently and learn differently. I do not like the testing our current generation are subjected to. The tests are used to inform about national standards and highlight school failure or success. These tests are not designed to engage children, raise self esteem and ignite imaginations. Tests can damage self esteem. Their necessity must be given careful thought, and this must come from teachers.

Time for change

There are children with so much potential, children who learn differently, who are not being properly engaged, inspired and nurtured. Children with such amazing potential, who deserve a better start to education, are often let down by the system. I do not want to hear of those children who 'slip the net'. This simply must not happen. Children deserve better. Education must move forwards, adapt and change.

Sharing, adapting and inventing

Observing that things should change is just a starting point. The next step is to become inventive and create solutions. Changing things in education involves hard work, determination and an ability to swim against the tide.

To facilitate change for our visual learners I've put together this book of ideas, examples and strategies based on my training and classroom experience. It's filled with the many tricks that are up long-serving special needs teachers' sleeves, because every child should have access to specialist teaching. I want to show how strategies like Intensive Interaction, the Picture Exchange Communication System (PECS), Makaton, Attention Autism and TEACCH can involve, engage and enhance education for our visual learners.

I will highlight strategies and resources which can improve the attention and ability of our visual learners. Additional resources to accompany this book are available to download from www.jkp.com/catalogue/book/9781849055987. These resources will help teach children who learn visually to read, write and communicate some of their new ideas.

I hope to enable children who learn visually to reveal what they *can* create when their learning style is correctly catered for.

Note: For ease of reading children will be referred to as 'he' and teachers as 'she'. Children's names have been changed to protect identities.

Chapter 1

Visual Learners are in *Every* Classroom

Preventing a Learning Difference From Becoming a Learning Difficulty

All our knowledge has its origin in our perceptions.

Leonardo da Vinci (1452–1519)

Toddlers are using touch screen devices; school children socialize via games consoles and argue through Apps. Teenagers are surfing social networks, uploading photos and creating visual 'my ideal life' scrapbooks for *all* to see. They can contact favourite celebrities directly via Twitter and achieve instant fame through 'viral' YouTube videos.

Travel back less than 20 years and *none* of these things were happening. The world is changing fast. The techie skill set that our children will have acquired by the time they finish school is impossible to imagine.

Gaming

We must look at how children are learning outside of school, and they are *constantly* learning. I watch our sons playing Minecraft, the speed at which they navigate and create. They are accessing a never-ending pile of interactive virtual building blocks. They are busy building a whole world. This is a world that teachers *need* to see. Minecraft can be a really motivating teaching tool. We will investigate further in Chapter 6.

Technology

The Director for the Organisation for Economic Co-operation and Development (OECD) Directorate of Education and Skills, Andreas Schleicher, explained:

We live in a fast-changing world, and producing more of the same knowledge and skills will not suffice to address the challenges of the future. A generation ago, teachers could expect that what they taught would last their students a lifetime. Today, because of rapid economic and social change, schools have to prepare students for jobs that have not yet been created, technologies that have not yet been invented and problems that we don't yet know will arise. (Schleicher 2010)

Children can now search the internet for facts – they have so much information at their fingertips. This wondrous pool of information contains other hidden dangers. Children must have some factual knowledge in order to sift information and distinguish good sources from bad. Children need to understand that *anyone* could publish *anything* online. They need to know that as soon as they put a comment or an image on the internet it will be there forever. They need to be taught how to navigate in a safer way because the parameters are constantly shifting. They must be taught to think for themselves – to analyse and work things out.

No matter how much training teachers are given, the majority will not be able to stay ahead of students, who are so driven to know about new technology. The teacher must facilitate children in their learning and be willing to ask questions. In Information Communication Technology (ICT) the tables turn and the teacher becomes the learner. Embrace this! While the child explains, enjoy their enthusiasm. Listen and question, because while they teach they develop skills to explain their ideas, which will serve them well later in life.

Lessons

Our lessons must be attention-grabbing, visual, exciting and immediate if they are to compete with all the visual devices our children have access to. We must be more child-led, exploring natural curiosity and keeping the creative spark alight. Never mind a clipboard grading us as 'outstanding'. How many 'likes' would our last lesson achieve? Who are we teaching *for*?

Visual learners without labels

Children who learn visually do not always come with a label, but there are visual learners are in every class. For them to achieve their best, teaching styles must adapt.[1] Consider these statistics:

> Approximately 20 to 30 percent of the school-aged population remembers what is heard; 40 percent recalls well visually the things that are seen or read; many must write or use their fingers in some manipulative way to help them remember basic

---

1   Read more about this on FamilyEducation; see www.school.familyeducation.com/intelligence/teaching-methods/38519.html.

facts; other people cannot internalize information or skills unless they use them in real-life activities such as actually writing a letter to learn the correct format. (Carbo, Dunn and Dunn 1986, p.13)

Animal School Fable

'Animal School' is a powerful fable about education written early in the 1940s by George H. Reavis, for The Public School Bulletin. It is in the public domain.[2]

> The Duck was good in swimming – better, in fact, than his instructor – and he made passing grades in flying, but he was practically hopeless in running. Because he was low in this subject, he was made to stay after school and drop his swimming class in order to practise running. He kept this up until he was only average in swimming, but average was passing, so nobody worried about that except the duck.
>
> The Eagle was considered a problem pupil and was disciplined severely. He beat all others to the top of the tree in the climbing class, but he always used his own way of getting there.
>
> The Rabbit started at the top of the class in running, but he had a nervous breakdown and had to drop out of school on account of so much make-up work in swimming.
>
> The Squirrel led the climbing class, but his flying teacher made him start his flying from the ground up instead of from the top down, and he developed cramps from overexertion at the takeoff and began getting Cs in climbing and Ds in running.
>
> The practical Prairie Dogs apprenticed their offspring to the Badgers when the school authorities refused to add digging to the curriculum.
>
> At the end of the year, an abnormal Eel that could swim well and run, climb and fly a little came top.

Each of the animals are failed by a set system, where their learning styles and strengths are not taken into account. The message is that if we are to set our students up to succeed then education must be individual and respect that individuals excel at different things. There is not one way to teach or to assess that will suit everyone.

Apply this to a literacy lesson: the most creative, imaginative child may never get to share their story if the teacher is only focused on seeing them use the perfect cursive font. The child's hands may become achy and they may feel demoralized and disheartened looking around at their peers, who seem to find handwriting so easy. Their brilliant idea is lost because they cannot present it in the 'normal' way.

---

2   http://strengthsbuilders.com/the-animal-school-a-fable.

Every child must experience the freedom to explore, create and show what they can do. It is up to us teachers to invent new ways.

This quote, which is often attributed to Albert Einstein sums the story up brilliantly: 'Everyone is a genius. But if you judge a fish by its ability to climb a tree, it will live its whole life believing that it is stupid'. This 'Animal School' fable is still so relevant today and makes an important point in a simple yet brilliant way. I believe it is a must read for all those involved in education.

There are many adaptations of that animal fable. The important thing we must remember is that different children have different strengths, and if we push children too much in their less able areas we may dilute their abilities. Of course we want to encourage well-rounded, adaptive children, but teaching involves balance. Teaching is not about creating children who meet every target, but about helping children achieve their personal best. We want them to leave our class feeling confident and happy. Great teaching involves instinct, intuition and unconditional love.

Each child will have their own unique learning style and potential motivators. Awareness of how to gain attention and sustain interest will allow a teacher to engage her 'audience'. A non-engaged learner may follow a set of instructions, but they will not be achieving their potential.

Spotting a visual learner

So how do we know when a child is a visual learner? Is there a set of common characteristics? In 1999 Linda Kregar Silverman, a licensed psychologist who has been studying learning differences for over 40 years, created a useful comparison chart (Table 1.1).

Table 1.1 Visual-spatial learner characteristics comparison

The auditory-sequential learner	The visual-spatial learner
Thinks primarily using words	Thinks primarily in images
Has auditory strengths	Has visual strengths
Relates well to time	Relates well to space
Is a step-by-step learner	Is a whole-part learner
Learns by trial and error	Learns concepts all at once
Progresses sequentially from easy to difficult material	Learns complex concepts easily; struggles with easy skills
Is an analytical thinker	Is a good synthesizer
Attends well to details	Sees the big picture; may miss details
Follows oral directions well	Reads maps well

Does well in arithmetic	Is better at maths reasoning than computation
Learns phonics easily	Learns whole words easily
Can sound out spelling words	Must visualize words to spell them
Can write quickly and neatly	Much better at keyboarding than handwriting
Is well organized	Creates unique methods of organization
Can show steps of work easily	Arrives at correct solutions intuitively
Excels at rote memorization	Learns best by seeing relationships
Has good auditory short-term memory	Has good long-term visual memory
May need some repetition to reinforce learning	Learns concepts permanently; does not learn by drill and repetition
Learns well from instructions	Develops own methods of problem solving
Learns in spite of emotional reactions	Is very sensitive to teachers' attitudes
Is comfortable with one right answer	Generates unusual solutions to problems
Develops fairly evenly	Develops quite asynchronously (unevenly)
Usually maintains high grades	May have very uneven grades
Enjoys algebra and chemistry	Enjoys geometry and physics
Masters other languages in classes	Masters other languages through immersion
Is academically talented	Is creatively, mechanically, technologically, emotionally or spiritually gifted
Is an early bloomer	Is a late bloomer

Source: Silverman (2002). Chart originally created in 1999, reproduced with permission.

The list in Table 1.1 will immediately highlight areas of our current curriculum that could cause a visual-spatial learner difficulties.

Let's start off with reading. The visual-spatial learner is more likely to learn to read whole words and must visualize words to spell them. Imagine them in a phonics lesson with a class of auditory-sequential whizz kids, who sound out words with ease.

Ron Sandison is diagnosed with autism. He now works full time in the medical field and is a professor of theology, but he would have struggled with a phonics lesson: 'Phonetics was my weakness, and I was unable to spell a word by sounding it out. Teachers must use learning styles that fit the child's strengths' (Sandison 2014).

Moving on to handwriting – we find that the visual-spatial learner may have difficulty creating perfect handwriting and be much better at keyboarding. They are sitting amongst a group of children with the neatest handwriting, who have no issue with practising writing letters again and again.

Teachers must account for and cater for different learning styles. The content of a lesson must be suited to the individual child so that the individual can excel at learning in their own unique way. Yet the system persists in making children who do not even process sounds in the same way as other children sit through phonics instruction.

Teachers have a duty to create an environment with resources where every child can achieve, where they can all feel wonderful about themselves. Children learn at different rates in different ways.

Teachers as leaders

Dr Maria Montessori, founder of the Montessori schools, explained: 'A leader should feel a great responsibility for the orders he issues. A leader, therefore, is not somebody with a sense of great authority, but someone with a great sense of responsibility' (Montessori 2009, p.225). A teacher is a leader of a class of children. They do not have absolute freedom about their lesson content. They will have been told what they need to cover, but that should not stop them from looking out for each individual child.

Currently, there are schools where all children are taught phonics, but for some it simply doesn't work. Consider, for example, a child who has Down's Syndrome and is learning to sight read motivating words at home. He may recognize initial sounds, but cannot make 'blends', however hard he tries. What will continued attempts do to his self esteem? Then there is the child with autism who might not process sounds in the same way as other children. He holds his hands over his ears when the class gets too noisy. This child cannot read nonsense words through sounding them out, but he knows what is on the timetable from a written list. He is reading words that other children can't, but he has learnt to do this through other methods. What effect would teaching him to sound out non-words have on his attitude to reading? There is no one method of teaching reading that can suit every child. Children learn differently.

Teachers *are* leaders and have the 'responsibility' to stand up for these individual, brilliant children and ensure their sparkle does not get dulled down by taking part in years of whole class instruction if it is not relevant or helpful to them.

Responsibility

What if an officer has received orders to lead his army across a fast-moving river? The river is not so deep that the army cannot walk across, but the officer knows that some of the men are not strong swimmers. If they were to lose their footing they could be swept away. He looks out across the river and thinks about how he would feel if he could not swim well. He has an order, but he also has a responsibility. The officer will need to make a choice. Does he follow the order and hope the men will be okay to cross, does he find a way to get them across safely, does he think of another way to get them to where they need to be or does he think of a different task for these soldiers? The officer is responsible for his individual soldiers just like the teacher is responsible for her individual learners. If a soldier drowns because the officer did not think about him as an individual, it is the officer's fault.

If a child who could potentially cope is let down, if they wind up throwing chairs because the lesson hurts their ears and frustrates them, if the teacher knew the child and knew that they would not cope and if that child gets excluded from the class or school, the teacher must accept some responsibility. No matter what the orders are from above they are the leader in their own class.

What happens when needs are not met?

Parents who know that their child's needs are not being met start to look to other schools. They wonder if a child would be better suited to a special school if the mainstream school is not meeting their individual needs. These children often do not have severe learning difficulties, but they do have learning differences. They may have communication difficulties and anxieties, which mean they need to access specialist teaching, but this does not mean they are suited to learning in a school for children with severe learning difficulties (like the one where I teach). They need specialist support, but they also need stretching – they need peers to socialize with, compete with, learn with and see as role models. They will need some specific supports, accommodations with visual structures and preferably 1:1 staffing to ensure they achieve their potential best. They need accommodations for their learning style, but these should mostly be achievable in a mainstream school.

Parents come to our school with children who we know do not have learning difficulties, but learning differences. They are searching for a school to meet their child's needs, and it breaks my heart knowing that we cannot provide this place, but neither can we really suggest a good alternative.

Home schooling

Children know when their teachers are not supporting or stretching them enough. Parents are left in a difficult position when school cannot seem to get it right for their child. Do they stand by and watch their child suffer in education? Do they watch that wonderful, eager 'want to know' spark disappear?

Recently the actress Emma Thompson and her partner Greg Wise have spoken about why they are creating a home school for their 15-year-old daughter, Gaia. In an interview with *The Telegraph* (Sawer 2015) Wise explained, 'She loves learning and she's terribly focused and hardworking, but she didn't like the sausage factory of formal education. I've no argument with that'. Wise said he felt that 'home schooling made sense in a world where the nature of jobs and careers is changing at a rapid pace – requiring a more flexible approach to educating children'. People are becoming more aware that change is urgently required. Wise states, 'I read a fascinating statistic recently that said 60 per cent of the kids at school will go on to do jobs that haven't yet been invented'. Gaia now has a purpose-built home school in her garden and tutors to inspire and guide her, but most parents embarking on home schooling do not have this sort of financial freedom. The home schooling will literally take over their homes and lives. It's a big step (if it was not part of their original parenting plan).

Over 60,000 young people in England and Wales are currently home schooled (Sawer 2015). Many parents take on the role of teacher because they feel that the education system will not meet the educational needs of their child. They have been let down. Problems may be linked with children experiencing bullying, anxiety, lack of flexibility, pressure or simply a lack of understanding of their individual needs. Home schooling can be wonderful, but it is sad that so many parents are left feeling that they have no alternative. They experience an inadequate education system failing their child and realize that they must step in.

Creativity

In his lecture titled 'Do schools kill creativity?', which has become the most popular TED Talk[3] of all-time, with over 34 million views (at this time), Sir Ken Robinson points out that schools are preparing children for academic futures, but this is not suited to all children:

> Many highly talented, brilliant, creative people think they're not because the thing they were good at at school wasn't valued or was actually stigmatized. (Robinson 2006)

Going to university and getting a degree is not what *all* students should aspire to. A degree is no longer a promise of a job. It can hinder people from getting a job because they are seen as over-qualified. Many university students graduate with huge debts and no idea what to do next.

---

3   TED is a non-profit organization devoted to spreading ideas in the form of short, powerful talks. See www.ted.com/about/our-organization.

Jeremy Stuart, a documentary filmmaker, who, along with Dustin Woodard, made a movie about home schooling called *Class Dismissed*, says:

> It used to be that you had to go to a special institution to get information about a subject, but we live in the technology age and you can find anything you need on your phone. The whole paradigm has shifted. It's no longer about how to access information, it's about how to use the information, how to sift through it to determine how to apply it to your life. That's incredibly empowering, and schools are not doing that. (Quoted in Tanz 2015)

Sir Ken states in his talk that creativity is as important a subject as literacy. I believe that creativity should be viewed as integral and vital to every single lesson. Teachers should be allowed to follow their instinct, diverge from those topic-based curriculum plans and engage children with what motivates the children at that moment.

CASE STUDY: Going off plan

A while back, according to my plans, I was going to be teaching a personal, social and health education (PSHE) lesson linking with our curriculum topic. We were going to be looking at 'What to wear in different weather and for different situations', which is important and a discussion worth having, but there was something else on the children's minds.

In our next timetabled session we were going to have to split the class: half of them were going horse riding and half of them were staying at school to do yoga. Not ideal at all and quite confusing. We'd had to do this because there were not enough horses and not enough time for them to take turns. Two of the children were not happy. One girl who was going horse riding really didn't want to. One boy who was staying to do yoga wanted to go horse riding. Both children had Down's Syndrome and were developing some great communication skills through a combination of Makaton, PECS and speech (there is more information on Makaton in Chapter 13 and PECS in Chapter 11).

What a great opportunity to get these children to think, to problem solve and to communicate. And what about the other children? If two of them were verbally challenging this split group decision, what were the others thinking? We needed to explain splitting the group visually so that there was no confusion. Using a felt board, I quickly created a visual to explain the split group. I used our timetable symbols for 'horse riding' and 'yoga'. I placed the photos of the four children who were riding below the riding symbol and the four who were staying for yoga below 'yoga'.

Ginny, my reluctant rider, examined the visual. I waited, wondering if she would think of a solution. Ginny came up to the visual. She lifted her photo off and swapped it with Eddie's (the boy who wanted to go). Eddie beamed! He clearly thought that Ginny had come up with an excellent solution. The outing forms were already all completed, but it was possible to do a last-minute swap. I was torn. On the one hand they had communicated and problem solved on the other; if I let them get away with swapping, what would happen next week and the week after? I explained my thoughts. They had been brilliant and needed to be rewarded for their communication and problem solving. Communication and negotiation are amazing life skills and must be encouraged. I would change my plan and let them have their way, but in future weeks the chart would be up high. There would be no more swaps. What an opportunity we would have lost to develop communication, cooperation, problem solving and thinking skills if we had simply stuck to the original lesson plan.

A plan is just a plan

Teachers should not fear going off plan if a better learning opportunity presents itself. Plans are plans, but children are living, breathing, creative people, who deserve to have their questions answered and original ideas explored. They need teachers to take responsibility for their best interests, and who are willing to fill in an evaluation box stating what was done instead and justifying the change.

We want to support children in developing their abilities to question, to speak up for injustice and to suggest alternatives. These are all creative qualities. Our most creative inventors, artists, musicians, explorers and innovators would be just the type of personalities to question. They would be the 'Marmite' students, who teachers would either completely love or be driven up the wall by. Be the teacher who 'gets' these brilliant children.

There *is* currently a system and many boxes to tick, but there are ways around the things which stifle education. We may want change on a grand scale, but we must keep our main focus on those in our current care. Find ways around the tick boxes if those boxes suggest teaching in a non-motivating way. Teaching is a vocational profession and we must follow our instincts to keep the spark alive and protect self esteem. Be prepared to stand up, speak up and lead your children in a way that inspires and sparks their curiosity. If we could all have one year in one class with an inspiring teacher who just 'got' us, what a huge difference it would make to developing minds, self esteem and potential. I learnt early in my teaching career that if you are speaking up for children then you must know that you are on the right track. Keep speaking up. They only have one shot at this and *you* could be their great white hope.

Adapting

There seem to be more and more children who learn visually. Is this evolution? Is it linked with how our techie world is changing? Or have these children been in classrooms all along?

Mainstream teaching must adapt or this generation of children will not achieve their potential. Our teachers are currently not accessing the training or being given the preparation time required to differentiate for every child. This needs to change, but in the meantime my aim is to provide a very quick, easy-access teacher-to-teacher introduction to the visual tools we SEN teachers have up our sleeves so that teachers are aware of some of the ways to support, differentiate and include *every* child.

But in order to make best use of these tools, in order for mainstream teachers to become more 'special', they will need to be allocated either less black and white paper work or more resource making, investigating and creating time.

Visual learners can quickly become demotivated, bored and lose confidence. They may be labelled 'lazy', 'disorganized' or 'clumsy'. These words are like glue – negative stickers in the child's mind, which can hold them back. It's up to us to build every child up and make them believe in themselves. Help children paint positive, creative, happy futures.

In this book we will look at ways to help *all* children with a visual learning style. There will be a particular focus on visual strategies which help children who have learning difficulties and physical disabilities which affect communication. We will look at some of the many tricks SEN teachers know, that *all* teachers need to know. School budgets restrict teachers from going on specialist courses, but where does that leave those mainstream children who need these strategies to achieve their best at school?

We cannot expect teachers to read everything about every condition or convince headteachers to invest in sending them on every amazing course, so my plan is to provide a visual learner toolkit for literacy and a series of signposts, experiences and examples (lessons my SEN children have taught me). I will highlight some of the amazing training that is available so that parents and teachers can investigate and invest further.

This book will aid the inclusion of *all* children, from those who need visual supports due to a specific diagnosed condition or learning difficulty, to those with physical disabilities, to those many children being taught in an unfamiliar language and to those who are gifted and need more visual input to sustain interest and spur their creativity.

Tricks, training and experience

There are many tricks I've learnt along the way from training and experience. The way we engage children from the start is so important. We must gain every child's attention and show that *we* are excited about what is about to happen. What are we going to find out? Anything is possible!

SEN teachers are trained to be adaptive, to use children's interests, incorporating lots of visuals and including practical hands-on learning experiences to make lessons exciting and memorable. SEN teachers also know that they will need to repeat a lot and follow familiar structures but keep things exciting at the same time.

Mainstream teachers do not have access to all the constant SEN training that we SEN teachers get, but they do have an ever-growing number of SEN children to include. It can make a huge difference to these children when lessons are presented in a more structured, visual way. Without visuals, a child's attention drifts, learning opportunities are missed and behaviours linked with boredom and communication difficulties are more likely to occur. If these things lead to challenging behaviour or missed learning opportunities, the children are being failed. How frustrating, when all that the excluded child might have needed was greater awareness and a shift in teaching style.

In my school many of the teachers will stay on for hours after the children go home and our happiest tasks are creative. We enjoy making lovely new resources, creating beautiful displays and adding numerous photographs to our annual reports. We put a lot of love into our resources, and while we do this we speak about the achievements and antics of our students.

Mainstream teachers have more marking than we do in special schools, more boxes to tick, more tests and exams and more black and white piles of paperwork. Teaching is a very different job in special education and in mainstream, but with more SEN children being recognized and kept in the mainstream system it is time for a shift.

Potential difficulties visual learners face (why adaptations are necessary)

Below is a list of some of the difficulties visual learners can face when their educational needs are not catered for:

- Visual learners can find verbal instructions (without visuals) difficult to process and recall.

- They may find organization difficult, forgetting homework and messages, and misplacing things.

- They may get frustrated easily. They can see exactly what they want to say, but their words don't come out.

- They may seem to tire more easily and have a shorter attention span if not motivated by the topic.

- They may disrupt the group due to lack of interest, frustration or covering up.

- They may find it difficult to learn things in the same way as other children because they process differently.

- They may suffer from low self esteem when not having 'the same' learning style leaves them feeling 'stupid'.

- They may forget simple messages or information from a previous lesson.

- They may find it difficult to unlearn (for example, correcting incorrect spellings or letter formation).

- They may react badly to failure or change in routine as they have a perfect picture of what should happen.

Possibilities (why adapting is essential)

The visual thinker might be the child who will one day change the world. They have the potential to invent, to create, to problem solve or to think outside the box.

The visual learner deserves to reach their potential. Teachers and school leaders who do not relate to this way of learning must incorporate more visuals into their lessons and presentations. They must adapt assessment methods so that these children are able to see what they can do.

Abilities

Visual learners often have the ability to piece information together, problem solve and free think. This learning style, if correctly nurtured, can benefit the world. Many of the greatest inventors, artists, scientists and entrepreneurs shared this learning style. The world is changing and people are evolving.

Visual learners may 'think in pictures' (Grandin 2006a). They may have an incredible ability to map ideas and make connections. Being a visual learner is not a learning disability, but it is a learning difference. Making lessons visual and creative will help more children sustain interest and be more likely to achieve their potential.

Teachers cannot be expert in every condition and specialist strategy, but they can try to cater for all learning styles. Adding visuals and hands-on multisensory experiences to lessons will even the playing field and enable so many more children to fulfil their potential.

Chapter 2

Learning Differences and Disabilities

Autism Spectrum Conditions, Dyslexia, Dysgraphia, Dyspraxia, Down's Syndrome, ADHD, Cerebral Palsy and Physical Disabilities Affecting Communication

The secret of education lies in respecting the pupil. It is not for you to choose what he shall know, what he shall do. It is chosen and foreordained and he only holds the key to his own secret.

Ralph Waldo Emerson (1803–1882)

In this chapter we will take a closer look at some of the conditions often associated with visual learning styles. Different approaches suit different children. There is no one method. I will provide ideas and signposts, but it will be up to you, the parent or teacher, to decide which ones may help individual children. There will never be one glove fits all, but ideas and experience add to our toolkit, helping more children to achieve their potential.

Exceptions

Not *every* child with any of these conditions will be a visual learner. We must also be aware that conditions can co-exist. For example, a child may have a diagnosis of Down's Syndrome and autism or be gifted and dyslexic. They may have adapted to a visual learning style due to having a physical disability such as Cerebral Palsy or an undiagnosed learning difference such as dyslexia. Conditions may be undiagnosed and invisible to the unqualified eye. *All* children benefit from multisensory opportunities in lessons. Opportunities to see, hear, touch, smell and do gain attention and make experiences memorable. Each lesson should be an inspiring experience. We must think of where children are coming from. Settle down and watch some children's TV. Observe how the presenters use pictures, props, movement and sound effects to gain attention. We need to raise the bar if we are going to get today's child to attend.

Parents whose children are diagnosed with a learning difference or disability often become reflective about *their* experience of education. Learning differences often run through families. Parents look back and think about how their learning differences were missed.

I cannot cover every condition here, nor will we look at the conditions themselves in depth. There are many books and websites filled with information about individual conditions. What I can do is share my teacher toolkit so that other educators can pick up my experiences and observations and use them as teacher tools to help other children.

If you are teaching a child with a specific diagnosis I recommend looking at the blogs of people who live with these conditions and the blogs of teachers and parents investigating and innovating to support them. There is a wealth of fantastic free information available online. I will highlight a few brilliant pieces I have found, but these are only a selection. There is so much more freely available to read online.

In special needs schools many of our strategies are multisensory and visual because research and experience have shown that children are most engaged by this approach.

Autism spectrum conditions

I started teaching children with autism back in 2000 when I worked as a home tutor. Autism is a vast spectrum condition and not every child with autism or Aspergers Syndrome will be a visual learner. Even the diagnostic criteria for autistic spectrum conditions (ASCs) is shifting, so I will not attempt to define autism in this book.

Children with autism can do very well in mainstream school and end up with some incredible careers. There are no limits!

Children with autism can also find school (mainstream or special) extremely difficult. They can suffer extreme sensory overload, anxiety (making teaching new skills difficult), communication difficulties (they may process sounds differently and not develop speech) and fine motor difficulties (making writing much harder to master).

Teaching children with ASCs for so long has made me passionate about supporting their success. When a child has a learning difficulty associated with their ASC, visual supports can make the world of difference.

Visuals are important. We use visuals for timetables, individual schedules, to show behaviour expectations and to develop communication skills. We incorporate visuals into every lesson and every routine. The more visuals, the more structure and the less waffly teacher talk the better, because when these children are able to process our expectations they are less anxious. My first book, *Colour Coding for Learners with Autism: A Resource Book for Creating Meaning through Colour at Home and School* has a CD-ROM at the back containing hundreds of new visual supports (Devine 2014a). I am passionate about supporting these children and improving the support they get in school.

The autistic author Judy Endow explains:

> People with autism are often visual thinkers. It is not something we decide, but rather the way our brain handles information. We do not know when we are little that most other people think with words rather than with colors and pictures. This makes it difficult in school as delivery of information quickly becomes language-based as pictures drop away after the first few years. This dramatic change in materials in the United States occurs at the third-grade level when text-based instruction becomes predominant.
>
> For me, it was hard to think about or understand ideas that were not concrete ideas. Basically, if my brain could not translate the words I heard into a concrete picture in a few seconds, as a young child I would not be able to pick up the meaning of the words being spoken. Even though I did not understand the meaning, I was able to repeat the words. For example, when prompted I could repeat the teacher's instruction to use quiet voices even though I had no idea what the words meant at that moment because no picture popped up in my head to equal those words. (Endow 2013, p.34)

As I said in my first book:

> We know that children with autism like order, that they are often very visual and that they can be quite literal. They deserve beautiful resources and symbols that make sense. If a picture does not explain visually, it is pointless and the child will stop looking to the pictures for information. (Devine 2014a, pp.198–199)

Visual systems are so important to children with ASCs, providing emotional as well as educational support. For these children too much verbal language can be impossible to tolerate. When a child with autism is experiencing anxiety, the last thing they need is lots of verbal input. We reduce language. We use visuals. We wait. Too much language can cause them anxiety and physical pain. So visuals are not only essential for comprehension, but for their physical comfort and emotional well being.

Being stricter, louder, unpredictable or unfair will create anxiety, resistance and a fight or flight response. We can gradually stretch these children by slowly increasing our demands. We respect their need to feel they are succeeding; we teach with empathy. Frustration and overload can result if our expectations seem overwhelming. We keep our teacher demands secure within their comfort zone, but continue stretching them. Think of a flower growing. The stages appear seamless, but when filmed and speeded up we see them happen. Seeing progress in a child with autism can be a bit like this. Small steps, then at the end of an academic year we look back and go: 'Wow – how far they have come!'

> Teaching to the learning style of the student may make an impact on whether or not the child can attend to and process the information which is presented. This, in turn, can affect the child's performance in school as well as his/her behavior. Therefore, it is important that educators assess for learning style as soon as an autistic child enters the school system and that they adapt their teaching styles in rapport with the strengths of the student. This will ensure that the autistic child has the greatest chance for success in school. (Edelson n.d.)

Dr Temple Grandin was diagnosed with autism as a child and the family doctor suggested an institution. She went on to gain university degrees, write numerous books and develop a new system for slaughtering livestock (which has been taken on by most of America).

Grandin is an inspiration to so many parents who have children with an autism diagnosis. She was pre-verbal and had huge sensory issues, but she has achieved so much. If she can do it, they can do it. Believe it. They can! One of her many books has been made into a Hollywood film. She explains, 'I think in pictures. Words are a second language to me. I translate both spoken and written words into full-color movies, which run like a VCR tape inside my head' (Grandin 2006a, p.3).

Haley Massara is an adult with Aspergers Syndrome. In an article called 'Off the beat: Alternative wiring, or living with Asperger's', she recalls finding a copy of Temple Grandin's book and being surprised at the similarities between her own perception and that described by Grandin:

> The next morning, I mentioned Grandin's thought process – this way of 'seeing' things – to my parents over breakfast. My mother's reaction was immediate: She thought it was fascinating. But for my autistic father and me, Grandin had managed to put something intangible into words; many of the ideas and mental processes she described were startlingly familiar, even if we'd never thought of them as anything but business as usual. (Massara 2015)

Children with autism often have a visual learning style, but they may also need the visuals to support social learning and for their physical and emotional well being. Using visuals can be a support strategy for children with autism because they cut down the need for too much language. We must understand how vital it is when supporting children with autism that we reduce and simplify teacher talk (especially if they show anxiety).

I will highlight how many visual supports are structured, but autism is such a wide condition that to get an in-depth understanding of the individual 'whys' it will be necessary to read other sources.

Dyslexia

Dyslexia is still often missed and may not be diagnosed at all.

Children with dyslexia can be extremely bright and have very good verbal skills, but they may struggle with reading, writing, spelling, maths and organization.

Adults with dyslexia will often turn things around by using their creative skills to their advantage, but they should not have to reflect on a time in education where their learning style was not understood. If we cater for these children, teaching to their strengths and adapting to remove their difficulties, they may achieve so much more. If nothing else they will have much happier memories of their time in school.

Children with dyslexia may be labelled lazy, which may damage their already-delicate self esteem.

These children can benefit greatly from many of the methods used for teaching in special needs schools. Rather than write out words again and again to learn the spellings, they may respond better to tracing textured letters with a finger, writing in sand, using coloured bricks to build up words or sentences or by adding a physical activity such as throwing a ball or playing word games.

The letters themselves can be an issue for children with dyslexia. They may visually flip, mirror and move. Specialist fonts such as 'Dyslexie' can help counteract this. The Dyslexie font uses slight changes between similar letters to help dyslexic readers not to confuse them. It was developed by a graphic designer, Christian Boer, whose own dyslexia inspired him to develop a helpful solution. It is currently free to download for home use.

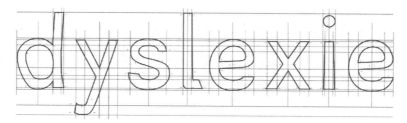

Figure 2.1 *The Dyslexie font*

Coloured acetate overlays, printing worksheets on to coloured paper or glasses with coloured lenses can all help reduce visual distortions for the child with dyslexia who is learning to read.

Many children with dyslexia learn to read through single word recognition rather than phonics.

It may be that children can make progress with reading and spelling when taught using a morphological approach.

Show them a list of words and get them to look for what they have in common. For example:

like
likely
liked
likened
likening
unlike
unlikely
dislike
disliked.

The students look for the base word (commonality) and they find the word 'like'. They learn about the common use of the prefix, for example 'un', and the 'suffix', for example 'ly'.

> Morphological awareness is the recognition, understanding, and use of word parts that carry significance. For example, root words, prefixes, suffixes, and grammatical inflections (e.g., –s or –es for plurals) are all morphemes which can be added or taken away from a word to alter its meaning. (Dyslexia Help 2015a, para.2)

The morphological approach also examines the history of the words, which adds to interest and aids memory.

Dr Neville Brown and his son, Dr Daryl Brown, who run the Maple Hayes Dyslexic Specialist School, are currently developing a groundbreaking dictionary for people with dyslexia based on this approach.

School headteacher Daryl Brown explains:

> It is not that the dictionary we all know and love is wrong – it works for many people but, quite simply, is completely inaccessible for dyslexics.
>
> We teach literacy using an entirely different method to phonics, instead using the 'morphological approach' which was developed by my father over 30 years ago. This bypasses the requirement to learn words by sounding them out. Instead we use icon meaning cards to visually represent words or parts of words. (Quoted in Halifax 2015)

The entrepreneur Richard Branson, who also has dyslexia and attention deficit disorder, is an example of a modern-day visual thinker. He left school at 16 and recalls in an interview:

> I couldn't always follow what was going on, so I didn't find the lessons interesting and became distracted. My teachers thought I was just lazy because back then, people didn't understand as much about dyslexia as they do today. (Branson 2012)

Branson uses his learning style to his advantage now as it allows him to simplify things, which is part of the success of his Virgin brand. He states that:

> Over the years, my different way of thinking helped me to build the Virgin Group and contributed greatly to our success. My dyslexia guided the way we communicated with customers. When we launched a new company, I made sure that I was shown the ads and marketing materials. I asked those presenting the campaign to read everything aloud, in order to test the phrasing and the overall concept. If I could grasp it quickly, then it passed muster – we would get our message across only if it was understandable at first glance. (Branson 2012)

Branson famously admitted how his team have learnt to support his visual learning style when he admitted how someone had to explain the difference between *net* and *gross* profit at a meeting because he did not understand what the figures he was looking at meant to the company. 'It's important for young children who have discovered they are dyslexic to see that successful people can get through it' (Branson, quoted in Goodman 2013).

Dyspraxia

Dyspraxia can affect a child's fine and gross motor skills. They may show immaturity in developing and organizing their movement or difficulties and delays in speech. It has been called 'clumsy child syndrome'.

Dyspraxia may impact on a child's self confidence as they struggle with things like balance, sports, organization and communication (things their peer group seem to find easy). The child may fall up stairs and struggle with ball skills.

Dyspraxia can make handwriting more difficult. When handwriting is developing at a different pace and a child is struggling, this may be a sign of dyspraxia or dysgraphia (which we will look at next). This child must not be put down or seen as lazy. Teachers should accommodate and be aware. These children find handwriting more difficult.

Dr Younger of the New York University Medical School said in a *Mail on Sunday* article: 'In the majority of children and young people with dyspraxia, we cannot find the cause so the basic treatment is occupational therapy – teaching them to make a plan for their actions and rehearse their movements' (Churcher 2008).

The actor Daniel Radcliffe (famous for playing Harry Potter) has always been open about his dyspraxia. He wanted to act from the age of five, but he revealed: 'My mother said, "Oh no you don't."' When he was nine she allowed him to audition to play David Copperfield because she saw his confidence needed a boost. Radcliffe is quoted in Churcher (2008): 'I was having a hard time at school in terms of being c**p at everything, with no discernible talent.'

When young people like Daniel Radcliffe who are part of children's current culture share their experiences of education with learning differences they do a great service. Daniel Radcliffe or 'Harry Potter' believed other people perceived him as talentless. Luckily he did not let it stop him from using his talents to achieve fulfilment.

Jake Borrett was diagnosed with dyspraxia when he was 18. He is currently studying English Literature and Creative Writing at the University of Hertfordshire, and aspires to be a professional writer. He writes a wonderful blog sharing his poetry, thoughts and experiences. So to explain more about dyspraxia I will hand over to Jake, who I believe is well on his way to achieving his ambitions:

Gross motor skills

Many with Dyspraxia will have some problems with gross motor skills. These skills are ones that use large muscles to create body movements, for example walking, running and maintaining balance.

I have often found playing sports like athletics and football a real difficulty. This was a particular issue each year at primary school when we had Sports Day. We were all required to take part in games like throwing beanbags into hula-hoops and had to enter into running races. Often I would miss the hoop or not win the race, but I still tried despite there being some disappointment.

Schools should give students a choice of what events they would like to take part in. It is not correct to force anyone into something they may not have the self-confidence to do. Teachers, families and friends need to give this support so those with the condition have the self esteem to perform any games they would like to take part in.

Fine motor skills

Similarly those with Dyspraxia generally have problems with fine motor skills. These involve small muscle movements, such as using cutlery, handwriting and playing musical instruments.

These do impact me in everyday life. It can be frustrating not being able to do something the first time. I remember trying to learn how to tie my shoelaces on holiday just before my eleventh birthday. Before this I would always wear shoes with Velcro straps. My parents would show me how to tie the laces but my mind just could not get around to doing it properly. The loop was either too small, way too big, or the laces would not fit together.

Over time I gradually got the hang of tying shoelaces. I will admit that even now I do have occasional problems with them. They often do come loose after a while. Still I am glad to have learnt. So it is important to have someone patient teaching you because it will take time. Then again there is nothing wrong with having Velcro straps or slip on shoes if you just simply cannot get it. What is important is feeling good about yourself no matter which option you pick.

Clumsiness

Those with Dyspraxia generally have a lack of awareness of their body position. This can result in bumping into, tripping over or spilling things.

Since I could crawl I would often bang myself into objects around the room causing an 'egg bump' on my head. This clumsiness still follows me now. It is amazing the amount of objects that I have dropped, broken, spilt or bumped into. Interestingly is that it is believed that many do have a good sense of humour. So if you ever see one of us fall over or drop something you may find us laughing about it afterwards. Well, as long as we were not badly hurt or that object was not worth a fortune.

Forming relationships

It can be quite difficult to form relationships. There may be isolation within the peer group or those with Dyspraxia may unfortunately be rejected by others because of their differences. Those with the disability may sometimes misinterpret what someone is trying to say or how that person is feeling, which could cause alienation.

Of course this is not always the cause. Those with the condition often display positive attributes such as being kind, empathetic and forgiving. It is these which often shine through and help build close bonds with those around them.

It did take me quite a while to find people I wanted to be friends with. Still they are there no matter the troubles I may be facing and I cannot thank them enough.

Speech, language and words

Those living with the condition may experience issues with speech, language or words, either in the form of talking or writing. Organising, planning and proofreading can also be affected.

Throughout primary school I hated English and would often get low grades. Because of this my secondary school placed me and a few others in something called 'Learning Support'. Instead of learning a second language, like French or German, we spent the time improving our literary skills. Thanks to the utter dedication of the staff during those three years I began to enjoy the subject and my grades increased. Now I am studying English Literature and Creative Writing at university.

Of course I still have difficulties, but those dedicated people helped me to thoroughly like English, which is something I would have struggled with otherwise. (Borrett 2014)

Always curious, I asked Jake to elaborate on any visual approaches that had helped and he wrote:

When it comes to visual approaches to learning, Learning Support at my secondary school often provided us with visual aids to help understand syntax, language and spelling. This often allowed us to associate words with pictures. In addition to this, as part of my Disabled Students Allowance at the University of Hertfordshire I have been provided with learning toolkits including 'Dragon Naturally Speaking', 'Olympus Sonority', 'Audio Notetaker', 'Inspiration' and 'Read & Write'. The tools provide some very insightful ways, both visual and otherwise, to help me plan and structure my English Literature assignments, but also to help organise my daily routine and notes. (Borrett 2015, personal correspondence)

Dysgraphia

Dysgraphia is a condition that causes trouble with written expression. The term comes from the Greek words *dys* ('impaired') and *graphia* ('making letter forms by hand'). Dysgraphia is a brain-based issue. It's not the result of a child being lazy. (Patino n.d.)

Dysgraphia is not as widely recognized as dyslexia and again is often not picked up by parents or teachers:

Dysgraphia may not be as widely discussed as dyslexia, but it's surprisingly common. Dysgraphia can manifest itself as difficulties with spelling and grammar, poor handwriting or trouble putting thoughts on paper. (Griffin n.d.)

Imagine how it feels to be given a list of weekly spellings to write out three times, when each word causes frustration. Each word is a visual 'not good enough' marker. The child knows it takes them longer and they are aware that despite their best efforts the writing in their book is larger and not so well formed.

Imagine seeing a peer group easily writing in that cursive style used in most primary schools as children prepare for doing joined-up writing. Many adults do not do joined-up writing. Many adults would rather type up a note than handwrite it because they like having the use of 'spell check' and 'grammar check' and being able to quickly edit mistakes.

In schools for children with learning difficulties we rarely start off using a cursive style. We are thrilled if the child begins to form letters. Only once they are writing and showing signs of transitioning to a mainstream school would we start introducing a cursive font. Mainstream teachers start off with this font, but that does not necessarily make it right. We must adapt our teaching styles to the child and let them achieve their best and know that we believe their best is amazing and sticker-worthy.

If we are sending out a letter to parents we do not usually handwrite it. We type the letter, we use those tools and we proof-read it.

The way to improve writing is to practise, so I'm not suggesting that we remove handwriting tasks, but that teachers must be aware of these children and nurture them so that they feel good about their efforts. Rather than only praising those who produce the perfect handwriting, remind the class that people have different skills and talents. It is important to try to do things to the best of their personal ability, but not to compare what they do with others. One child may be brilliant at handwriting, but another may have exceptional problem solving skills. The approach to teaching these children is so important. An empathic teacher can make the child believe in their 'can dos', which puts them on the path to success. A teacher who only sees the 'can't', who only praises those who tick boxes, will be creating another trip wire for the child with dysgraphia.

A child with dysgraphia may have the ability to think of the most incredibly creative story, but when it comes to writing it down it would take them hours. A child with dysgraphia may ask a teacher if they can write a poem instead of a story. A good teacher will allow a child to express themselves creatively so that they do not become frustrated and shut off from developing their ability to create. What a wonderful thing when a child wants to write a poem. They are not looking for a short cut. Or perhaps when it comes to creative writing the child with dysgraphia could dictate 'Agatha Christie style'. She was known for dictating her many famous novels.

Agatha Christie

The author Agatha Christie is believed to have had dysgraphia:

> In spite of excellent reading and problem solving skills, she had difficulty with spelling, arithmetic, the mechanical aspects of writing, and foreign language

learning. This disability, variously called developmental output failure, dysgraphia, writing backwardness, and/or arithmetic/writing disability, obviously did not prevent her from becoming one of the most popular writers in the English language. (Siegel 1998)

If you are teaching a child with dysgraphia, tell the class about Agatha Christie. People have different strengths and different ways of expressing themselves. Our responsibility to children with dysgraphia is to allow the Agatha Christies to become the Agatha Christies.[1]

CASE STUDY: Creative thinker

I recall when teacher training teaching a class of six- and seven-year-olds in a mainstream school. One wonderful little boy really struggled with handwriting. The poor handwriting meant that he was always grouped with the children who were struggling to keep up. His handwriting was holding him back in all subjects.

That same little boy came alive when we had carpet time with his hand shooting up with ideas for different adjectives. While the rest of the group would use the word 'big', he had a bank of amazing words – 'gigantic', 'enormous', 'expanded'. What if the class were asked to write these words down? His list would not have been so extensive. I made sure he had lots of opportunities to show this ability and incorporated this creative vocabulary-building time into all of our literacy lessons. It improved the other children's opinions of this child and got them trying to think more creatively, which would also improve their writing skills. I could almost see this boy plump his young feathers as his self esteem improved.

We must recognize children with dysgraphia and nurture their strengths.

Down's Syndrome

A diagnosis of Down's Syndrome is often predicted before birth or given very soon after birth:

Down's syndrome is a genetic condition caused by the presence of an extra chromosome 21 in the body's cells. Down's syndrome is not a disease, and it is not a hereditary condition. It occurs by chance at conception. (Down's Syndrome Association n.d.)

---

1   You can learn about a learner's experience with dysgraphia here: www.teenink.com/nonfiction/ perssonal_experience/article/409433/my-life-with-dysgraphia.

People with Down's Syndrome are known to often have a visual learning style:

> Research suggests that people with Down syndrome learn better when they can see things illustrated. This finding has been demonstrated across a number of areas of development including the acquisition of language, motor skills and literacy. This suggests that teaching will be more effective when information is presented with the support of pictures, gestures or objects. (Down Syndrome Education International n.d.)

> Studies suggest that the processing and recall of spoken information is improved when it is supported by relevant picture material. This information has led to educators stressing the importance of using visual supports including pictures, signs, and print, when teaching children with Down syndrome as this approach makes full use of their stronger visual memory skills. (Down Syndrome Education International n.d.)

I love teaching children with Down's Syndrome literacy for many reasons. Thinking about their wonderful reactions lifts my heart and makes me smile. Children with Down's Syndrome are often natural actors and love getting up and acting out a story with masks and dressing up. They love sensory stories and being part of the action, and make gathering all those props seem so worthwhile.

Children with Down's Syndrome are usually great at sustaining attention in group activities when they are fun and visual. They benefit from 1:1, fun, visual activities when learning to read individual letters and whole words. They are brave about learning and willing to attempt new activities. When motivated and supported they can make amazing and exciting progress.

Learners with Down's Syndrome require an individual interest-based approach with huge amounts of praise, rewards and motivators.

We will look at some great examples of children with Down's Syndrome learning, and examples of what these young people can achieve when their learning styles are correctly catered for and they are allowed to develop their own talents.

The Down Syndrome Association of Orange County list some 'myths and truths' on their website. The first 'myth' they list relates to the idea that people with Down's Syndrome have learning delays. They state:

> Standard IQ tests do not measure many important areas of intelligence, and you will often be surprised by the memory, insight, creativity, and cleverness of many with Down Syndrome. The high rates of learning disabilities in students with Down Syndrome often mask a range of abilities and talents. Clearly, educators and researchers are still discovering the full educational potential of people with Down Syndrome. (Down Syndrome Association of Orange County n.d.)

Dr Julia Pewitt Kinder, family practice physician, author, national speaker and consultant on Down's Syndrome, is keen to dispel the myths associated with having Down's Syndrome:

Parents of babies with Down syndrome should expect their children to have fulfilling and independent lives. The possibilities for children with Down syndrome are endless, and the best thing anyone can do to help maximize the potential of a child with an extra chromosome is to expect success and to refuse to place limits.

Myths and misconceptions about Down syndrome unfortunately persist, and individuals with Down syndrome may be judged based upon outdated notions instead of getting to know the person and their amazing abilities. Here are truths about Down syndrome:

- It is possible for individuals with Down syndrome to have normal IQ. Most people have cognitive delays that are mild to moderate, not severe.

- Some individuals with Down syndrome are completely healthy with no chronic medical issues.

- 80% of babies with Down syndrome are born to moms under the age of 35.

- Mom's age does not cause Down syndrome. The cause is unknown.

- Developmental milestones can be reached on time or ahead of time.

- The tongue is not enlarged; the oral cavity is small.

- Tongue protrusion and open-mouth posture can be prevented.

- Poor speech does not indicate lower intelligence. Speech can be difficult in people with Down syndrome because their muscles are weak.

- Down syndrome is not rare; it occurs in about 1 of every 800–1,000 live births.

- Down syndrome is the most common chromosomal variation.

- Life expectancy is around 55 years.

- Children with Down syndrome are not always happy and loving, but experience all the typical moods of any child.

- Children with Down syndrome are more like other children than they are different.

Because of new therapies and improved methods of teaching, better health care, and determined families, teachers, and therapists, children with Down syndrome are achieving the same goals as any other child, and growing up to be successful adults.

(Kinder 2015, personal correspondence)

What might the child with Down's Syndrome achieve with the right supports? The short answer is that they could achieve anything. There are athletes, actors, academics, teachers and photographers. They may have greater obstacles to overcome, they may need to have additional support, but adults with Down's Syndrome are doing great things. I could fill a book with success stories of young people with Down's Syndrome.

Oliver Hellowell is a young photographer, who has a huge worldwide following of people who love the way he zooms in on details and captures landscapes and wildlife in a unique and beautiful way. He explains:

I'm different from other photographers, I like the framing and the composition, and having the camera on the ground looking up. I don't do people, I do landscape and wildlife, especially birds. I like Bence Mátté, Ben Hall and Andy Rouse – they're amazing. (Quoted in Goleniowska n.d.)

More detail about Oliver and his lovely mum's journey will follow towards the end of this book in Chapter 19.

Children with Down's Syndrome respond well to very visual, enthusiastic teaching. I recall advising a newly qualified teacher to be 'Mr Tumble' (a Makaton signing CBeebies character). Use lots of signing and visuals, and incorporate drama, role play, fun and individual motivators. Up the volume a bit and use very clear speech, only including the necessary words. Microphones can be a great teaching tool. The teacher can use a microphone headset, and the added volume can really help some children. Similarly they love hearing their own voices in microphones, which may help develop speech. Makaton signs illustrate words, adding interest, and help develop communication and promote understanding. Use a child's name to gain attention. The child with Down's Syndrome may have hearing difficulties, so do be aware. Makaton and PECS are amazingly effective for speech development (see Chapters 11 and 13 for more details).

Repeat and repeat and be over the top with praise. The visual structures of TEACCH can help with independence. Motivate and motivate. Use those special interests!

These children love to be told how wonderful they are. They love drama and fun. They love helping so pretend you have forgotten something for the lesson and see them jump up to go get it. I've found these children *love* the structure of our Attention Autism sessions (see Chapter 14 for more details).

Smile, exaggerate, praise, make full use of signing, gesture and modelling (showing as well as telling) and speak clearly – make everything you do an opportunity for communication and developing independence. Be fun and enjoy, enjoy. These children are *all* fabulous to teach.

Cerebral Palsy and physical disabilities affecting communication

Children with Cerebral Palsy and other physically disabling conditions can be visual learners for a different reason. Their understanding of language may be absolutely brilliant and their hearing can be incredible, as can their ability to process, to listen and to unpick meaning.

It is when these children have communication difficulties that they may need to adapt to using visuals to aid their communication.

Visual systems on Augmentative and Alternative Communication (AAC) devices can allow a non-verbal person with physical disabilities to communicate. They may use their finger to tap, their chin to control or their eyes to navigate through categories and pictures to communicate.

When I was a child, my cousin Louise, who was born with severe physical disabilities, got an AAC device she operated with her chin. It was amazing to suddenly be able to hear more from her than 'ummm' (yes) and 'nnnnn' (no). We could ask questions that required answers other than 'yes' and 'no' and she would navigate through her pictures to respond. This meant so much to us all.

Communication and inclusion

Always speak to the child, not over them or about them. Always be extremely, genuinely positive about what they *can* do and what they *will* achieve. Have high expectations. Provide them with the means to communicate. Teach them to use a smile for 'yes' and a frown for 'no'. Let them see the power communication can give them. Smile at these children, joke with them and love them. Become someone who fights their corner.

Ensure that they are seated in an inclusive way and they can see the action. We got our whole class beanbags because one child needed to sit in a specially moulded Pea Pod beanbag chair.

Sensory stories and story massage

Sensory stories allow children with physical disabilities and profound and multiple learning difficulties (PMLD) to enjoy stories by adding sensory elements such as a water spray for rain or warm ginger-scented play dough for the gingerbread man. Music and massage can also help create meaning and sustain interest (see Chapter 9 for more about sensory stories).

Materials and parachutes

We use large pieces of material sewn on to long rods to build a picture for stories, assemblies and whole school drama. At harvest, for example, we'd have material with autumn leaf prints and gold and brown colours. These materials can be great for children who have a tendency or a physical disability which causes them to always look up.

Parachutes can be another great teaching tool for story time or song time. You can add other elements like autumn leaves or coloured tissue paper.

Switches

Using communication aids such as switches can be a great way to get a child with a physical disability to realize that they *can* join in. Switches like Big Mack have a large surface area and allow a message of 20 seconds or less to be quickly recorded. For example, when we do our school council meetings, one of our students with PMLD comes with her class contribution to the discussion recorded on a switch. I then record a message back on to the switch which she can share with her class. Chapter 12 has more information on using switches.

In his wonderful book *Ghost Boy*, Martin Pistorius, who was trapped in an unresponsive body after an inexplicable illness when he was 12, recalls how he felt when the switches that would operate his computer arrived:

> The switches I'll use to operate the computer have arrived and I've started practicing with them, knowing they are so much more than nuts and bolts, discs of plastic or networks of electric wires. Talking, chatting, arguing, joking, gossiping, conversing, negotiating, chittchatting: these are all within my reach now thanks to the switches. Praising, questioning, thanking, requesting, complimenting, asking, complaining and discussing: they are almost at my disposal too. (Pistorius 2011, p.53)

If you have a child with communication difficulties, fight for them to get the chance to communicate and don't be afraid to try again if a previous teacher says it didn't work. Look at the story of Martin Pistorius who defied all predictions when he started to be aware of the world around him. Look at how he felt when he was given the chance to show what he could do. That initial switch trial was based on the belief of one person, who saw a flicker of comprehension in his eyes. You could open a door to a whole new world and completely transform a life.

Changes

Change the lighting, change displays, change the music to link with the lesson, change the location. All of these things add interest and build anticipation.

If a child is not motivated to use the switch to join in with songs or discussions then get something that really does motivate them. With adapters, switches can be used to operate most of those funny dancing toys, multisensory equipment and lighting, or for switching on more practical equipment like hairdryers or juicers. They can also be linked with software for cause-and-effect activities on the computer.

Attention deficit disorder (ADD)/attention deficit hyperactivity disorder (ADHD)

Children with ADD/ADHD will be absolutely fantastic learners when they have the right teacher, who 'gets' them, respects them and knows how to support them. These children can be amazingly creative, inventive and exciting to teach, but with the wrong approach they can disengage and disrupt, creating a series of negatives, which lead to low self esteem and potential exclusion. The current statistics are that there is a child with ADD/ADHD in *every* class.

Children with ADD may be labelled 'lazy' or 'wilful' and may not get the diagnosis as quickly as those with ADHD because they do not display challenging behaviours.

When children with ADD try, it can actually make it harder for them to concentrate. Top American psychiatrist, author and brain-imaging expert Daniel G. Amen, MD, explains:

> The harder many people with ADD try, the worst [sic] things get for them. Brain-imaging studies show that when people with ADD try to concentrate, the parts of their brains involved with concentration, focus and follow-through (prefrontal cortex and cerebellum) actually shuts down – just when they need them to turn on. (Amen 2014)

Teaching should be broken down and stepped so that learning is more gradual. Lessons should seem more like fun than 'hard work', because the idea of 'hard work' hinders 'hard work'.

These children benefit from many of the same visual structures and supports as children with autism (see Chapter 16). They like to be able to see expectations and schedules and know how long activities will last. Timers can be helpful; visual schedules, and visual prompts for organization can also make a big difference. These children benefit from a clear structure and lots of positives. They may need to take breaks, fidget and be forgiven if they speak before putting up a hand.

These children also benefit from having teachers who know their attention span, their interests and their individual triggers. They may have strong emotional ups and downs. ADD has been around forever and is not due to poor parenting or poor teaching, but good parenting and good teaching will make the world of difference to the child with ADD. Protecting their mental health through listening and providing emotional support and consistent, fair reactions is so important.

Unpredictable ADHD

In a blog post titled 'The Lotto numbers are easier to predict than someone with ADHD', Niall Greene writes:

> For those without ADHD try and imagine wakening up in the morning in your nice warm bed at home and getting ready to go to your job knowing that before the end of the day your life could be turned upside down and everything lost due to a condition that you seem to have little power to control. That's not an exaggeration of what it's like to have ADHD. I've experienced it myself on many occasions and have heard others with ADHD describe the same scenario. I think it's caused by a combination of frustration, impulsiveness, denial of how severely the ADHD is affecting the person and the arch enemy of every ADHDer **BOREDOM**. (Greene 2015a)

Learners with ADHD may need to be told to focus on one activity at a time. Sending multiple homework assignments home in different books may result in none of them coming back completed. I'd compare it to handing a child six balls and telling them to juggle. They throw the balls up in the air, knowing they won't be able to catch any of them. But if you start with one ball and get really, really into juggling, they may build up and end up being the most brilliant juggler. Children with ADHD are known for having short attention spans, but they can also become hyper-focused. Teach with awareness of this hyper-focus and try to make it into a positive strength for the child.

Beth Kaplanek, volunteer president of the board of directors for Children and Adults with Attention-Deficit/Hyperactivity Disorder (CHADD), says, 'Teachers can make all the difference with how a child feels about [himself or herself].' Kaplanek recalls how her son Chris, now 18 years old, struggled in school because of ADHD and learning disabilities. She credits a special teacher with helping her son believe he could achieve in school: 'She was the most caring teacher, and she would point out his successes whenever she could. The best thing a teacher can do is to look for the small milestones with kids with ADHD' (quoted in Weaver Dunne 2007).

Oppositional defiance disorder (ODD)

ODD is often linked with ADHD and deserves a mention here as it is another condition where visuals can have an impact.

Niall Greene recalls:

> I happened upon the **Break Glass Fire Alarm Box** and I fully understood that if I broke the glass with the drumstick I would be in trouble and yet I just couldn't resist. It was like the **DO NOT PUSH THE BIG RED SHINY BUTTON** that you see in cartoons and in my mind I was thinking 'you won't tell me'.
>
> The consequences of my actions didn't seem to click until the siren of the alarm went off and all eyes turned to me. For the next hour I had to listen to an angry music teacher, caretaker, and fireman lecturing me on my irresponsible behaviour. When they asked me why I did it I gave the most honest answer I could at fourteen which was 'I don't know'. I asked myself that question many times afterwards. (Green 2015b)

When a child has ODD traits, visuals telling them *not* to do something, or authority figures who represent 'being told not to', are like big red flags being waved in front of a bull. If you are teaching a child and you suspect ODD, think very carefully about how you place your demands. If you show these children respect and ask nicely rather than tell, explain the reasons for the request before the request itself and use lots of positive visuals, then they are much more likely to be able to learn.

Chapter 3

Gifted Visual Learners

Past and Present

The knowledge of the world is only to be acquired in the world, and not in a closet.

Lord Chesterfield (1694–1773)

'You have a gifted child' should surely be music to a parent's ears. But anyone who parents a gifted child will know that the gifted tag comes at a cost.

Gifted children

There's a common misconception that the gifted child is the one who is blessed with amazing intelligence – they're the one who can pick up a violin and just play, the one who will never have to study, whose hand shoots up eagerly with every answer at the tip of their tongue... That the gifted child is the one to whom everything comes easily and who will always do well. When gifted children are grouped into special classes, other parents of children with special educational needs (SEN) may see them as less deserving of additional support and less in need of accommodations. They do not see that the giftedness is a 'special educational need'. The giftedness can even create a learning difficulty.

Giftedness is truly a double-edged sword because children who are gifted can find school and later life extremely difficult. They can have difficulties with making friends, organizing themselves and being on time; they can experience sensory issues and often have poor handwriting or spelling ability. They may be seen as obnoxious for pointing out teacher errors, they may be put down or they may have self esteem that is extremely fragile and absorbs every negative comment.

Gifted children are more likely to be moved from school to school, with nowhere truly able to meet their individual needs. Giftedness may be misdiagnosed as another learning difference, or a gifted child may have a dual diagnosis, making things even more complex.

Gifted children are not those who were born to the parents who will push and push them to achieve. Often they have parents who would much prefer they go and kick a ball in the park or talk about what happened on *The Simpsons*. These children not only feel that they do not fit into school, but they stand out in their families too. All of these issues can add up to later mental health issues.

Gifted child traits

In an article titled 'What is a gifted child?', David Farmer states:

> The word 'gifted' has been defined differently by different academics and practitioners and is often considered by many to be an unfortunate term, but it has become generally associated with a child whose potential in one or more areas of skill would place him or her in the top 2–5% of children of the same age. (Farmer 2007)

The authors of *Misdiagnosis and Dual Diagnoses of Gifted Children and Adults* have pulled together a useful list of the social and emotional characteristics of the gifted child:

- Unusually large vocabularies and complex sentence structure for their age
- Greater comprehension of the subtleties of language
- Longer attention span; persistence
- Intensity and sensitivity
- Wide range of interests
- Highly developed curiosity and limitless questions
- Interest in experimenting and doing things differently
- Tendency to put ideas or things together in ways that are unusual, not obvious, and creative (divergent thinking)
- Learn basic skills more quickly, with less practice
- Largely teach themselves to read and write as preschoolers
- Able to retain much information, unusual memory
- Have imaginary playmates
- Unusual sense of humour
- Desire to organize people and things, primarily through devising complex games.

(Webb *et al.* 2005, pp.4–5)

Hidden giftedness

We might imagine the gifted child to be the one who has their hand up and knows all the answers. We think of the musical prodigies, the children who speak multiple languages and can recite Pi. We do not think of the child who doesn't answer a single question during a whole lesson, who stares dreamily out of the window and who might put their shoes on the wrong feet. We do not think of the child who is bouncy and hyper, the child who everyone believes has undiagnosed ADHD. We certainly don't naturally link poor handwriting, distraction or challenging behaviour with giftedness.

The gifted child may not demonstrate their gifts at all in the classroom. Stephanie S. Tolan uses the metaphor of a cheetah to explain how a child's giftedness can become hidden in a school:

> The cheetah is the fastest animal on earth. When we think of cheetahs we are likely to think first of their speed. It's flashy. It is impressive. It's unique. And it makes identification incredibly easy. Since cheetahs are the only animals that can run 70 mph, if you clock an animal running 70 mph, IT'S A CHEETAH!
>
> But cheetahs are not always running. In fact, they are able to maintain top speed only for a limited time, after which they need a considerable period of rest. (Tolan 1996)

Tolan points out that

> certain conditions are necessary if it is to attain its famous 70 mph top speed. It must be fully grown. It must be healthy, fit and rested. It must have plenty of room to run. Besides that, it is best motivated to run all out when it is hungry and there are antelope to chase.
>
> If a cheetah is confined to a 10 × 12 foot cage, though it may pace or fling itself against the bars in restless frustration, it won't run 70 mph. (Tolan 1996)

You can see where she is going with this...

The gifted child does not come with a label stuck on their head. Their giftedness might not reveal itself to the teacher through schoolwork. In fact they might be infuriating to some teachers. Reports may highlight that the child is not achieving their potential – that they are 'lazy' because they are not handing in homework, daydreaming instead of listening in class and not doing the same beautiful cursive writing that they should be capable of.

Poor handwriting

The expert psychologists who wrote *Misdiagnosis and Dual Diagnoses of Gifted Children and Adults* reveal:

In our experience, the majority of gifted children have poor or mediocre handwriting. The explanation is generally simple; their minds simply go much faster than their little hands can write. Additionally many gifted children simply consider writing to be an unimportant skill. For example, if you can read what they write, and the purpose of writing is to communicate, why does it have to be an art form? (Webb *et al.* 2005, p.141)

Non-conformist rule testers

The gifted child may test rules and boundaries. They may put their creativity and problem solving skills to the wrong use and end up in the headteacher's office too often. They may frustrate teachers by disrupting when they are bright and should know better. The important thing is not to break a gifted child's spirit. Go with the giftedness, celebrate it and show you get it. Ignite their interest and have empathy for their individual needs.

The gifted child may be extremely non-conformist and appear difficult to teach, but when the gifted child has a teacher he respects and enjoys he can be the most wonderful, helpful and cooperative student.

Low self esteem and underachieving

Gifted children are not so rare, and it is our responsibility to nurture them, inspire them and support them.

The NSW Association for Gifted and Talented Children states:

Too many of today's gifted and talented children have poor self esteem or are tragically underachieving. They suffer from varying degrees of emotional, social, and educational deprivation and distress due to a lack of understanding of, and provision for, their needs by those responsible for their care.

Gifted and talented children may come from low socio-economic backgrounds, or from aboriginal, multi-cultural, physically-handicapped and learning-disabled populations.

Returning to that wonderful cheetah metaphor, Tolan rightly criticizes *all* schools for restricting gifted children:

Even open and enlightened schools are likely to create an environment that, like the cheetah enclosures in enlightened zoos, allow some moderate running, but no room for the growing cheetah to develop the necessary muscles and stamina to become a 70 mph runner. Children in cages or enclosures, no matter how bright, are unlikely to appear highly gifted; kept from exercising their minds for too long, these children may never be able to reach the level of mental functioning they were designed for.

A zoo, however much room it provides for its cheetahs, does not feed them antelope, challenging them either to run full out or go hungry. Schools similarly provide too little challenge for the development of extraordinary minds. Even a gifted program may provide only the intellectual equivalent of 20 mph rabbits (while sometimes labeling children suspected of extreme intelligence 'underachievers' for NOT putting on top speed to catch those rabbits!). Without special programming, schools provide the academic equivalent of Zoo Chow, food that requires no effort whatsoever. Some children refuse to take in such uninteresting, dead nourishment at all. (Tolan 1996)

Jacob Barnett

Kristine Barnett, author of *The Spark: A Mother's Story of Nurturing Genius* (2013), took her son Jacob Barnett out of his special needs school when the teacher showed that her expectations were so low she believed he would most likely never read. Instinct told her that she could reach her pre-verbal son Jacob, who was diagnosed with autism.

Jacob is now 15 and enrolled at Purdue for a PhD in quantum physics. He has given a TED talk,[1] published many articles and is tipped to be a future Nobel Prize winner.

Barnett explains how Jacob's education at home was led by his individual interests:

I would tell parents of any child to not be afraid to 'jump in' to their world. Do things with 'muchness'! To me this philosophy helped me very much in bringing out the colorful way that Jacob sees the world. I surrounded him and immersed him into the things that he loved and was drawn to as a child. I did not worry so much if they neatly lined up with any educational plan. I just set out to find what makes him truly happy and to do those things with him. Doing this gave me a peek into his mind and what I saw there was spectacular! (Quoted in Seaberg 2013)

What can teachers do?

First we must try to identify these children. We must keep in mind that 'not all smart children are gifted, and not all gifted children are geniuses' (Webb *et al.* 2005, p.2).

---

1   For more about the history of TED talks, which are free online videos or podcasts, see www. ted.com/about/our-organization/history-of-ted.

We must show them that we recognize and respect their brilliance and rebuild the bridge that may have been damaged by past teaching. We begin by building trust, getting to know exactly what will inspire the gifted child to want to learn *with* us.

Gifted and talented children, like all children, must be provided with educational structures, programs and provisions which motivate them to develop their talents and assist them to perform as closely as possible to their optimum levels. These structures, programs and provisions should also be designed to minimise the ill-effects arising from any lack of identification of gifted and talented children or from any lack of recognition of their special needs. (Farmer 2007)

The darker side of giftedness

In January 2015 Marcello Di Cintio wrote a startlingly brilliant article called 'For gifted children, being intelligent can have dark implications'. The case study that follows is discussed in Di Cintio's article and illustrates the difficulties gifted children can face.

CASE STUDY: Reed Ball

Reed Ball started playing Monopoly with his family at age three – and beat them. In the early 1980s, he was one of the first kids to have a 'portable' computer, a 10-kilogram Amstrad PPC512. Reed brought it to class until one of the school's bullies knocked it out of his hands and down a stairwell.

Reed was a math whiz, and used to correct his teachers' science errors. When they warned him he would get lead poisoning if he kept stabbing at his own arm with a pencil, Reed replied, 'Actually, it is graphite.' Just before he graduated from high school in 1991, Reed developed software for a major oil company that converted old blueprints into working documents. He began his studies for a degree in mathematics that September, but flunked out a year later. Then, when he was 21 years old, Reed Ball swallowed a bottle of sleeping pills. He died quietly with his pet kitten, Solis, beside him and his computer still on.

'Reed never fit in,' says Jennifer Aldred, one of his longtime schoolmates. 'My heart broke for him.' Aldred recalls Reed's math skills and his heavy computer, but what she remembers most about Reed was how he used to twist his slender body around the legs of his desk. He would tie himself into such knots that the caretaker would be summoned to rescue Reed by taking apart the desk with a screwdriver. (Di Cintio 2015)

Reed inspired his fellow gifted classmate Jennifer Aldred to follow a career in teaching gifted children:

> I will never know more than they do. They need teachers and programs that focus not on the magnificence of their brains, but on the fragility of their hearts. Unless their heart is intact, no learning can happen. (Di Cintio 2015)

CASE STUDY: Eli's answer

Eli was causing quite a storm in his little village nursery. The staff had never had a child like him. He seemed to enjoy creating chaos. Antics included throwing sand in other children's faces at the sand tray, knocking over brick towers, riding the tricycle directly into other children, tripping up, winding up, unnecessary noises during story time. The list of negatives went on…

His use of language was advanced. He was not afraid to ask questions loudly and his knowledge (especially of dinosaurs) was amazing. He was really bright.

'Was Eli ever quiet?' I asked. The teacher said he would sometimes spend long stints alone in the book corner. He loved looking through each book taking in every detail. He had a particular fascination with one book. I flicked through the book (*Don't Be a Bully Billy: A Cautionary Tale*) and saw what could be a problem. The story went through all the times when the central character 'Billy' bullied other children and ended with him going off with the aliens in a space ship. This story could be confusing. Eli was either getting ideas or trying to use it as a Social Story. The pictures only showed unfavourable behaviours and the book was not going to help Eli get it right.

I suggested that the teacher remove this book as it was not helping and replace it with Social Stories, which clearly illustrated behaviours people want to see at school. They could also use visuals to show Eli how to behave at the sand pit, on bikes and teach him how to build bricks and turn take with another child. They should praise other children getting it right in an obvious way so that Eli could learn the expectations.

I caught up with Eli's mum who told me about some of the things that Eli was finding difficult at nursery. Why did he hate going in so much? Eli's mum said that the teacher had stopped Eli from drawing pictures, telling him to scribble instead. 'Scribbling is how you learn,' the teacher had said.

Eli hated nursery and said the teacher was 'stupid'.

A month later I met with the teacher to see if things had improved. I asked her about the writing too, expecting her to say that of course she did not tell a child who wanted to draw to scribble, but she nodded, saying that the other children scribbled and Eli should be doing that too. The teacher then said that Eli was still looking at *that* book and still disrupting. She had not implemented any of the suggestions I'd made. It was as though she'd never heard them… I asked why and she explained that they could not do things differently for *one* child.

Sadly sometimes you realize that the best thing to do is move the child to a place that has more understanding of SEN children and a willingness to meet their needs.

Happily we found this setting for Eli and he has been supported brilliantly ever since. (Devine 2015)

CASE STUDY: A brilliant child with autism at a school for severe learning difficulties

Hal found school really difficult. He would ask to go home often, and his anxiety when demands were placed on him could result in the classroom furniture being thrown and turned over.

Hal had started off in a mainstream primary school and they did not cope well with his anxieties. This resulted in challenging behaviours and Hal being sent home. Hal had learnt to see home as his sanctuary, where he could get away from school.

Hal had not learnt to write because he could not cope with lessons or the idea of his writing not being instantly perfect.

Hal was extremely clever and had an incredible memory for facts. He had an amazing imagination and ability to create complex creations using construction toys, but there were never enough pieces for him. My instinct when I met Hal was that we needed to build trust. I'd have loved to start teaching him to read and write, but there was a lot of fixing to do before that could happen. Reading and writing would have to wait until we had built trust. My instinct was that Hal needed more to construct with. We sat together at the computer looking for the perfect construction materials. Hal was enthusiastic and told me about Mobilo®. I'd never heard of it. Together we chose a big set and I ordered it. Hal loved the Mobilo and could have used more and more… If only class funds would stretch!

As I taught cookery to the class Hal said that he did not see the point. I totally understood. Why would he want to learn to make a sandwich when there were military strategies to discover? I explained that I knew he could make a sandwich, but I wanted him to learn to sit with his classmates and that we might need some creative ideas for what to put in the sandwich.

When it was playtime Hal wanted to do research. I explained that he needed to have breaks from research to keep his mind working brilliantly. Hal was a wonderful, gifted boy and his behaviour had led him to a school for children with severe learning difficulties. How I wished I could create the perfect school for Hal and other children in his situation.

Fragility

Gifted children find following the teacher's directions difficult – they may be extremely verbal and they may interrupt, contradict and refuse to follow. They may disrupt and not seem to deserve extra support and care. But gifted children are also fragile. They *do* have special educational needs. These children need to be nurtured; they need teachers who will learn with them and enjoy them. They need to develop their talents, but most importantly they need to learn resilience because it's resilience which will allow gifted children to become our international 'treasures'.

Lessons from our past

The history of education reveals how things evolve yet constantly move in circles.

Lord Chesterfield (1694–1773) wrote a series of instructional letters to his son. In one of these letters he wrote, 'Learning is acquired by reading books; but the much more necessary learning, the knowledge of the world, is only to be acquired by reading man, and studying all the various editions of them' (Chesterfield 2007).

Before we assess or adapt our current teaching methods, let us hear the amazing voices of past visual learners. Let us learn from them.

Gifted 'greats'

Through history there are countless examples of famous 'greats' who are now believed to have had undiagnosed learning differences. Psychologists have gathered evidence and put together profiles linking so many famous figures with conditions such as dyslexia, autism and ADHD. Many of our famous 'greats' are also documented as not having had a happy start to education. They may have had teachers who did not understand, engage or tolerate children with differing needs. These 'greats' were not the high flyers or over-achievers with glowing report cards. But they *were* the creative sparks, the live wires, who would make history.

Parents use these historic achievers as positive role models. Their profiles are both interesting and inspirational.

I believe that the achievements, problem solving abilities and creativity of many of these famous figures hint at giftedness combined with a visual learning style. Gifted visual-spatial thinkers will learn differently. Many may be given a dual diagnosis or perhaps even be misdiagnosed. With this in mind let us take a look back through history. Let us take a small selection from the many, many examples and read some of their insightful reflections. Let us imagine how they were viewed in school. Let us begin by learning and ensuring that the difficulties past gifted visual learners encountered are not still occurring in today's classrooms.

Leonardo da Vinci (1452–1519): Dyslexia?

The multi-talented artist, inventor, engineer, scientist and writer Leonardo da Vinci may not have appeared to have had such a bright future ahead of him when he was at school. Apparently da Vinci had strange spelling and a habit of writing backwards.

He also had amazing ability and was able to create incredibly detailed drawings.

Da Vinci is quoted to have said, 'There are three classes of people: those who see. Those who see when they are shown. Those who do not see.'

Did da Vinci's teachers see a gifted, visual learner or did they get hung up on his odd spellings? No matter what his learning differences were, no matter what his teachers' views were, da Vinci learnt to use his strengths. He had the determination and strength of will to keep learning, to practise and to make an amazing contribution to our world.

Da Vinci went from strange spelling and backward writing at school to being regarded as a genius. Da Vinci is quoted to have said, 'Learning never exhausts the mind.' Was da Vinci bored at school, exhausted learning things he didn't want to know about and desperate to escape and learn things of interest to him and relevant to developing his art? Da Vinci is also quoted to have observed, 'Study without desire spoils the memory, and it retains nothing that it takes in.' Look back at secondary school. How many lessons did we all sit through, learning sets of facts for exams, but taking away nothing useful or memorable? Were we really *learning*?

Thomas Edison (1847–1931): ADHD and dyslexia?

The famous inventor Edison was described as 'difficult' and hyperactive when at school, but he also had a huge thirst for knowledge.

Edison spoke up for other children who might be full of bounce, saying that education had to change:

> The mind of a child is naturally active, it develops through exercise. Give a child plenty of exercise, for body and brain. The trouble with our way of educating is that it does not give elasticity to the mind. It casts the brain into a mold. It insists that the child must accept. It does not encourage original thought or reasoning, and it lays more stress on memory than observation. (Quoted in Hakim 2007, p.1)

Niall Greene wrote a wonderful blog post-referencing Thom Hartmann's book *Attention Deficit Disorder: A Different Perception*:

> Those with ADHD are the Hunters of society... Scientists recently found a gene called DRD4 and some believe that it may back some of Hartmann's ideas. This gene, also known as the Thomas Edison gene because those with the gene tend to have unusually high intelligence and although not limited exclusively to those

with ADHD, has been found in many people displaying ADHD Traits. DRD4 is seen to have been a critical asset for the survival of ancient humans. If you were alive 10,000 to 50,000 years ago and happened to have this particular gene your chances of survival in the wild would have been greatly enhanced. If a family was hungry the hunters needed to be able to think outside the box, scan aggressively and be able to notice everything around. Today this is what is known as distractibility and is typically seen as a negative trait. (Greene 2015c)

Edison found a way to manage his learning differences, developing his great gift for problem solving. What better inventions could there be to excite a visual learner than the photograph, the motion picture camera and the light bulb?

So are schools now supporting talents? Not according to Greene, who states:

In my personal and professional experience the modern day school system as well as many adult work learning colleges and universities are failing to meet the needs of countless potential modern day Thomas Edisons. (Greene 2015c).

Alexander Graham Bell (1847–1922): Dyslexia?

Alexander Graham Bell, who would revolutionize communication, did not show the teachers 'typical' signs of future brilliance when at school. He had trouble with reading and writing and he was eventually home schooled by his mother. Was this because she saw that her creative, dyslexic son needed a different approach and that by staying in the school system he was losing his spark? Perhaps she instinctively knew that his self esteem needed to remain intact if he was to fulfil his potential. Bell's mother's approach must have been successful because he was able to put his gift for problem solving to great use as an adult by changing the way the world would communicate. He invented the telephone.

Today we still hear of many children for whom a school is not working out or able to meet their 'individual needs'. There are bright children who are too academically able for special needs schools and too non-conformist for mainstream. Was Bell like this?

Bell once commented, 'When one door closes, another opens; but we often look so long and so regretfully upon the closed door that we do not see the one that has opened for us.'

School may have closed the doors to Bell, which must have seemed quite tragic when he was such an eager learner, but then his mother started home schooling him. Working together, they took his education to another level.

Schools should be able to cater for, include and stretch children like Bell. Bright, boisterous live-wire children need other children to spark them and help them develop social skills. Education is about experiences, developing the abilities to relate to others and to cooperate. Children need other children to learn about these things. But many parents are still being forced into home schooling because a suitable placement cannot be found.

Henry Ford (1863–1947): Dyslexia?

Henry Ford, known as founder of America's industrial revolution and founder of the Ford Motor Company, preferred hands-on learning to reading. His different learning style did not hold him back or hinder his incredible success. Many people with learning differences become more adaptive and inventive. Ford once stated, 'Obstacles are those frightful things you see when you take your eyes off your goals.'

Knowing that differing learning styles such as dyslexia can run in families, it is interesting that Ford has a great-granddaughter called Anne who writes and speaks about her daughter's trouble with learning. She was also formerly chair of the board of the National Center for Learning Disabilities.

Ford is quoted to have said, 'You can't learn in school what the world is going to do next year.' How insightful and delightful is that quote!

Pablo Picasso (1881–1973): Dyslexia?

Picasso was open about his difficulties at school. His father encouraged him to develop his skills at painting. I love Picasso's quotes. They point to a rebellious original, who refused to be pinned down: 'If only we could pull out our brain and use only our eyes.' Picasso also once said: 'Painting is just another way of keeping a diary.' What a wonderful visual diary he left behind for the world to work out.

Albert Einstein (1879–1955): Aspergers Syndrome? Dyspraxia?

Einstein did not reflect on his school years in Germany as a time when he was sparked, inspired and stretched. Rote learning and authoritarian teaching styles did not suit Einstein, but he did want to further his education and go on to university.

Einstein left his school in Germany when he decided to follow his parents to Italy.

In order to gain the qualifications to get into university, Einstein needed to complete his formal schooling. This was when Einstein found the school which catered for his visual learning style. Einstein attended a school in Aarau where the visual teaching style was based on the philosophy of the educational reformer Johann Heinrich Pestalozzi. Pestalozzi 'believed in encouraging students to visualize images' (Isaacson 2007, p.55).

Einstein loved Aarau. 'Pupils were treated individually,' his sister recalled. 'More emphasis was placed on individual thought than on punditry and young people saw the teacher not as a figure of authority, but alongside the student, a man of distinct personality.' It was the opposite of the German education that Einstein had hated. 'When compared to six years' schooling at a German authoritarian gymnasium,' Einstein later said, 'it made me clearly realize how superior an education based on free action and personal responsibility is to one relying on outward authority.' (Isaacson 2007, p.55)

Einstein has been posthumously diagnosed with dyspraxia by some psychologists and with Aspergers Syndrome by others. Reading about his life and reflections on his schools leads me to believe he was also another of our gifted visual thinkers. Einstein observed, 'We can't solve problems by using the same kind of thinking we used when we created them'. Schools were originally created for children who would live in a very different world. Schools taught sets of facts from books. Information was not available at the click of the button. There was no internet, no mobile phones, no Twitter… Einstein's observation is so crucial.

But Einstein did find a school where the teaching finally sparked him, rather than frustrated him. So let us delve further into the philosophy behind this school and the education model thought up by Pestalozzi that got such applause from Einstein.

Let us look at was happening in the Aarau school. Let us see if the educators of the past found answers which we can still apply today.

Chapter 4

Visual Teachers

Past and Present

Even if I knew that tomorrow the world would go to pieces, I would still plant my apple tree.

Martin Luther (1483–1546)

Learning from past educators

In Chapter 3 we looked at gifted 'greats' from our past. Education does go in circles. The longer you teach for, the more you see this. I wondered if way back there was a teacher who was already finding solutions and new ways of teaching. Albert Einstein had chanced upon a school that suited his learning style. Let us look further into this man, Johann Heinrich Pestalozzi, and the theory behind the school that suited Albert Einstein.

> Pestalozzi's method was used by the cantonal school in Aarau that Albert Einstein attended, and which has been credited with fostering Einstein's process of visualizing problems and his use of 'thought experiments'. Einstein said of his education at Aarau: 'It made me clearly realize how much superior an education based on free action and personal responsibility is to one relying on outward authority.' (Quoted in Isaacson 2007, p.65)

Johann Heinrich Pestalozzi (1746–1827)

Johann Heinrich Pestalozzi was a Swiss social reformer and educator. He believed in the education of the whole child, in seeing each child as an individual and that education should not be elitist, but open to everyone. Pestalozzi was heavily influenced by Jean Jacques Rousseau. Rousseau insisted on 'knowing the child before attempting to teach. And knowing the child means freeing the child from the rationalistic constraints of education. It is this point that has influenced nearly all subsequent education writers, including Montessori, earning Rousseau the appellation, "Father of Modern Education"' (Kirkpatrick 2008, p.53).

Pestalozzi's approach has had massive influence on education, for example, his influence, as well as his relevance to education today, is clear in the importance now put on:

- The interests and needs of the child

- A child-centred rather than teacher-centred approach to teaching

- Active rather than passive participation in the learning experience

- The freedom of the child based on his or her natural development balanced with the self-discipline to function well as an individual and in society

- The child having direct experience of the world and the use of natural objects in teaching

- The use of the senses in training pupils in observation and judgement

- Cooperation between the school and the home and between parents and teachers

- The importance of an all-round education – an education of the head, the heart and the hands, but which is led by the heart

- The use of systemised subjects of instruction, which are also carefully graduated and illustrated

- Learning which is cross-curricular and includes a varied school life

- Education which puts emphasis on how things are taught as well as what is taught

- Authority based on love, not fear

- Teacher training.

(Johann Heinrich Pestalozzi website n.d.)

Pestalozzi's theory would form many of the fundamental ideals to shape good teaching practice, but has the theory continued into practice? This list sounds incredibly familiar to the way we now teach in schools for children with special educational needs (SEN) and it is clearly visible in the Montessori approach, but is it still holding true to what is happening in our mainstream schools? I hope so.

In her book *Creativity for 21st Century Skills: How to Embed Creativity into the Curriculum*, Jane Piirto writes:

Darwin saw evolution as a branching tree. Einstein pictured what it would be like to fly next to a beam of light. 'If a person could run after a light wave with the same speed as light you would have a wave arrangement, which would be completely independent of time.' Einstein learnt to make visual thought experiments at his high school in Aarau, which was run on the Pestalozzi theories that, 'Visual understanding is the essential and only true means of teaching how to judge things correctly.' (Piirto 2011, p.90)

Pestalozzi, the 'father of pedagogy', is also known to have believed in studying teaching as a subject in its own right. Education is a separate branch of knowledge. Initial teacher training is just the starting point to a teacher's training. Teachers continue to learn from their students, from other teachers and from the many professional courses they attend.

Maria Montessori (1870–1952)

Dr Maria Montessori was an education innovator, influencer and believer in children. She was academically gifted, highly intuitive and curious. She became interested in how the environment influences a child's learning, and this led to her life-long passion, which had a transformative effect on education.

> Maria Montessori was profoundly influenced by Friedrich Froebel, the inventor of kindergarten, and by Johann Heinrich Pestalozzi, who believed that children learned through activity. She also drew inspiration from Itard, Seguin and Rousseau. She enhanced their approaches by adding her own deeply felt belief that we must follow the child. One does not teach children, but rather creates a nurturing climate in which children can teach themselves through creative activity and exploration. (Kennedy n.d.)

When she started working in a mainstream nursery Montessori found alternative ways to get the most out of children, inspiring them to *want* to investigate, create and explore. She knew from her experience engaging children with learning difficulties that there were other ways to approach educating children.

Part of the Montessori approach is not to stream children by age, but to group them together in a three-year age mix. Thinking of our own children's school transitions in the mainstream system, this makes a lot of sense. One of our children made friendships with children in the year below and the other two like to play with older children. They make these links during preschool, but once in infant school they are put into year groups. Montessori believed that children benefit from having a three-year age range. This way the younger children have older role models and the older child has a chance to develop greater self confidence, catch up, reflect on the stages of learning or develop leadership skills.

In special needs schools children are not usually grouped by age, but by ability and learning style. Rather than pool children together we think about the individual child and which group of children they will work best with. We think about role models, friendships and individual needs.

Montessori teachers spend significantly less time teaching to the whole class than mainstream teachers traditionally do. They spend more time travelling around interacting and engaging children 1:1 or in small groups as the children become involved in exploring and creating their individual projects.

I have a wonderful cousin, Carrie, who is a teacher at a Montessori school in Colorado, USA. We are passionate about our teaching and often share ideas via Skype. We have both observed so many similarities between the Montessori approach and the way we teach in special needs schools. It is interesting to me that Montessori began shaping her ideas for changes in education when teaching children with learning difficulties.

Montessori was ahead of her time – an inspirational voice. Her starting point was not to raise grades, but to observe children and see how they learn. She realized just how incredible children are at building on their own learning when they have well-chosen resources and the freedom to explore and create. 'Education should no longer be mostly imparting knowledge, but must take a new path, seeking the release of human potentials' (Montessori 1966).

We need to teach children to have the confidence to take a leap, to make connections and to get creative so that they can really make a difference to the world.

Montessori schools are always popular. Maybe it would be as well for decision makers in education to go and observe some Montessori school teaching and special needs teaching and see if this leads to considering adaptations to mainstream teaching. Maybe a lot of the methods which would engage our new, highly visual generation are already working in some schools?

Teaching styles

Good teaching will involve a balance – catering for visual, auditory and kinaesthetic learning styles. All styles should be properly catered for when teaching a mixed group. It is also true that knowledge of the individual child will give that child the power to achieve their personal best. A good teacher will be aware of exactly what the learning styles are of individuals in her class so that she can play to their strengths. She will adapt her style and questioning to increase confidence and provide a level of stretch that suits the child.

Empathic teachers

A good school needs a balance of skills, and also a balance of teaching and leading styles. We all recall the teacher who 'got us' and the teacher who sidelined, ridiculed or bossed us.

The teacher, author and education consultant Sue Cowley recently published a blog post titled 'You cannot be serious':

> When I think back over the education I had myself as a child, and the education my own children have so far received, it's easy to highlight the kind of things that got us learning. It has never really been about the systems schools use, or the methods teachers choose. It has always been about people: the great, beating heart of humanity. The teachers who got me and my children learning (and, perhaps more importantly, sustained our love of learning) were warm, kind, funny, approachable, caring, strict when needed, flexible when required, clever, creative, imaginative, inspirational and all those other wonderful attributes that the best teachers have. But they were always, always first and foremost flesh and blood human beings. They were people who could have some fun when the situation merited it, because they did not take themselves too seriously. (Cowley 2015)

I was intrigued and contacted Sue Cowley to ask if she had a visual-spatial learning style, and she responded: 'I do tend to "see" things such as words, numbers, ideas in my head, and I'm quite strong spatially, as I originally trained to be a dancer' (personal correspondence).

Visual teachers

Are current trends in classroom requirements limiting our visual learners by deterring teachers who also have visual-spatial learning styles from staying in the classroom? Teachers now have to adhere to so many tick boxes that they have to provide multiple plans and cannot go so much on instinct and child interest as they could in the past. This 'tick box culture' has now crept into special education, but it seems there is a lot less creative freedom in mainstream schools. Teachers are observed regularly to ensure they fit with exacting standards and tick boxes. They are measured by their students' ability to tick academic boxes, but they are not given the time or freedom to adapt to learning styles.

A teacher with a visual-spatial learning style might be an ideal fit for the child with this same learning style, but are schools conditioned to allow these teachers freedom to keep doing what they are good at? Adults who are visual-spatial thinkers 'are the ones who question the rules...'; they are also the ones 'whose thinking is likely to be particularly inventive... Others view them as disorganized or scattered in their work. Their tendency to leave tasks incomplete is not likely to be viewed as acceptable, at least not by methodical teachers or bosses' (Webb *et al.* 2005, pp.20–21). Oh, how I can relate to that!

The way teachers are currently expected to work does not fit so well with the character traits of the visual-spatial thinker. Schools need teachers who will follow set expectations, but they also need those who want to invent, to push boundaries and to create. Children need these teachers. We must ensure the inventive, creative, problem solving, non-conformist teachers remain in our schools, which may mean shifting some expectations and listening to teachers whose ambitions do not include climbing the career ladder. These are the teachers with a vocation who want to stay in the classroom directly guiding and shaping the children they care for so completely.

I am a visual-spatial thinker. I am constantly inventing, thinking of new angles, adapting, going off plan and suiting lessons to our individual children. I am very lucky to teach in a school where my curiosity and creativity are encouraged and seen as an asset. Our headteacher does not fear a new idea (which is lucky, as our teaching team have a lot). As well as classroom teaching I have been given the role of 'Research Co-ordinator'. I get to investigate my ideas and share them with the Research Co-ordinators in other special schools. I get to sift through education magazines and, when something might help advance teacher practice, I photocopy the article for the other teachers. I love this role.

In special needs schools we have smaller classes and are more led by individual ability, interest and learning style. Our planning has to be adaptive and our resources are most often handmade to link with interests.

Are our visual-spatial thinking teachers more likely to be found in special needs schools, where they have more freedom to invent? If that is so it seems a terrible shame that the many mainstream children who share this way of thinking are missing out on having those teachers who 'get them' because those teachers do not fit inside the mainstream box.

Sue Cowley also observes:

Maybe it's just me, but it feels like education has gone all po-faced in recent years. We seem to believe that everything must be measured, analysed, specified, standardised, turned into data that someone can input into a spreadsheet. We have started using words like 'metrics', and phrases such as 'opportunity cost'. We have begun to talk like accountants and economists. We pick apart the minutiae of this method or that method, claiming that research will tell us exactly which one to use. I read entire blog posts about teaching, that do not contain the word 'children'. We seem to have lost sight of the fact that learning is slippery, complex, nuanced, elusive and uncertain. (Cowley 2015)

The authors of *Misdiagnosis and Dual Diagnoses of Gifted Children and Adults* explain, 'When an intense, sensitive, and visual-spatial gifted child is put with an auditory-sequential teacher or parent, the interaction can be like mixing oil and water' (Webb *et al.* 2005, p.20).

Our differing visual learners who are coping enough to tick those academic boxes are being educated in that oil–water mix.

All teachers must teach so that the visual learner has an equal chance of excelling. They must ensure that schooling does not turn a learning difference into a learning disability.

Think of that old tradition in nursery schools where children bring things in for 'Show and Tell'. Hold on to those words. As children progress through education they continue to require both the 'show' and the 'tell'.

Are you a visual teacher?

Teachers must first understand their own learning style to ensure they do not teach children who learn like them brilliantly, but fall short when it comes to learning differences. We are bound to relate our own experiences of learning to the way we teach. We will present ideas to children in the way that worked for us. This could cause problems and must be addressed.

So the first thing is to do a little self assessment. Are you (the teacher) a visual-spatial learner? The quiz below was created by Linda Silverman and is a quick tick box way to self assess.

Are you a visual-spatial learner?

		Yes	No
1.	Do you think mainly in pictures instead of words?		
2.	Do you know things without being able to explain how or why?		
3.	Do you solve problems in unusual ways?		
4.	Do you have a vivid imagination?		
5.	Do you remember what you see and forget what you hear?		
6.	Are you terrible at spelling?		
7.	Can you visualize objects from different perspectives?		
8.	Are you organizationally impaired?		
9.	Do you often lose track of time?		
10.	Would you rather read a map than follow verbal directions?		
11.	Do you remember how to get to places you visited only once?		

		Yes	No
12.	Is your handwriting slow and difficult for others to read?		
13.	Can you feel what others are feeling?		
14.	Are you musically, artistically or mechanically inclined?		
15.	Do you know more than others think you know?		
16.	Do you hate speaking in front of a group?		
17.	Did you feel smarter as you got older?		
18.	Are you addicted to your computer?		

If you answered yes to ten or more of the above questions, you are very likely to be a visual-spatial learner.

Source: Silverman (2002). Reproduced with permission of the author.

Research

In a blog post titled 'Why your students forgot everything on your PowerPoint slides', teacher Mary Jo Madda, Associate Editor for EdSurge, who previously taught middle school maths/science and, most recently, served as an Education Entrepreneurship Fellow at the Harvard Innovation Lab, explains that teachers should not be reading from PowerPoint slides because having both written and verbal information at the same time overloads the student. She points to research that shows written visuals hinder success whereas pictures help:

> Richard Mayer, a brain scientist at UC Santa Barbara and author of the book 'Multimedia Learning', offers the following prescription: Eliminate textual elements from presentations and instead talk through points, sharing images or graphs with students. Other studies, such as a separate Australian investigation by Leslie *et al.* (2012), suggest that mixing visual cues with auditory explanations (in math and science classrooms, in particular) are essential and effective. In the Leslie study, a group of 4th grade students who knew nothing about magnetism and light learned significantly more when presented with both images and a teacher's explanation than a separate group which received only auditory explanation. (Madda 2015)

Picture a teacher handing back work to a class. There's a student in the room who has put their heart into a piece of creative writing. They are expecting a great comment about their original take on the subject. The teacher hands them an essay covered in angry red pen. They see fail after fail after fail, and so do the rest of the class. That red pen may as well be a great big sign saying 'CAN'T'. But underneath all that red pen there is something amazing that a good teacher would have spotted. There is an original idea.

In a blog post titled 'A dyslexic author's writing tips for dyslexic kids', the children's author Tom McLaughlin suggests that young people with dyslexia should 'never be afraid to think visually'. He goes further, advising: 'If anyone goes at your work with a red pen, grab it off them, snap it in two and throw it out of the window, then ask them to read what you have written, rather than correct it. Corrections can come later, when you have bought them a new red pen'. Brilliant advice Mr McLaughlin! Children with learning differences do not need a red pen pointing out errors. They need teachers who see their brilliance.

McLaughlin states, 'Being able to spell has nothing to do with being a good writer. Being able to know how a car engine works, doesn't make you a racing driver. It's about having something to say. It's about feeling the wind in your hair' (McLaughlin 2015).

When a child does not reach milestones or fit into social norms, when these differences are first flagged up or when a child is given a diagnosis, what most parents will now do is go to an internet search engine, such as 'Google', and type in the symptoms or the diagnosis.

Parents are opening the door to a minefield of information and personal experiences. They will find medical information, blogs written by parents and reflections of adults who live with that condition. The internet provides a never-ending pool of information. A lot of it is wonderfully helpful, but there is also the incorrect, the exploitative and the negative.

When a child starts school many parents will already have, through research and personal experience, gained expertise in their child's specific condition because that child is their world.

It is generally recognized that mainstream teachers are not given access to training to teach children with specific learning differences. A mainstream teacher will not know everything about every condition. That would not be possible. Teachers learn on the job. They are constantly learning, and the best teachers learn most from the children they teach.

That said, a newly qualified teacher can be quite brilliant. Teaching is a vocational profession, and many will start off with the most incredible instinct, empathy and passion. They listen and learn quickly, which helps every child in their class achieve their best. They love each individual child and children instinctively pick up on this.

Not every teacher will have experienced teaching a child with Down's Syndrome or autism and not every teacher will know how to spot the child with dyslexia or dysgraphia. Even if a teacher knows a bit about the labels, all children are individuals – they are all different, and there is no *one* way to teach them.

However, there are strategies that every teacher should have up their sleeve. There is knowledge every teacher should have. Every teacher should at least have an understanding that these different learning styles exist. They must know that there will be children whose attention will wander if they give lengthy explanations; there are children who need to get up every so often to remain focused and children who will recall lessons better when they have been an active participant; and there's the child who will remember a diagram with pictures of kings, but not be able to process a long list of names. Then there's the child who cannot learn something unless they know the reason it is being taught. These children need to see the point in listening, to know how it will help them in life. There's the child who needs to know the exact expectation of the teacher and will experience extreme anxiety if a demand is not in their zone of comfort. And there's the child who immediately clocks a difference on a visual schedule and will not be able to focus on anything else without an explanation for that change. They may not show or tell it, but they *feel* anxious about it.

A condition or diagnosis does not make a child a visual learner, but if a child is diagnosed with a condition commonly associated with having a visual learning style there are strategies which are likely to help.

Teacher knowledge of different approaches will enable more children to reach their potential, and complete education with their self esteem intact. Whatever a child's learning style, our first priority must be to build confidence and protect children's self esteem.

Henry Ford is quoted as having said, 'The man who thinks he can and the man who thinks he can't are both right. Which one are you?' It is up to teachers and parents to help the boy grow up to become the man who 'can'. My grandfather Stanley Quenet, who was a chief engineer, had a mantra: 'If he can do it, I can do it.' He repeated it so often that it has stayed with all his grandchildren and we will pass it on to his great-grandchildren. What a wonderful, positive legacy to leave!

Chapter 5

First Impressions!

How We Introduce Literacy Can Help Develop a Positive Attitude to Learning

Education is not the filling of a pail, but the lighting of a fire.

William Butler Yeats (1865–1939)

Keep up with expectations

Advances in technology constantly up the ante, raising children's expectations, and we teachers must embrace this as an exciting new challenge. Children expect colour, entertainment and excitement on a grand scale. It is up to us to ensure that they get the same feelings of anticipation when they see us lift up a book as they do when they discover a new App for their iPad.

Ever-improving technology creates incredibly high standards. Children today are used to fast-moving computer games with amazing graphics. At home they may access a DS, a Wii or an iPad. Look how the pace and colour in children's films has changed. They don't *do* long pauses where nothing happens or expect to sit through the credits without additional entertainment. Can teachers compete with this and make the big book seem as alive, interactive and exciting? We gain their attention by being as bright and exciting as the presenters they see on television. We must make them want to watch while remembering there is a delicate balance to be struck. We must also retain their respect by being 'real'.

Before we can expect a child to communicate creative thoughts through speaking or writing, we must first gain their attention. We must seem so interesting and entertaining that we sustain their interest and enthusiasm for the next stage. The spotlight is on. Our initial expectation will be that the children become engaged and involved by what they see.

The storyteller's hat

First, I suggest investing in an outrageous storyteller hat (the bigger, bolder and more outlandish your hat is the better). Maybe you could be a storyteller with a big top hat covered in letters? Choose something fun that will spark the children's imagination. The idea is that, rather than tell the children it is time for literacy, the hat will become a visual cue.

Figure 5.1 *A great storyteller hat is likely to get the children's attention*

I have a 'Mad Hatter' top hat from a fancy dress shop, which I decorate to match my story. Invest time in choosing an exciting hat and learn to love it. View the hat as a costume that will help transform your literacy lesson into street theatre.

Put on your hat and get out your box of tricks and you will spark the children's interest so that they will come to you. Get support staff to gasp excitedly and point you out and then come and sit around you. Their anticipation and excitement will help create the mood. Explain this to them before you begin. The silly hat and mystery box should spark the children's attention. They must want to know what you are about to do.

A box of tricks

Next you need some props to match your hat. You will need a box, a bucket or perhaps a sack (depending on your chosen theme). Decorate it with coloured paper or paint to make it extra interesting. You could fill it with clues to your story – for example, for Goldilocks and the Three Bears you could have a bowl, a little chair, a blonde doll, etc. Or you could add things that all begin with the same letter.

Save the magic theme as this can be a fantastic starter for 'knowledge and understanding of the world' or science. In science you can wear a magician's hat, wave a wand and create potions in a cauldron.

Watch an episode of CBeebies' *Something Special* on YouTube and see 'Mr Tumble' to get an idea of the sort of characters children like. Be fun and animated with minimal speech and more action.

Building interest and encouraging good sitting

Choose a child who is sitting well to take something from the box. Say out loud, 'Hmmm, I'm looking for someone who is doing good sitting.' Use Makaton signs for looking and sitting and have a visual showing a child sitting as you are hoping that they will sit. Adding signs and symbols offers the child who has trouble processing language additional visual cues. They will also learn by watching what support staff and other children do. You have become a character, and they are much more likely to comply because they want what is in your magic box.

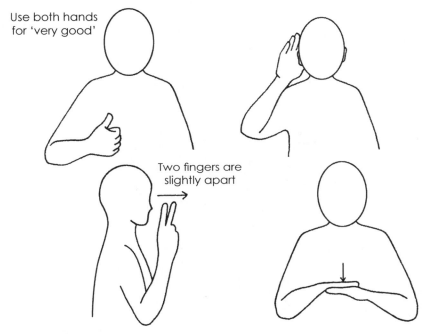

Figure 5.2 *Makaton line drawings of signs for 'good', 'to listen', 'to look' and 'to sit'.*

Figure 5.3 *Symbols for 'good looking', 'good listening' and 'good sitting' by SEN Assist (available to print: http://senassist.com/resources.html)*

The children will soon get to know your expectations, but you are not telling them what to do in an authoritarian teacher way. You are not setting 'rules', but following them. You cannot choose the child who isn't sitting with the group because you *have* to choose someone who is doing 'good sitting'. Speak your thoughts aloud, following your gut instincts (if you think a child just needs a little extra prompt): 'I'd love to choose Jimmy. If only he was sitting well I could. It would be sad if anyone had to miss getting a turn.' Allow the non-cooperative child time to process, and if your activity is engaging enough they should come and join the group. Do not engage with the child any more if they do not join in, but give the other children lots of attention and praise. More than likely Jimmy will decide to join in, but if he doesn't, have a support assistant ready to redirect him to something else. Do not create a conflict. If Jimmy is not motivated by your mad hat or your box of tricks, think of something else that *will* spark his interest. What does he like? If you have a resistant learner it is worth investing time in thinking about what would make him really want to have a look or take a turn.

Figure 5.4 *This mystery box was made from an A4 paper box with a hole cut in the lid. It was covered in coloured paper.*

Select a child quickly and let them feel for an item in the box. Do not let the child keep the item because this will create a distraction. Have a set place for them to add their item to a display. I still remember the letter tree with hooks for hanging different things that began with that letter in my preschool. These are age-old teacher tricks. You can buy magic hats, resource sacks and sets of props if you have the budget. If there is no budget then get creative. Cover boxes in wrapping paper and make a hat. Maybe you have great sewing skills or could enlist the help of a crafty classroom assistant or friend?

I have a set of coloured boxes I bought in a charity shop. Each one is a different size and colour. I put small things in the box to link with our term's topic. If, for example, our topic is 'journeys and transport', the little boxes will contain cars, trains and helicopters. To add interest I will include really motivating little toys like a tiny remote control car from Disney's *Cars* film. Find props in charity shops or on eBay. Think of things that will motivate individual children: a light-up sensory toy, a tank and toy soldiers, a wind-up Thomas the Tank Engine. They have to really want to see what's in those boxes. Motivation is the key! If some of the class are pre-verbal they may use the Picture Exchange Communication System (PECS) to choose a certain box (there is more information on using PECS with pre-verbal children in Chapter 11). The children will ask for a specific box using their method of communication. Mystery will spark their interest. They want to know what is in the box, and by being the one who gets to choose they become the director and somehow take ownership. The following week you can also assess the children's recall by having the same items in the boxes. But the week after that pre-warn them that the items and order might change. When you open a little box anticipate the contents as you would when opening a really exciting present. When you see the contents gasp in excitement, giggle, enjoy… Shut the box again – add to the anticipation, build up the moment. Have staff on board doing this as well. Have you ever seen how quickly a crowd can form when people stop to watch a performer or sales person? If you see someone else is interested you stop to look. If everyone else is walking past we make the assumption that there is nothing worth stopping for. With support staff we can create the same effect – staging interest as a sales person or street performer might. You will need to tell support staff to act excited before the session begins and explain why.

Some children can find sitting on the floor for too long really challenging, especially when part of a group. We are not only expecting the child to focus on the book, but to do this with a heap of other distractions. Other children may be causing sensory disturbance with their various noises, smells and wriggles. There may be visual distractions such as colour, light or other children's hair. So how do we get past this? How do we get the child to focus on the story and listen to the words?

We know that sitting on the floor with the whole class is not easy and that the book is not motivating them to stay put. So maybe we should flout convention and introduce the story without the book.

Most children are motivated by visual technology. If we are lucky enough to have an interactive white board or plasma screen then the visual learner will be so much more engaged if we present our story on the big screen. We can scan the pages of the book and add our own simplified text (as often big books can be very wordy). If we have a symbols program we might want to add symbols to some words as this will highlight that the words have meaning.

We may choose to ask our wriggly child to be the page turner because by doing so we will instantly remove the sitting issue. Our aim for the lesson is that they take in the story. Sometimes we get distracted and focus too much on the art of sitting still. If the child is able to sit for small amounts of time we can ask children to take turns to click the screen to turn the pages.

Figure 5.5 *A child using the computer to turn the pages*

If you have the budget, a video camera can be attached to the white board and you can instantly put your big book on the screen for the children to see. Once the camera software is installed you simply focus the camera on the page and it will show on the big screen. Text that is too wordy can be covered with simplified text. Point to words as you read and the children will see this projected on the screen.

If you don't have a white board then get some old boxes and use the cardboard to create a big book. The important thing is to make it bright and visual, and adapt language so that you use high frequency words. Often visual learners start reading by learning the pattern of individual words rather than sounding out words using phonics. Let the wriggly child stand up and be your page turner or 'help' by using a pointer to follow the words. Giving the child who has trouble sitting still a job to do will be so much better for their self esteem and help them get the most from the lesson.

CASE STUDY: Tom

Diagnosis: Autism

Turning the tables (literally)

Tom was a brilliant bouncy boy. We had two horseshoe-shaped tables in our classroom. The idea was that the teacher would sit in the middle of these with the students around her. The shape of the combined table allowed all children to reach the teacher, which was great when it came to using the Picture Exchange Communication System (PECS).

Tom always chose to sit at the flat bit and did not want to sit on the curve. The difficulty with this was that when we came to use the white board, or if I was modelling an activity for the class, he couldn't see. Tom was adamant though. If he was going to sit, he wanted to be at the end.

My support staff were aware that sometimes Tom needed to get up to bounce. Rather than try to keep him at the table I had asked them to give him the freedom to get up, go bounce and then return. This worked. He always came back, but the end of the table thing was more difficult. He needed to be able to see what was going on if he was going to learn.

That's when I realized there was a very simple solution. Before the next lesson I turned the horseshoe-shaped tables around. Tom came in and sat happily at the flat end and the other children happily sat around the curve. There was no sitting battle and everyone could see.

If a child is struggling to meet your expectations, evaluate what your expectations are. Is there a way to compromise? Sometimes there is an incredibly simple solution if we just stop and have a think.

Story time

Imagine a class of 30 children. The teacher has just read them a story about Red Riding Hood. Twelve of the children were listening intently taking in what she was saying.

'Who was the main character?' asks the teacher. Twenty hands shoot up.

'What did she wear?' Fifteen hands.

'Where did she go?' Ten hands.

One of the children has upped and left and is in the book corner. Another couple lost interest and are now being 'taught' in an adjoining room.

I'd describe this as a black and white lesson.

So let's add some colour...

The same teacher tells the same story, but this time she uses a big book with big pictures. Maybe she has puppets or other props. She hands out puppets so that some of the children have to hold them up when they see certain characters. After the story she gets children wearing masks and costumes to role play the story in front of the class. Everyone will get a chance to be in on the action. The children are peppered with smiles and praise.

She asks the same questions, but responses are much, much better. She has added a layer to her teaching and catered for more of the children.

Now let's make this lesson even better... The teacher starts off by drawing a schedule mapping out the lesson into three or four parts. She includes some sign language or Makaton at the start. Let's give the pre-verbal child who knows the answers the chance to show it with a visual communication system such as PECS. Let's give the child who finds it difficult to focus on the distant big book a smaller version of the same book with symbols above the words and a teaching assistant to encourage them to follow the words with their finger. Let's add some sensory elements – the children can feel the wolf's shaggy fur coat and experience chopping with a cardboard axe.

Suddenly the teacher is doing something amazing. She is including *all* the children. The only way a teacher can achieve a differentiated, inclusive lesson is by being aware of different learning styles and including the strategies to involve every learner.

Some children will be auditory learners, some visual and some more kinaesthetic, so when we teach a group we must cater for them all and allow strengths to develop.

Teachers fill in those evaluation boxes, but the good teacher does not stop at that written evaluation. The written evaluation ticks a box. Good teachers will reflect on lessons and judge them long after they have taught them. They will think about the *least* engaged child and try to work out how they could include them better. They will reflect, revise and adapt accordingly. Even the best teachers make mistakes, but they learn from them, improving each time.

Loving literacy

Whenever we introduce a new activity we must ensure we do it in such a way that sets *every* child up to succeed. First impressions are important. These children need a teacher who understands their individual issues and prioritizes happiness and wonder over ticking boxes. Observations and meeting targets are part of the teacher's job, but we must never lose sight of what really matters. Be overly positive, celebrate each victory and raise children's self esteem, because if they believe they *can*, they will.

The child's first impressions are important and there may not be a second chance. Before we begin to teach reading or creative writing we must first spark the child's interest. Children are used to such high levels of stimulation, visual effects and fun. Create a box of magic tricks and become a storyteller. Once we have their full attention they can embark on our adventure through a book. Along the way they will learn to use their imagination, create and communicate. As their self esteem soars they may develop their writing, typing or drawing skills to give their ideas permanence. We must always set the child up to succeed, by enthusing about what they can do and sparking their imagination. A child does not need to read to enjoy a story or do perfect handwriting to make one up. We must instil a love of the arts and build self esteem, then we will see what children can create. We must prepare amazing lessons and get it right from the start. If we can inspire a love of literacy by focusing on interests and 'can dos', the child could develop a love of books which will last them a lifetime.

CASE STUDY: A NEW CLASS

I remember my son, Donovan, going to school for his taster day in preparation for going up to Year 2. The children all have the opportunity to try out their new classrooms and spend the day with their new teacher. His new teacher, Mrs Stocchetti, greeted him with a warm, energetic smile and told him to give his book bag back to me. 'We don't need book bags today,' she said. 'Today we are just going to have fun.' Donovan seemed to grow an inch taller as he skipped through the classroom door. Thank you Mrs Stocchetti! I walked home happy as can be, knowing that for the next academic year our little man was going to be in the best hands.

Sir Ken Robinson rightly points out, 'Really good teachers inspire curiosity, provoke, set puzzles, stir the imagination and excite people so that they will learn' (quoted in Thought Economics n.d.).

We must engage children from the outset and make them want to learn along with us. First impressions are *so* important!

Chapter 6

Motivation to Learn

Finding out What Motivates the Individual Child Can Be the Key to Engaging Them to Want to Learn

The distance is nothing when one has a motive.

Jane Austen (1775–1817)

Getting to know what a child likes can be absolutely key to motivating them to learn. If a child likes trains, Disney princesses or sharks, we can use this in so many ways to spark interest, draw them in and make learning fun.

CASE STUDY: A farmer's son

I once tutored a child who was struggling at school. His mother was having great difficulty getting him to complete the mountains of homework he was bringing home. The first thing I wanted to know was what the boy liked. His mother couldn't really think of anything. When pushed she explained that he was a farmer's son. He liked the animals and being out on the farm, but couldn't see the point of school work. So there we had it. The animals and the farm, I explained, could be his motivator.

We needed to associate school tasks with farm tasks and show him that there was a point. We needed to get him thinking creatively about stories linked to animals or practical solutions to make the farm work better. We had to praise him for getting things right and build his self esteem. Learning had somehow become a negative, mundane task with a focus on a long list of 'can't dos' and 'not good enoughs'. He was on a slippery slope to not caring and needed picking up with fistfuls of positives and possibilities.

Motivation is key

A motivator removes the 'work' element from learning. We must begin by getting *every* child wanting to explore. We don't give them a pencil and expect them to immediately devote hours to forming letters correctly. We pick up the pencil and get excited about the possibilities. We talk about stories which are relevant to them. Think adventure and excitement and creating the atmosphere where the child wants to learn.

There is so much focus these days on ticking boxes and assessment, but when it comes to teaching children literacy we must not miss the vital point. We want to inspire them and get them thinking, because many of the greatest writers, inventors, thinkers and creators were not held back by not having perfect handwriting. We need to teach the practical skills, but we must not get bogged down in it.

These children are growing up in a completely different era, where in most jobs they will have access to computers which already highlight spelling mistakes and grammar errors.

We want the children to feel free to express themselves, to know that what they think and say excites us, that they are free to develop new words and safe experimenting with original ideas. Motivation is such a vital key to unlocking a child's creativity!

The greatest motivator

We must spark curiosity because being curious is the greatest motivator. Don't tell a class that they are going to learn about adjectives. Instead, bring in the most exciting up to date toy or gadget. Start to explore it excitedly. Make sure support staff know to come over to look and show interest. Think about how crowds form in market places. People get interested when they see other people interested. Tell staff you've borrowed the gadget and you only have it for today, but you want to write to the headteacher and convince him that you need one for the play area. Maybe a child will pipe up and say, 'I don't want one. It's rubbish.' Smile brightly and ask what they would want. Use the opportunity for a discussion. We must engage with our bright, non-conformist learners. They challenge things to test you. Enjoy the tests. Use them to engage the other children. Do other children have different ideas? What other gadgets are there like this? As great new words are used, write them on a big sheet of paper. Say, 'What a brilliant word.' Children will want their word written on the paper. See them try to outdo each other with creative thinking.

What was the plan behind this lesson? Where is the structure? What are the 'learning outcomes'? How can we know? A literacy lesson is a journey. Some of the most exciting journeys take us in new directions along paths less travelled.

The 'Genius Hour'

In a fabulous article called 'Creative confidence builds a strong future', Leigh Ann Whittle suggests:

> You know about setting time aside for math and science and even arts and crafts. But have you ever thought of building a Genius Hour into the day? More than just a time for kids to play, Genius Hour is an opportunity for students to follow their imaginations and build creative confidence – an important aspect of childhood development. (Whittle 2015)

What a brilliant idea! I'd love to add 'Genius Hour' to our timetable. Modern schooling is often accused of stifling a child's natural curiosity. If we had a set lesson where the sole aim was getting children to invent and create, then teachers would start to see just how much children *can* achieve when they are motivated.

Teaching with a cardboard box

I love sparking children to be creative. Whenever there is a delivery to school I make sure we get the cardboard box. A cardboard box can become literally anything. We've had rockets, buses, boats, secret hide outs, shops, stables. Children love to see a cardboard box transformed. I recall one Christmas when our boys ended up making cars out of the big boxes the presents arrived in. They spent ages decorating, discussing and then sitting in them delighted as we pushed them around the room. They got more out of the boxes than the presents. In our high tech world some parents may not incorporate this creative play into children's lives. It's up to teachers to ensure all children have this opportunity to create – to be a part of making something big and fun.

Figure 6.1 Hours of fun when a cardboard lawn mower box becomes a boat

Language development

- *Colours* – Children choose the colours to paint the box. Involve pre-verbal children in the discussion. Let them choose colours using pictures, switches, reaching or eye pointing.

- *Turn taking* – Being able to turn take is an important skill for speaking. Physical turn-taking games help children walk through the process. Let them take turns inside the rocket while the class count down: 'Ten, nine, eight…', or in the boat sing 'Row, row, row your boat…'

- *Role play* – Use boxes for role play. Make houses for the Three Pigs, or paint a bridge for the Three Billy Goats and stick it to the side of a table.

- *Puppet theatres* – Use a box to create a puppet theatre with scenery or a small world farm. I recall watching one of my techie students totally engrossed in creating an enclosure for his small world box farm.

- *Cooperation* – The children must learn to move around each other, to share the art supplies and to agree on what the box should be.

- *Sequencing* – Children must think about the order in which they do things. You could photograph the children as they progress and see if they can order these photos. They will be so much more engaged if they have been involved.

- *Requesting* – Do not have all the resources to hand. Make sure they either need to request the glue and the sticky tape or think about where the things are located and go and get them. Give them problems to solve themselves.

- *Commenting* – You can model all sorts of amazing language with your comments and encourage other children to make positive comments. Incorporate an abundance of verbs and adjectives in a clear voice.

- *Positional language* – What could be better than a box boat or castle for building prepositions such as 'on', 'in' and 'under' into the discussion? Be a bit silly. Make them laugh.

- *Encourage self assessment* – Is there anything they could do differently next time? Why? Teach them that mistakes are okay. It's through mistakes that we learn.

Moving on to Minecraft

The cardboard box idea is great for learners aged 3–6, but as children get older they are exposed to more high tech entertainment and gaming, particularly if they have older siblings.

I had just written the heading above when I realized our son Donovan (6) was standing behind me looking intrigued.

'Mummy, why have you written "Minecraft" in your book?' he asked.

'I'm going to suggest that teachers use Minecraft in their lessons.' Donovan's eyes lit up. 'Do you think that's a good idea?' Hugely enthusiastic nodding followed. 'Would you like your teacher to come in and talk about Minecraft or ask you how to build things?'

Next Donovan got his Minecraft book. 'I could show her how to make a cake. I could show her what to do. The instructions are here in my book.' Suddenly I knew my book had got a little street cred in Donovan's eyes. Isn't this what we want for our lessons? For the children who are old enough to assess lesson content to go away thinking, 'That was kinda cool.'

Minecraft (a computer game where people dig and construct using bricks) is a *big* motivator for children. It is also an amazing creative tool, with a never-ending supply of different building blocks and huge possibilities. We would be silly to ignore its potential as a teaching tool.

In June 2014, BBC News visited Holy Trinity School to show teachers using Minecraft in a literacy lesson. The literacy teacher explained how watching his own son, who was a reluctant reader and writer, prompted him to introduce Minecraft to his literacy lesson as a way in to teaching creative writing. One of the children explained why it was such a great motivator: 'Some games you've got to stick to boundaries, but on Minecraft you can go anywhere you want.' Santeri Koivisto, founder of TeacherGaming, stated that MinecraftEdu is going into 200 new schools internationally every month (BBC 2014).

Diane Main is a teacher at the Harker School in San Jose, California. She has been using MinecraftEdu with her students for the past two years. Her students have made amazing progress, especially when they can follow their individual interests. Main commented:

> When you have opportunities for creativity and more open-ended situations, it allows kids to figure out that they can try things, they can do things differently – there's not one formulaic way to do well in this class. A student told me after the class that he learned that first option [to solving a problem] isn't always the best option. And that's something you can't teach kids – they need to have the opportunity to experience it themselves. (Quoted in Ossola 2015)

YouTube videos

Most recently our boys have started wanting to watch YouTube videos of other people playing Minecraft. Why? Who are these teenage gamers becoming famous with the next generation? They are making money through videoing themselves playing games. What sort of example are they setting children? Having fun and making money. How dare they! But wait, is that not the best thing: making money doing what you love?

Chinese social philosopher Confucius wrote, 'Choose a job you love, and you will never have to work a day in your life'.

Are these Minecraft video gamers potential role models? Should we be talking about them in our lessons, if we know they are current and relevant to the group of children we are teaching?

I once heard a teacher complain that a child with autism was so absorbed in the 'Minecraft world' that he wasn't listening in her lessons. Hmmm, I wondered. Is that because Minecraft is more interesting, engaging and stretching than your lessons? Maybe that teacher should have taken the boy's interest, investigated and used it. Maybe after school the boy was busy home educating.

A child's individual motivator is our way in. If there is something that motivates a whole class we should use it.

Lego® education

Lego has always had amazing potential to teach visual learners. We've all been using it for years to explain concepts such as addition, fractions and measures in mathematics.

Lego therapy

Lego has now become so much more. When I attended parents' evening recently the teacher told us about the amazing success of their 'Lego therapy' sessions for building confidence, communication and self esteem in the children involved. Children are carefully grouped to increase confidence and raise self esteem. One child gives instructions encouraging speaking and leadership skills, whilst the other listens carefully and tries to follow them. The children have to communicate, listen, engage and cooperate to construct their Lego. What a fantastic idea!

Lego® spelling and sentence building

As our children start to outgrow their huge Duplo® and Lego collection I've been eyeing up the possibilities. I believe that a Lego brick should be eternally multifunctional, so I prefer to use sticky tape to apply letters and words. This way bricks could be restored to normal bricks or given another function.

Top ten tips for Lego or Duplo spelling and sentence building

- Use different-coloured bricks to highlight vowels. For example, have all the letters of the alphabet written on individual blue bricks, then use yellow for vowels. Use the bricks to make words.

- Use two different-sized Lego bricks so that a tall letter 'l' is on the side of a larger brick than a short letter 'a'.

- Teach upper and lower case letters with a small 'a' on one side of the brick and a capital 'A' on the opposite side.

- Draw words on a white board or paper and get children to build them. Use words linked with their high interests.

- Create your own reading rods using Lego so that children can copy sentences (again linked to high interests).

- Use different colours for adjectives, verbs and nouns. You could prepare these with the students in a lesson. If they are part of making them they will enjoy using them more.

- Get children to create a sentence and select the right colour for adjectives, verbs or nouns.

- Use longer bricks for longer words. Get children enthused about using a longer brick in their sentence.

- Teach alliteration, having two words with the same start on either side of the brick.

- Build silly sentences. Children pick adjectives, verbs and nouns from a pot and construct a sentence.

Figure 6.2 *Letters written on Duplo® to encourage letter recognition and High Frequency word building*

Lego® StoryStarter

Lego have created an amazing new kit for engaging visual and hands-on learners. The Lego Education website explains that StoryStarter is

> a hands-on tool that also inspires students to collaborate while creating and communicating their stories. It is an innovative way of teaching a wide range of essential skills, including:
>
> - Literacy skills, improving writing, language, and reading abilities.
>
> - Communication skills, including speaking, listening, and presentation capabilities.
>
> - Collaboration skills and pupils' ability to work in teams.
>
> - Comprehension skills and enabling pupils to compose new stories or analyze existing ones.
>
> - Integrating the use of digital tools via the unique StoryVisualizer Software.
>
> (Lego Education 2015)

Figure 6.3 *Children create a story together using Lego®*

Animation

Creating animations can be a great way to engage visual learners. It allows them to see their story become a film.

Animation can be used to encourage creativity and get children thinking up exciting stories without having the pressure of writing them down.

As well as Lego StoryStarter animations, there are some great animation software packages that children can use with modelling clay. The model does not need to be complex. In fact the simpler the better – a blob with pipe cleaner arms works well. The children could each create a monster and plan a monster party, or get each child to make a scare scene inspired by the film *Monsters Inc*. The children can create their own scenery, which again will involve discussion. Get the children working in pairs or small groups so that they need to plan and cooperate with each other.

Get them to analyse their completed animations. What mistakes did they make? What could they improve? What did they enjoy?

SEN Assist motivators

When we came to develop the Fairy Tales, which are described in more detail in Chapter 17, I knew that the first thing we wanted a child to do was select their individual motivator. Together we came up with 48 individual motivating characters based on what children like and sorted them into four categories – animals, transport, fantasy and people.

Exit CD

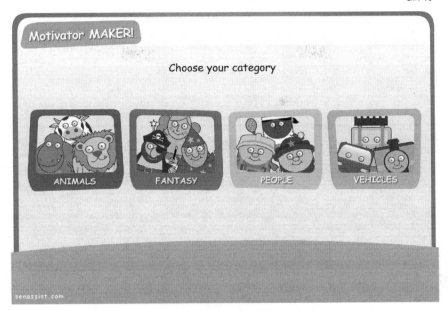

Figure 6.4 *Categories screenshot*

The first thing we wanted the child to do was select their motivator. Rather than saying 'Come and do some work', the teacher could say, 'Come and choose your favourite character.' Immediately we had something that would personally motivate that child. They had taken ownership and it was now their activity.

Their character would stay on the screen at all times, and when they completed a task it would give them a 'roar', a 'yay!' or a friendly 'toot'. A child's motivator can be surprising. I recall a little girl who chose a swimmer. When I mentioned this to her mother she told me how much her daughter loved swimming. I had no idea. Another pre-verbal nine-year-old boy consistently chose the blue fairy. From those 48 different characters he chose that blue fairy every single time. I would never have made that link, but he loved that fairy. When I included it in non-computer tasks he clearly recognized her and was motivated to complete them.

Figure 6.5 *More screenshots. The top one shows the 'Fantasy' motivators; in the bottom one, the child selects the 'Blue Fairy' motivator*

Once we know what motivates the child we can use this in oh so many ways. We can theme their schedule, their worksheets, the area where they work. Why do we decorate children's bedrooms with what they like? We want them to feel happy in their own space. We want them to enjoy being there and feel safe. When a child comes to school we want them to feel like this too. The classroom should be a happy, comfortable, safe feeling place.

We must take care to get the balance right because we do not want to overdo the motivators and cause a huge distraction. It's one thing to have a picture of a princess, but another to have every different princess covering the walls. We still want the child to be able to focus on a task.

CASE STUDY: New Year's resolutions

It was the first day of the autumn term and we were talking about New Year's resolutions.

I was asking the class and staff in turn about what they hoped to achieve in the next year. I was using the prompt 'I will try to...', with symbols on a sentence strip to add structure and some pictures of 'be kind', 'share', 'work hard', etc. I presented Callum with the picture cards to choose. He pushed them away. He made an attempt to get up from his chair. Callum could not balance enough to stand or walk without aids due to his Cerebral Palsy, but he could bear weight. I took his hands and helped him to stand, and seeing the determination in his five-year-old eyes I realized he was giving me an answer. I said, 'Callum will try to walk?' His smile said it all. 'And we will do everything we can to help you,' I resolved.

From then on everything I asked Callum to do had a connection to helping him walk. As Callum had no speech I had been trying so hard to motivate him to use pictures to communicate. He would usually react in much the same way as he had in that lesson. He'd push them aside and look away. I got Callum a four-button communication aid. I added the symbol and recorded 'walker', 'wheelchair', 'help' and 'more'. Callum had a lot of specialist equipment. He had a walker, a wheelchair and standing frame. When we transitioned anywhere I would show Callum the buttons and ask, 'Callum wants walker or wheelchair?' Every single time Callum determinedly pressed 'walker'. He never pushed this communication device away. He used the walker to go everywhere. We had some hairy moments in the town centre! All the time Callum's muscles and balance were improving and he now saw the purpose of communicating.

My next step was to try to get him a more comprehensive Augmentative and Alternative (AAC) device. I was so convinced he could use one now that we had sparked his interest. I was told in order for him to access such a device I would need to prove he could.

I asked my husband Quentin to help by creating a series of activities on the interactive white board. The first one was for Callum to press letters to correctly order his name. Callum would stand up from his chair and walk the short distance to the interactive white board (without his walker). When he selected the correct buttons his photo would appear.

Callum loved this activity. Quentin added other 'games'. The children would select the day of the week and weather. Callum consistently got it right. Callum was observed doing this, and everyone agreed that he needed access to a highly expensive communication device.

Callum took to the device straight away and wanted to explore it constantly. He pressed the buttons all the time, enjoying all the new noises he could make. It was wonderful to see him so excited by his new voice, but he needed to learn when to talk and when to listen. Taking away the device was not an option. Our usual visuals, requests, rewards and praise of other children were not working. Callum kept pressing and pressing buttons. We were secretly delighted, but held back our smiles. I discussed our new noisy Callum with my classroom assistant after school. What would we do if one of the other children decided to continually sing and talk during lesson time? The next lesson when Callum was pressing all his buttons, talking and singing non-stop I said, 'Quiet now. Callum must let other children listen.' There was a naughty twinkle in his eye. He was deliberately challenging us and having fun being able to. I loved seeing this spark, but we needed to regain some order for the rest of the class to learn.

I showed Callum a 'quiet' and 'good listening' symbol. Callum would have five minutes outside of the class if he couldn't follow this. Callum had clearly understood, but he did not want to stop. I did a countdown and sent Callum out of class. As he pulled himself up with his walker and walked towards the door, I felt incredibly proud. At the start of the academic year Callum had shown no interest in communicating and had always been pushed in a wheelchair, and there he was walking out of class independently because he had been talking too much.

Callum is 16 now and still at our school. Whenever I see him, walking along with occasional wobbles, but no walker, with his iPad at his side, I feel so proud and happy. What a determined little boy he was and how brilliantly he stuck to that New Year's resolution.

Charting progress on wall displays

CASE STUDY: A reading reward chart

In Year 4 of junior school our son's teacher introduced a visual reading reward chart. Each child had an aeroplane on the wall. Parents were to record daily reading in their child's reading records, which made the aeroplanes travel. I knew nothing about this until the night before parents' evening when I asked if there was anything I could say to the teacher. Was there anything that bothered him? Was there anything I could say that would make school better? That's when our son told us about those aeroplanes and how his had fallen off the wall. He had looked everywhere for it, but it was completely gone. He *had* told the teacher, but she'd said it didn't matter. I knew how much this would matter to our visual (and competitive) son.

So at parents' evening I mentioned the aeroplanes. The teacher said it didn't matter because they still had a written record. But when you have a visual learner with a competitive streak it's important to understand that charts like this on the classroom wall really do matter.

A warning about wall displays

Kathleen Jasper, a teacher, educator and author for the ConversationED website, wrote a blog post titled 'Shaming students one wall at a time', recalling 'an enthusiastic teacher' showing her around a school:

> My smile faded as I looked to my left and saw a huge bulletin board that said, *Ribbit Reading Progress*. On this bulletin board were 15 or so frogs with five segments. Some frogs were colored in a mosaic pattern – the head was green, the right arm was purple, left arm was green, right leg was purple, left leg was orange. I saw two or three frogs where the entire body, head and legs were green. Two frogs were completely orange. I knew right away, the orange frogs were the losers.
>
> Even though I knew the answer, I asked, 'What's with the frogs?'
>
> Proudly she said, 'It shows their reading progress. When a student can read a passage fluently in a minute, they color part of the frog in. Then we post the frog on the board so the kids can see their progress. If they improve, they get to go to the treasure box in the front office on Friday.'
>
> I took a breath and said, 'Let me guess, the green frogs are the winners and the orange frogs are the losers?'
>
> 'Well, I wouldn't say *losers*,' she said defensively. 'They just need more time and more remediation. And we use orange not red, because we feel red is a little too abrasive. We don't want to break anyone's spirit.'
>
> I smirked and said, 'Don't you think the owners of the orange frogs feel like losers when they look at this wall?' (Jasper 2014)

Libraries

Libraries are a fantastic resource and should be used so much more. Where else can you take children and tell them they can choose whatever they want? Take a child to a library with a big box. Tell them to put in it whichever books they like. Anything at all, as long as it's *free* (otherwise you might end up with a load of DVDs). Pick up books you think they might like and say, 'Oh look! A Spider-Man comic book', have a look and then put it back. Do not be tempted to force any books on them. Get out all the books in the box (you may need to use a couple of library cards). The box of books will be a good way of finding motivators.

Stickers and rewards

A great teacher should inspire children to want to investigate and create, but there is nothing wrong with using stickers, stamps or other rewards as long as they are used in the right way. Stickers, certificates and stamps are a visual way of saying that you are happy with a child. Stickers can also show parents that a child has done something good, which adds an extra positive layer.

A lot of children are really motivated by rewards, but some have no interest in them. Know these children. Get to know the best way to show them that you are really happy. Ask them.

Reward charts

Reward charts and token boards can be a great motivator for children who like to have a visual structure to break down expectations (particularly children with ASCs or ADHD).

Teachers use tokens or reward boards, but these must be used correctly. I've seen teaching assistants using tokens and forgetting about them, then suddenly adding them all at the end of a lesson or suddenly giving each child one for a tiny thing when they sense a meltdown is about to occur. Showing the child your expectations on the token can really help. This means everyone is clear of the expectations before any structured work begins. See the token board in Figure 7.2 (page 104).

Figure 6.6 *A token board with transport tokens*

Wows

In our nursery class we have a wall of 'wows', which are written whenever a child does something that makes us go 'wow'.

Photographs

We also have an 'I can...' display of photos of the children showing what they can do. At the end of each term we take the photos down and add them to the children's scrapbooks, creating a permanent record of positive 'can do' moments.

I like to add photos to the children's home/school books showing what they have done in the day. This is really good if you have a child with communication difficulties because it will get a conversation started at home, when their carer sees the photo and can talk about what they see.

Praise

Praise can be the most brilliant motivator, but it must be 100 per cent genuine or a child will see right through it. Your positive comments will stick. They may even stay with a child through life. Do not just direct praise at children. Tell other staff and parents about them when you know that the child is in ear shot.

Explain your praise

Think about how you word praise so that the child knows what they have done well.

> James did the most amazing sharing trains at choice time. He played so well with Isaac. He let Isaac have the Thomas train even though that's his favourite. What a good boy. I was so happy with James.

Or:

> Connor did something brilliant today. He went to his visual schedule and saw we were going to do art. He went to the art table and there was no chair. Connor went and got a chair from the stack and took it to the table, then sat down ready for art. I was so happy with Connor. What a clever boy!

While you relay these moments to another teacher or parent the children will be listening. This is so much more meaningful and memorable than a 'good boy'.

Use visual thumbs-up signs

When we were developing resources for *Colour Coding for Learners with Autism* (Devine 2014a), we created a host of visuals for thumbs-up symbols. These could be printed out and put up in areas where the children are likely to show the behaviour. When you say 'Good sand play Charlie', you can point to the thumbs-up symbol with a picture of a child at the sand tray. This allows the child who did not process your language, or who was too absorbed in sand play to hear, to get your meaning. They can have a look at the image combined with the thumbs-up and know that you are seeing something good. They will then link the way they were behaving with a positive. Next time they are at the sand tray they will look and note that visual, remembering the positive praise they got. They may try to get it again. Be sure to give it.

We must use whatever motivates the individual child. We must also learn to stand back and allow them the space to get creative. We should observe more and then we will learn more.

Chapter 7

Teaching Writing Right

Setting Them Up to Succeed, By Stepping
Learning to Meet Individual Needs –
Sandpaper Letters, Stamps and Pencil Grips

*Writing, the art of communicating thoughts to the mind through the eye,
is the great invention of the world…enabling us to converse with the
dead, the absent, and the unborn, at all distances of time and space.*

Abraham Lincoln (1809–1865)

Imagine a class of children standing on the side at the deep end of a swimming pool. They are all at an age where they are 'expected' to be able to swim. The instructor assumes that the teacher has done the checks, got those parental forms and that, when they say jump in and swim to the other end, all the children will be able to do this; but this is not the case. One of those children is new to the school. The deepest water he has experienced is up to his chest. He can swim, but has never experienced being out of his depth.

When the instructor says 'jump' the children jump, but the boy sinks to the bottom. He struggles up for breath, and when he surfaces he is met with angry eyes. The boy scared the instructor, and despite his relief the instructor is angry. What would this experience do to the child's water confidence, attitude to swimming, self esteem and ability to learn?

When we teach a child to swim we take small steps. At the first stage we build their water confidence. We may use arm bands, rubber rings or other buoyancy aids. We motivate with toys that float or sink, or familiar songs and games. We do not expect children to be instant swimmers. We are happy to give them any support so that they look forward to swimming and see it as fun – something they can do.

But there are children who miss out on this early 'building confidence' stage. As they get older they become more self conscious and aware of their own safety. They can't swim, but are embarrassed to go and learn because it's something their peers can do. They do not want to try in public. These are all reasons why the earlier we teach any new skill the easier it will be.

So when we approach handwriting it can be useful to keep that non-swimming child in mind. We do not want to set children up to fail. No matter what age they are we must teach them at the correct level and pace and also be aware of that group of peers. We must protect children's self esteem at all costs, because if they believe that they can, they will be more willing to try. Belief and hard work combined will create success.

Children can become extremely disheartened by handwriting tasks. I look at the reams of cursive letters my sons have done at school and imagine how their hands must have ached. What a mundane way to learn, yet their school books show they were willing. My son Malachy wrote in his year book that he 'loved handwriting', so his teacher must have worked some sort of miracle. She instilled in him that there can be enjoyment in grafting towards perfection.

Often children are willing to keep on practising because they want to form perfect letters. Maybe there's the motivation of social sameness or being able to move from pencil to pen.

But what about the child who finds writing extremely difficult, whose lack of fine motor skills make forming perfect letters almost impossible? What about the child who has a strong desire for immediate perfection and cannot see that there are stages to learning? Often the children who are going to need longer to learn to form letters are the ones who feel the need for immediate success. Frustration and anxiety may lead to angry outbursts and outright refusal to even try.

Creative writing

The foundations for creative writing form early when a child first starts to think, move, manipulate and explore. Creative writing begins with feeling curious.

Look at a child who is entranced with watching sand pour through his fingers. What are they seeing? Do a Google image search of sand magnified. Really, if you have not ever done this – look! The colours and the shapes are amazing.

Is it the look of the sand, the feel of the sand? What is it about the sand? These are the questions teachers need to be thinking about when they watch children explore. Not what are my aims and objectives, but what are theirs? What gets the child's interest, sparks their curiosity?

As children's thoughts become more divergent and links are made with real life, a child's explorative play may veer more towards manipulating toys. Maybe they will play with dolls or cars or trains or dinosaurs. At this stage other children and adults will get what they are doing, make links and join in. Maybe they will start to role play, dressing up and getting creative with their language skills.

But maybe the child will stay with the sand, and perhaps while that sand pours through their fingers they are working something out, like capacity, or perhaps the sand has become their focus because they know it and they trust it.

These early stages of play are the time when teachers must observe, but if a child's play gets stuck they can intervene. Intensive Interaction (see Chapter 14) might help the child at the sand pit. A visual Social Story™ might help the child who keeps running up to the other children so fast he knocks over their brick towers or bumps into them, as might a trampoline to get out some of that bounce. Maybe a child's not sure what to do with other toys. An adult could sit nearby and model playing with the cars, speaking the story as they play.

Play is so important because it's through play that children's ideas begin to develop, where they work things out, make connections, try things, succeed and sometimes fail. You can have an idea without all the play, but you will not be able to share it with the world.

Creativity

Children do not need masses of toys to get creative, investigate and explore. I recall as children the hours we would spend in the garden making houses, using leaves for bowls and crumbly wood for chicken. I remember watching the bumble bees delve into the foxgloves, fascinated. I remember trying to make the world's longest daisy chain. This is the sort of freedom that allows children space to think up ideas.

Story building

The ability to build a story begins when the child decides to introduce more actions and interactions to their play. They are taking the dolls for a walk in the pram. One of them is crying. Why is she crying? She needs a new nappy. Oh no! We've left the nappies at home.

They are pushing the Thomas train around the track, but then a lion jumps out. The zoo keeper traps the lion in a big cage.

Adults can model having these sorts of ideas. The child becomes the storyteller. They start to think of characters, events and outcome. They start to get creative.

Books

Sharing books and stories, pointing at the words and looking at pictures all help develop story writers. Most of our greatest authors had childhoods filled with books. They would read and read, and while they were reading they were learning to question, to think, to step into someone else's shoes. See much more in Chapter 9.

Writing is so much more than handwriting, and it is vital that teachers remember this. You could have the best creative writer in the whole school in your class, but never discover it if all essays had to be handwritten. Even typing could hold some students back. Think of the famous author Agatha Christie (posthumously diagnosed with dysgraphia). She may have had trouble with handwriting and spelling, but this did not stop her telling stories. She was home schooled and recalled a happy childhood filled with lots and lots of undisturbed reading time.

Art

Allow children to develop storytelling before they can write by letting them dictate. If a child has done a picture of a stick person, ask who the person is. What are they doing? Are they going somewhere? Write these things down. Show them that they can tell stories. They can make you laugh or frown or even shock you with their imaginations.

Show the child a painting and ask them what they see. Develop this with lots of questions. Do this with a group and see what they come up with. Write their wonderful ideas on a big sheet of paper so they see you writing them.

Draw in front of the child and see if they suggest additions. Offer them the choice of colours; allow them to set the scene.

So how do we start teaching handwriting?

The first stage in teaching writing is so distant from those formal handwriting sessions. To begin, we create activities that will strengthen the muscles the child will eventually need to use to properly hold a pen. We create fun activities to involve the child.

Strengthening hand muscles

'Ideally, the first materials used are not markers and pencils but materials that allow children to strengthen the muscles in their hands needed to properly hold writing implements,' says Mara Guckian, early childhood specialist and managing editor for Teacher Created Resources. 'We add a tactile (kinesthetic) component when we practice shaping the letters with different materials. Shaping letters with dough, tracing them on textured paper cutouts, and writing in the sand or salt trays all help children internalize the shape of the letter, while developing their fine motor skills.' (Geiser 2013)

Some activities that strengthen hand muscles:

- pulling and rolling play dough

- rolling and stretching theraputty

- finding dinosaurs in a ball of theraputty

- threading or lacing string through card

- copying hand actions in familiar songs

- building bricks or Duplo®

- opening packets, zips or buttons

- sorting objects with child-size tweezers

- pressing buttons or switches for cause and effect

- sorting shapes, peg boards or puzzles.

Try to make all of these activities motivating. For example, if a child likes bugs, give the threading a mini beast theme, hide plastic mini beasts in the theraputty, sort bugs by category or colour using tweezers, catch plastic bugs in a net and use those little magnified collector pots to go on a bug hunt. The more relevant the activity is to the child's interest the more motivated they will be.

Even with highly motivating, themed activities, the child may benefit from a visual schedule. This does not necessarily have to have a set order. You could laminate and stick visuals for each activity on a board with Velcro. As the child completes an activity they post the image into a pot or post box. When all the visuals have gone into the pot then they can choose. You could present this on a 'Now and Next' board, as shown in Figure 7.1.

Figure 7.1 *Now and Next board*

The thumbs-up reward board in Figure 7.2 is another way to present activities. The child can see on the back the activities they will be expected to complete, and each one gets them closer to their chosen reward.

Figure 7.2 *Thumbs-up reward board*[1]

Theraputty

The internet has a wealth of visual ideas for using theraputty. Print the pictures of what you hope the child will do.

Please note that theraputty (at least the type I have used) can be extremely difficult to remove from fabric.

Crossing the midline

Amanda Masters, MS, OTR/L, who is a Clinic Occupational Therapist at TherapyWorks, explains what crossing the midline is brilliantly:

What is 'Crossing Midline'?
Imagine a line dividing your body into right and left sides. Crossing Midline includes any activity that requires one side to cross into the other side. Imagine using both hands to put on your shoes and socks, brushing your teeth, using your tongue to manipulate food from one side of your mouth to the other, combing your hair, reading, writing, etc.

Why is this important for brain development?
Crossing Midline all starts with crawling, which typically develops around age 7–11 months. Crawling is a very important developmental milestone. For many children, especially those with Autism, Dyspraxia (motor in-coordination), or

---

1   Figures 7.1 and 7.2 were created for *Colour Coding for Learners with Autism* (2014).

Dyslexia, they may have 'skipped' the crawling stage all together. Crawling is important because it works on upper and lower body dissociation, trunk/core rotation, weight bearing/weight shifting, reciprocal movement patterns, and dynamic movement transitions (i.e.: quadruped to side sit, quadruped to ½ kneel, etc.). This is also a precursor for Crossing Midline which is necessary for the brain to communicate across the corpus collosum, the thick band of nerve fibers which connects the two brain hemispheres. This is required for higher level skills such as reading and writing. In fact, research has shown that children with dyslexia have smaller, less developed, corpus collosums.

Symptoms

Children who do not Cross Midline often do not develop hand dominance which should be determined by age 5. Children who do not Cross Midline often show symptoms including:

- poor fine motor control (immature pencil grasp, poor manipulation skills)

- poor bilateral coordination (catching a ball, cutting skills)

- poor upper/lower body coordination (jumping jacks, riding a bike)

- poor right/left discrimination

- becoming 'stuck' in mid-reach and having to switch hands.

(Masters 2013)

For ideas and activities linked with this I recommend reading Masters' full blog post.[2]

Visual tracking and perception

When a child has difficulty with visual tracking or their individual perception is distorted or their processing is delayed, this can affect reading, writing, coordination and gross motor skills such as throwing and catching a ball.

Difficulties can also lead to lowering self esteem, frustration and even anger. Children may self preserve from feelings of failure by completely refusing to try.

An optometrist report may show that a child's vision is good, but they may not have accounted for perception. The child may process or interpret what they see in a different way, which affects how they respond.

It is the responsibility of the teacher to look out for these difficulties, communicate concerns to other professionals such as the school's special educational needs coordinator or refer the child to an occupational therapist or vision therapist.

---

2   www.therapyworkstulsa.blogspot.co.uk/2013/07/crossing-midline.html.

Observe what the child 'can do', be really positive and support them to develop skills at their own pace with a program carefully tailored to their individual needs.

The willingness to 'have a go' and an attitude of 'can do' are delicate essentials and must be protected if the child is to make progress.

If a visual child displays behaviours that suggest they may be experiencing visual distortions it is worth investigating. Adults with autism have reported extremes in perceptual distortions, such as not seeing things as whole or seeing faces differently. Imagine how frightening this would be to a child, who does not know that this is not how the majority of people can see.

Visual perception differences can drastically impact on learning to read, write and spell. Some people find that using a certain coloured paper or colour-tinted glasses can help.

Messy sensory

Messy sensory is a great way to start making marks and lots of fun too.

Model how to mark-make by squirting shaving foam into a tray and making a letter shape.

Cornflour and water make a really interesting mix, because when you touch the cornflour–water mix it feels hard, but then when you lift it it goes through the finger as a liquid. Fascinating!

Pour paint from up high on to the table or a tray. Let children swirl it (ideally with their fingers), but also have sponges or brushes. This can be printed by putting paper over the top (great for creating backgrounds for displays).

Sprinkle flour through a sieve and then make a letter 'S' for sieve. Always model what you expect the child to do. The child may decide to do their own thing. If they are mark making, exploring or experimenting observe and use your instinct. Sometimes a child needs us to guide, but sometimes they are more open to learning when we follow their lead.

Pre-writing

As your messy sensory develops maybe some children are copying marks such as straight lines or circles. They are pre-writing. This may be a good time to introduce some pre-writing sheets.

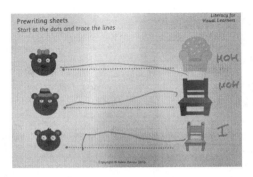

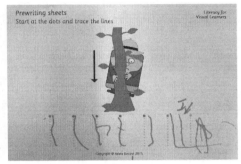

Figure 7.3 Pre-writing sheets based on 'The Fairy Tales' by SEN Assist

Handwriting Without Tears

Handwriting Without Tears is a multisensory way of learning handwriting developed by occupational therapist Jan Olsen. I discovered the Handwriting Without Tears resources when I was teaching at an autism-specific school and teaching a complex class. They were all at the mark-making, pre-writing stage, and for some the idea of writing caused real anxiety. The children responded brilliantly to the 'Get Set For School Sing Along CD' and we used the Mat Man song a lot.[3] The children and the staff really enjoyed the structure, and using drawing instead of writing to teach them seemed to get past some anxieties. I would model drawing Mat Man on a big flip chart and then the children would copy while the music instructed them what to do. This is a brilliant program for introducing handwriting. It is designed so that *all* children can be involved as it caters for all learning styles and uses fun, child-friendly language with images.

---

3   Available from http://shopping.hwtears.com/product/SING.

CASE STUDY: Finn

Diagnosis: Autism

Finn made it very clear he did not want to be in school. He wanted to be at home with his mum. He was a bright boy, whose vocabulary was impressive. He could talk at length in a very adult way about his high interest subjects. He did not see the point in learning to read or write. His mind was thirsty for knowledge linked to his personal interests and he resisted anything which looked like 'work'. So when Finn arrived at school and started to ask to go home I didn't ignore his request, but explained that it was not up to me. If he wanted to go home then perhaps he should write a letter to the headteacher. Why couldn't he go and tell the headteacher? I explained that headteachers are very busy people and the best way is to write them a letter so that they can look at it and respond when they are less busy.

I wasn't expecting Finn to 'write' yet. We sat together at the computer and he dictated the letter. I used a symbols program called Symwriter and as I typed I saw Finn looking at the words and symbols. Once the letter was written we printed it and then went to collect it from another printer.

I explained that we would need to put it in an envelope (because headteachers like letters to be in envelopes) and he could ask the office staff for one. Finn, who had such advanced, extensive vocabulary, asked me, 'What is an envelope?' I explained. We got the envelope and then I asked Finn to sign the letter (because the headteacher would need to know who it was from). I wrote 'Finn' in dots so he could overwrite it. Finn put it in the envelope and then overwrote 'M' for Matthew on it. I showed Finn where the pigeon holes were and he located the one which said Matthew.

During that morning Finn had learnt a lot. He had controlled his anxiety and frustration at being in school and learnt a way to address it and communicate exactly how he felt. He had transitioned through school calmly and communicated politely with office staff. He had extended his functional vocabulary and learnt what an 'envelope' was. He had picked up a pencil to try writing and then looked for the headteacher's name – reading – and read the reply (more reading). What if I had simply made Finn do his work as usual? How would this have made him feel or react, when he had arrived so resistant and anxious?

Finn got a reply later in the day. We read it together. The letter explained that it was the law that he should be in school, but if he wanted to take this further he could write to the education minister. Another letter followed and we waited for a response…

Finn kept asking if the education minister had replied. He suggested we email him as this would be quicker. Brilliant thinking, but I explained that a letter was more likely to get his attention. In time Finn did get a response, but it was not what he had hoped for. The education minister agreed that Finn would have to stay in school. Finn sighed as he had really hoped the education minister would see sense. Through this process Finn had learnt so many important things. He'd learned about another way to make a point and get an answer from an adult. He'd learned about letter writing, communicating and the purpose of reading and writing. He'd also realized that we were ready to listen to him and that his point of view was valued and respected.

By going off plan, I had the opportunity to assess his reading, writing, fine motor and language skills.

Sometimes we must forget what is on our immediate agenda, listen, learn and build a child's trust.

The child must *always* come before the tick box.

CASE STUDY: William

Diagnosis: Autism

William was always willing, but was struggling with some aspects of school. He would mark-make and try to form letters, but they would come out looking like a series of squashed circles and lines. As he was already happy to pick up a pencil and complete worksheets, we started off with pre-writing sheets linked to the W in William's name.

He found transition times difficult and was never quite sure what to do with himself, so during these times he would sit and practise writing. Pretty soon he was overwriting his whole name. Each time William did some work I taught him to write his name on the back.

I created handwriting sheets for each letter and William would practise and practise. I gave his mum copies for home as well.

I also suggested a number of those books which come with a dry wipe pen. William kept practising.

I wanted him to become more independent, but he was not yet ready to write without any guidelines. He could overwrite really well with dotted or yellow letters to guide him, but without these he reverted to his circles and lines (with the exception of some letters in his name).

I found some letter stampers online and bought some yellow ink to go with them. William learned to copy words using the yellow ink and stampers and then overwrite. He used this in other subjects too. Suddenly in numeracy sessions he was able to fill in the numbers independently by using his number stamps.

Through constant practice, the right structures, stepped learning and back-up from home, William made fantastic progress with his handwriting.

Figure 7.4 *A child traces letters following the dots*

Figure 7.5 *A child enjoys using alphabet stamps to copy long dinosaur names*

Multisensory handwriting

There are many ways to include the senses and practise writing letters:

- Shapes can be drawn using torches in the dark.

- Write in the sand or draw big faces.

- Use water to paint on fences, patios or big blackboards.

- Bury plastic letters in shaving foam or gloop.

- Hide the letters in a dark box so the children can feel them.

- Use play dough and cut out letters.

- Copy letter shapes with play dough.

- Use stampers or letter sponges to print letters.

- Make glitter letters.

- Make sandpaper letters (more information below).

Letter formation – sandpaper letters

A great way to introduce handwriting can be to use sandpaper letters. Sandpaper letters can be bought, but they can also be a DIY project. If time is short you may find a willing teaching assistant. Be very specific about how you want these, though. My teaching assistants have a giggle at how specific I am about how symbols are cut out, but I've learnt that being specific and having high standards is fine if everybody knows about it.

To make sandpaper letters you will need:

- fine sandpaper

- thick card (I use one colour for lower case and one for upper case)

- glue

- scissors

- a letter template (available online).

Method

1. Print the letter templates.

2. Cut the thick card into equal-sized pieces (somewhere between A5 and A6 depending on age and ability). Make sure that they are the right size for your letter template.

3. Stick the letter template to the back of the fine sandpaper backwards and then cut around it.

4. Stick the sandpaper letter to the card.

You do not need to start with every letter. You could select the easier letters to begin – maybe c, o, l, i, v and x. Start with three letters at a time. I usually start off with the letters in the child's name.

Begin the letter writing with a sound game linked with the child's interest like 'I spy', saying, 'I spy something beginning with "c"' or 'Can you spot a train?' Then say, 'Yay! Train begins with "t,"' holding up the 't' next to the train. Use the letter sound rather than the alphabet sound. Using Makaton signs will help with meaning. Say, 'Let's see what "c" looks like.' Show them the sandpaper letter 'c' and then model tracing over it with your finger. Help the child to do this hand over hand and always ensure that you start at the right place. You could add a spot to the correct place on the letter as an extra visual prompt.

Once the child is able to trace the sandpaper letter independently with a small physical prompt, you can start working on writing the letters. Open some salt and scatter it on a tray. The child might enjoy watching it pour. Do be aware that salt particles dropped from too high a height may hurt the eyes. Draw a 'c' in the sand. See if the child will try this with hand-over-hand help. As the letter is written say the letter sound. Praise each attempt, then rub it out by disturbing the salt and move on to the next letter. The next stage will be to get the child to trace the sandpaper letter, then model drawing the letter in the salt, saying it aloud – 'c'. Always be sure you are asking the child to do something they are ready for.

As a child's ability to stay on task builds, you may want to go through all the letters one at a time. Master all of the lower case letters first, unless you have decided to start with the letters in the child's name, as this will include one upper case letter.

Next replace the salt with a small dry wipe board and dry wipe pen. Again support the child and wipe out the letter after it is done. The act of wiping it out is important to children who find writing difficult because it is not immediately perfect (often those with ASCs). It means errors are not permanent.

In time you will increase the number of letters used. Make sure the child knows how many letters they will need to do. Maybe you could have the sandpaper letters in a pile and then place them in a 'finished' box, or just create another pile, turning them over when they are finished. We know that children with ASCs and ADHD particularly like to have a visual structure so they know how much they have to do before they are finished. Tasks seem more achievable when we can clearly see when they will end.

Children can quickly learn to form their letters incorrectly and it is so much harder for them to unlearn. The child shown in Figure 7.4 had got into the habit of starting in the wrong place when forming his letters, but was beyond using large sandpaper letters. Continually telling a child to change his writing will only lower their self esteem. He was trying so hard. By using a visual structure where each letter had a green dot where he should start and which faded in the correct direction, he was able to self correct this habit. He only needed to be shown to start at the dot once and he was able to form every letter correctly. By repeating this process he would learn the flow of those letters as a dancer learns a routine through repetition of the moves.

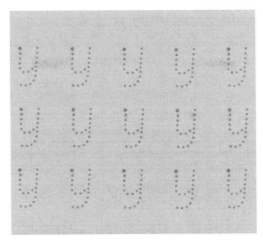

Figure 7.6 *Lower case letter formation sheet*

Pencil grip

A child will not begin by holding a pencil using a three-finger grip. Occupational therapists advise against interfering with the natural development of the pencil hold, which is linked to physical development.

Tracey Le Roux is a qualified occupational therapist (OT) and has set up a website called 'OT Mom'. She explains:

> When a child is made to use a 'proper' pencil grasp **before** the shoulder and arm muscles are **ready** to support it, you may find fine motor problems emerging, such as holding the pencil in 'weird' ways, messy work and even avoidance of drawing and coloring tasks. (Le Roux n.d.)

OTs are best placed to advise about additional supports for children with special educational needs, as conditions such as Down's Syndrome and ASC can affect the development of fine motor skills. The strengthening exercises previously mentioned can help. There are many pencil grips which can be used to encourage a threefinger grip and positioning of the fingers. There are also the chunky triangular-shaped pencils, which can help.

Give writing a purpose

The way we ask a child to write can make a huge difference towards their mental attitude. Rather than say to the reluctant writer that they must practise, I suggest hiding that practice and giving them a reason to write. Replace the chore with a reasonable and ideally fun function:

- writing lists

- plans

- maps

- sand

- magnetic letters

- labels

- instructions

- warnings

- letters

- naming.

Finger spaces

If a child struggles to remember to leave finger spaces between words, then a visual can help (this does work better for right-handed children as left-handed children end up with their hand over the finger). Create the visual with the child by drawing around their finger. Draw on the knuckles and nail to make it look like a finger. Write finger space on the back. This will last longer if laminated, but it could also be covered over with sticky tape. Encourage the child to place the finger between words as they develop this skill. They will not use this for long and the 'finger space' visual can be kept in their pencil case. If it is taken out and placed in eyeshot it can serve as a good visual prompt for them to remember.

CASE STUDY: Billy

Diagnosis: Down's Syndrome

I once went to observe a five-year-old boy with Down's Syndrome who was in mainstream school. He was being 'included' in a room alongside the classroom. The teacher showed us the special sand tray they had provided to help him learn to write his letters, but explained that the boy would not even try. She lifted his hand to guide his finger towards the sand, and he resisted. I picked up a pencil and drew a smiley face in the sand then handed the boy the pencil. He took it and tried to copy, drawing a squashed circle and dots in the sand tray. The teacher was amazed. She'd thought the boy's refusal was behaviour, but the resistance was due to a sensory issue with the sand.

Sitting for writing

Good positioning is so important, as when a child has core stability it can really help with handwriting. A child needs to have their feet on the ground for stability. If feet are dangling in class chairs, a block can be placed under to rest on. A wedged, textured cushion can provide additional positioning support. Using a wedge to raise the paper can help with focus, reach and control.

CASE STUDY: Natty

Hayley Goleniowska explains how she taught her daughter Natty, who is diagnosed with Down's Syndrome, to write.

The correct writing position is vital, so that your child has core stability, giving the strength to write.

We purchased a variety of *pencil grips* and played around till we found one that suited her fingers. We then found triangular pencils with grooves cut in them and we moved to those.

We began by using *dots* for Natty to trace over (you can find fonts that do this on your pc or you can create the dots freehand), letter shapes to colour in (free downloads are widely available online) and guided Natty's arm from the elbow to make the shapes to encourage errorless learning.

There are also letter tracing Apps for iPhones and iPads.

Natty liked the *Kumon* tracing books (available from Amazon) as they provide simple steps to writing in a fun, bright and interesting way.

Natty's teaching assistant made sure that she was *sitting in a stable position* at her desk. In order to have core stability and pencil control your feet must be grounded. At school Natty has a *foot wedge*, a *textured cushion* which stops her fidgeting and a *writing slope*. At home we used either a small chair and table, or later on a Tripp Trapp chair which has a built-in foot ledge. You could use cushions, books or a toilet step for your child's feet. We found a writing slope in IKEA for around £2.

To stop paper and slopes sliding around, cut a length of non-slip material (available from kitchen shops) to put underneath.

When Natty was showing signs of being ready to write independently, we introduced the *Ruth Miskin* flashcards (part of the *Read Write Inc* scheme), again a couple of pounds from Amazon. They show a picture within each letter and give you a catchphrase to remember how to write each one. For Natty's name we used:

- 'round the apple and down the leaf' for 'a'

- 'down the tower and across the tower' for 't'

- 'down the horn, up the horn and round the yak's face' for 'y'.

For the capital N of her name we just shouted 'up, down, up, STOP', which Natty adored.

Natty practised writing over countless differently printed towers, apples and yaks, before we removed the pictures altogether and simply repeated the phrases as she wrote.

Yesterday I found a scrap of paper on which Natty had written her name, independently, without a model, and without anyone even watching.

Practice at home

Natty is a great example of how much can be achieved when a child gets extra support at home. Writing is not a skill we are born with – it takes practice, and for some children it takes lots of practice. We're not expecting perfectly formed letters, but it will make such a difference to a child's self esteem if they are able to write their name on their work.

Do not make handwriting a chore, but if a child is having difficulties learning to form letters at the same rate as their peers, some home practice can really, really help. Speak to parents, and if they think their child would happily practise at home provide them with printed dotted letters and dry wipe tracing books. Progress will be so much quicker if the child gets extra practice.

Homework

First, we must understand that we might see a very different child at school to the one a parent sees at home. For some parents and children homework can cause absolute nightmares. Maybe they compartmentalize school and home? Maybe school takes so much out of them? Maybe they do not write the homework down because at the time they are convinced that they will remember?

Rather than applying negative labels like 'lazy' or 'disorganized', think of positive solutions. That 'lazy' child might not be doing the homework because they need to be told to write in the book or because they can't write as fast as the other children. Why not type up a list of homework, in order of priority, with tick boxes for them to tick off what's done? Are they overwhelmed? Don't give all the homework out on the same day. Do they need more support? Is the homework differentiated and suitable for them? *All* children *can* when we set them up for success.

The future's bright even if they don't handwrite

Adults may joke about their dreadful writing. When I handwrite the home/school diaries in a great big rush, I'm aware just how scrappy my own writing is. I prioritise and decide not to give the time to doing beautiful handwriting, when there is so much else to do.

If children really struggle with handwriting, do not despair. Do not let them feel any less because of it. Explain that writing is important, but then tell them about the other things that are important. Talk about something that they *are* good at.

The future has never looked brighter for non-handwriters. Keep on trying, but get them typing too.

In reality they will type much more than they will handwrite. The usual argument is that we will always have to fill in forms, but not so now.

There is now an amazing free App called SnapType (see Figure 7.7 on the next page) for filling in worksheets, which was devised by Amberlynn Gifford, an occupational therapy student at Springfield College in Massachusetts. I contacted her to learn more, and she explained:

> I had the idea during my field work session last year. I saw a student with dysgraphia struggle to complete his school worksheets. I thought there had to be a better way. (Personal correspondence)

Think of the child who is brilliant with numbers, but cannot write them on worksheets. Now they could take a photo of the worksheet, type the numbers in and then email it to the teacher. They could photograph the same worksheets the other children have and type answers in. Imagine the possibilities for the child who gets the story, but can't write the answers to comprehension questions. This App even does speech-to-text for those who have the ideas, but cannot type them. Brilliant! Brilliant! So many children can benefit from this.

A mother wrote:

> I can honestly tell you that I have spent many hours crying and hurting inside while watching my son struggle to write pages of sentences and spelling words and other homework assignments. He screams out with frustration. It's been so bad that I have stopped him and honestly wrote for him, left-handed to make it look more like a neater version of his because I could not take it anymore! Now, with SnapType, he completes his worksheets, shows off his intelligence and feels more confident than ever. (Quoted in Gifford 2015)

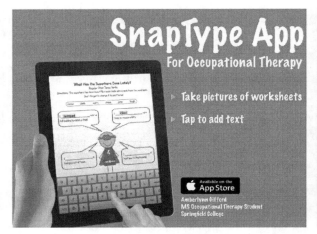

Figure 7.7 *SnapType App*

There are voice-recognition Apps such as 'Dragon Dictation' so that creative thinkers can dictate their ideas.

There are Apps like Pixton (see Figure 7.8) for creating visual comic books which can be personalized. Children can write stories which are more visual and less wordy.

There are too many wonderful Apps to list here, and the list is ever-growing and ever-changing. Instead I suggest you look at the OTs with Apps – Handwriting App List.[4] This list tells you a little bit about each App along with price.

It is our responsibility as teachers to keep researching, resource searching and creating solutions, ensuring that the children who *can* are given access to the problem solving tools, which are being created by our new tech-savvy generation of OTs, teachers and speech therapists. These tools are out there, and it's our responsibility to keep researching so that the children we work with have access to them.

---

4   www.otswithapps.com/ots-with-apps-mtool-kit-6-2-2013/ots-with-apps-handwriting-apps

Figure 7.8 *Pixton App. Reproduced with permission (www.pixton.com)*

Instruction does much, but encouragement everything.

Johann Wolfgang von Goethe (1749–1832)

Chapter 8

What's in a Name?

How Names and Labels Give Reading and Writing a Purpose

Words have meaning and names have power.

Author unknown

A child's name provides so many opportunities for improving literacy skills. The brilliant thing about a name is that it can get a child's attention and that learning to read, write and type it is functional. There are so many opportunities! When teaching young children or children with learning difficulties we quickly learn that repetition is essential for progression. We also know that learning must be purposeful. A child may not be willing to match a lot of black and white letters if they can't see a purpose. Names have purpose, and this makes them a powerful place to start.

Communication

When a baby first responds to their name they meet a developmental milestone, typically at around seven months. If they are not responding to their name by 9–12 months there is cause to investigate.

The article 'Developmental milestones: Understanding words, behavior, and concepts', which was reviewed by the BabyCenter Medical Advisory Board, outlines the stages in typical baby speech development:

As a newborn, she doesn't know the precise meaning of the words you use, but she picks up on your emotions – such as happiness, sadness, love, concern, anxiety, and anger. By the time she's 7 months old, she'll respond to her own name, and by 8 to 12 months she'll understand simple directives such as 'No' or 'Don't touch.' Around 24 months, she'll be able to talk to you in two- or three-word phrases. About the age of 3, she'll have a vocabulary of a couple hundred words and a pretty good sense of some of the rituals and activities of everyday life, such as food shopping, housecleaning, and knowing night means bedtime. (BabyCenter n.d.)

Teaching children with learning difficulties by using their name is a powerful way to gain individual attention. A child might not be aware that you are addressing them and not the group. They may not notice that you are looking at them when speaking; they may not realize that you are expecting them to respond. By using a child's name you make things personal and you will, hopefully, gain their attention.

Processing time

It is vital to be aware that not all children are quick to process information. It is important to speak directly and simply and to allow a long enough pause for the child to process and then react. This can make all the difference to the responses you get. Say, 'Johnny give me the book.' Then allow ten seconds for Johnny to respond before repeating exactly what you just said. Some children will take even longer. It is not that they are disobeying – they are just not quick enough to process. Similarly the command may be too much and may be reduced to 'Johnny, book'. Add a visual of a book and point to it. You may just get the book.

If you do not get the response you are expecting, break down the language, add a visual and allow the child time.

Oh, and when you get the book be over-the-top grateful. You want Johnny to be motivated next time.

Know their names

This might sound incredibly obvious, but learning the names of every child in the class quickly is essential to managing behaviour, gaining respect, building trust and knowing the individual children. How can you really know who they are if you don't know their names? Some teachers do find it difficult to remember the names of a class of 30, when they have so much going on, but forget the other things. Focus on what's important.

There are some tricks experienced teachers use to get to know names quickly. Some use labels; some will use tricks at registration: 'Today when I call your name I want you to tell me your name and something you like that begins with your initial.' The first child says, 'My name is Charlie and I like cheeseburgers.' And so on...

Or there are name games. One of my favourites is a memory game with a ball, described on the next page.

Name game

Teacher: 'My name is Adele and I'm going to throw the ball to Sam.'

Sam: 'Adele threw the ball to me. My name is Sam and I'm going to throw the ball to Lucy.'

Lucy: 'Adele threw the ball to Sam. Sam threw the ball to me. My name is Lucy and I'm going to throw the ball to Will.'

Will: 'Adele threw the ball to Sam. Sam threw the ball to Lucy. Lucy threw the ball to me. My name is Will and I'm going to throw the ball to Emma.'

This will not only help you learn the names, but will help other children, who may not have matched name labels to all faces. The repetition of this activity helps.

Learning classmates' names – circle time or registration

There are many opportunities for children to learn each other's names, and circle time or registration are two of the best.

If you are teaching in a mainstream school then it is important that every child has the opportunity to answer when you read out the register. A child with speech difficulties should still be given the opportunity to answer 'Yes Miss', whether this be with a visual 'Yes' sign to hold up or a switch with 'Yes' pre-recorded.

Circle time in special schools is a great learning opportunity for attention, focus, cooperation, sustaining attention, reading and communication. This is not simply the functional taking of a register to tick who's in school. In most special school classes they will take turns to sing to each child.

We use the children's photos with their name below. We might ask the child to point to their picture or to select a friend to say good morning to, or we might have photos pre-ordered (when there are competition or control issues). We sing to each child in turn:

'Johnny Brooks, Johnny Brooks where are you?'

Johnny may sing or sign or he may press a pre-recorded switch which sings back, 'Here I am, Here I am. How do you do?'

Another popular 'Good Morning' song is:

'It's time to say good morning, hip, hip, hip hooray.

It's time to say good morning and it's Johnny's time to say…'

Johnny will either say 'good morning', use a PECS symbol on a sentence strip or use a switch with the pre-recorded 'good morning'.

Or:

'Good morning Johnny. Good morning Johnny.

We hope that you are well today.

We've a busy day before us with lots of work and lots of play.'

We also incorporate a hat song into our circle time, which is great for getting the children looking at themselves in the mirror and another opportunity for learning names:

'Who is going to wear the hat, wear the hat, wear the hat?

Who is going to wear the hat? Who, oh, who will it be?'

The child is selected and they get to wear the hat, while everyone sings:

'Johnny is wearing the hat, wearing the hat, wearing the hat.

Johnny is wearing the hat, doesn't he look good'

Johnny then gets to see in the mirror.

It is very important that support staff show enthusiasm and join in with the singing. This should be a 'happy team' part of the day. You may need to remind them nicely. Also appreciate when support staff join in by thanking them.

Some children will hate this singing part of the day. Be respectful of this because they may have real sensitivity and your singing might cause them actual pain. Could you sing more quietly, let them try ear defenders or shorten the songs and the session? Do not remove the session or allow the child to completely opt out, but be sensitive and adaptive to the needs of every child in the group.

Reading names

Use names in print as often as you can so the children see them again and again. Have the children's names under photos on display. Their eye will be drawn to their own photo, and each time they look they will see their name, creating a visual link. Names can be used at registration time. Maybe they will be placed on a board or a child could be asked to sign in.

When making choices, get children to take their name and place it to indicate their choice. Our son's infant school recently adopted a system for children selecting their school dinners in the morning. They find their name and place it on the colour linked to their choice of meal. If there were a SEN child in reception who could not yet read their own name, imagine how helpful that daily activity would be in learning. A repetitive task such as this makes name recognition functional and the child sees all the other children doing it as well.

In our daughter's preschool the children are encouraged to get their name and put it on their chair at registration and snack times. There are so many opportunities to get children using their name labels. The more they see, handle and match them during the day, the sooner they will learn to read them.

Figure 8.1 *This simple colouring task helps develop name recognition and pencil grip*

CASE STUDY: Alexander (age 5) (the child with the long name)

Diagnosis: Autism

Alexander was attending a mainstream school. He was a bit more wriggly and squiggly at carpet time and did not always follow verbal instructions as well as his peers, but was mostly keeping up.

But writing was a bit of an issue. Alexander really struggled with pencil control and had developed a bit of an 'I can't' attitude as he saw his peers make progress.

I've always found that getting a child to attempt to name their work is a good starting point to developing reading and writing skills because they can see it has a clear purpose. Writing the letters of a name is less daunting and more meaningful than writing strings of letters one after another or copying lists of words.

The first letter of Alexander's name became our focus. I did not expect him to write the whole name instantly, but we practised his capital, 'A'. Alex mastered this quickly and moved on to 'l' (nice and easy).

At this point I sent an email to his mum about his progress. His mum emailed back, and when she mentioned Alexander she used the short form 'Alex'. I asked his mum if she would be happy for us to teach

Alexander the shortened form to name his work as it would make the task quicker to achieve and mean he could start to independently name his work. She was happy with this.

Alex struggled a bit with the formation of the 'e', but worked and worked at it, and then 'x' was easy.

It was wonderful to see the sense of pride and accomplishment Alex got from being able to write his name. His whole attitude to writing changed, and his 'can't' became a 'can with some work'.

Overcoming anxiety

A name seems like an obvious starting point in teaching writing, but it needs to be introduced in a positive, functional way rather than as a task. The constraints of fine motor skills can make writing genuinely difficult to master, which is why we take small steps. No one expects a toddler to be able to pick up a pen and write their name instantly. Ability assumptions should not be linked to a child's age or by what they can do in other areas. We know that all children develop differently, and it's up to us to tune in to their pace.

But what if you are not the first person to introduce a child to writing their name? What if it was all done wrong and you are working with a child to whom a name-writing task is like waving a red flag at a bull?

When a child has decided they can't do something and built a wall against learning, we are fighting against the tide. In this instance we need to take a break, build trust and approach things in a completely different way. We know they have the potential to write their name, but there is a mental barrier, so each time they see a pen and paper hackles go up. The answer is to stop asking them to write their name and focus on getting them to learn the letters and sequence. This may be through matching activities or typing on the keyboard.

CASE STUDY: Joshua (age 8)

Wanting to get it right

Joshua was the student every SEN teacher needs to have in the class. He was the one who you could rely on to run an errand such as taking the register to the office, to cooperate and to try his best. He was so desperate to please that we found ourselves willing him to occasionally go his own way.

I observed how Joshua wrote his name and noticed that he was consistently writing Jooouo. The J, o and u were all formed well enough to recognize, but he was making no attempt to write the other letters even when they were there to copy. I wondered if this was due to that desperation to please and get it right. He had learned to write some of the letters and he knew they were correct, so instead of risking failure he simply filled in the gaps with the letters he knew.

We started to learn the formation of each of those missing letters individually. Josh was so willing that with lots of practice he was soon writing his 's', 'h' and 'a' correctly. Next step he was given his name written in yellow or dots to trace each letter and get into the routine of writing each letter in order without filling with lots of os. By the end of the academic year Joshua was able to write his name correctly without looking at anything. We celebrated this achievement and praised him each time he got it right. This not only reinforced that his hard work reaped the praise, but the praise created protective layers, building his self esteem and confidence to go ahead and try new tasks.

When a physical disability stops a child being able to write their name

There are children who will not have the physical ability to control a pencil. These children can still be taught to name their work using a stamp. Personalized stamps are available to buy online. Being included in this way can make such a difference to the attitude of a child with physical difficulties. Giving them a name stamp shows that you know their physical restrictions and are thinking beyond them.

Chapter 9

Reading

Practical Strategies Including Teaching
Children Who Do Not 'Get' Phonics

There is creative reading as well as creative writing.

Ralph Waldo Emerson (1803–1882)

Why reading is important

Reading is such an important life skill. Once a child can read they can learn so much more in all the other subjects. Reading will help them achieve independence, raise their self esteem and give them the most amazing outlet for calm, contemplative enjoyment.

How do we begin to teach a child to read?

We begin by having beautiful, bright, high interest books available for them to lift up and explore. We create a cosy area with beanbags or cushions and blankets where children will want to sit. We model looking at the books. We read books with other children. We read books to their teddy bears or dolls. We smile a lot. We may have toys or props that link in with stories. We may have books with flaps to lift, buttons to press or interesting textures to explore. Our starting point is to get the child to see how we love books and spark their interest.

The hope is that this introduction to reading will have begun before a child starts school. We hope a child will have already been immersed in a wealth of happy literary experiences before they start school. It is never too early to start!

Rhymes

Use familiar rhymes like 'Round and round the garden', or songs like 'Row, row, row your the boat'. See if the child anticipates and fills in gaps.

Props

Use props when telling stories. Sound books can also add interest.

Sensory stories (bringing stories to life through sensory props)

I love the Anton Chekhov quote: 'Don't tell me the moon is shining; show me the glint of light on broken glass'.

As well as a multitude of props and puppets, there are sensory resources, massage and full sound effects. Reading a story is a bit of theatre with ample opportunities for audience participation. Children and support staff should *love* our sensory story sessions. They should all be involved and engaged. When a child sees that a story is on our visual schedule we want them thinking, 'Yay!'

Who can benefit from sensory stories?

The short answer is that *every* child can benefit from sensory stories. They add an exciting new element, which can lift the story off the page, but they do so much more than simply entertain.

The sensory story allows the child with profound and multiple learning difficulties (PMLD) to experience the story through any of their senses. They may respond to feeling a breeze when the wind blows, the touch of tickly bird feathers, the smell of green grass or hear the crackle and crunch of autumn leaves. Adding sensory elements involves these children and adds to their experience. The sensory elements can be vital to gaining the attention of the child with a disability, affecting their hearing or vision. Sensory surprises and sounds may spark the interest and help the child with attention difficulties to attend. As stories repeat, the child with sequencing difficulties may begin to predict what's next through the different sensory props in a way they could not from a stand-alone book.

Joanna Grace, special educational needs consultant and author of *Sensory Stories,* explains how sensory stories can be helpful to individuals with sensory processing disorder:

> Sensory stories offer the opportunity to practise interacting with stimuli in the safety of a story. Research has shown that stories hold a special power over us; within a story we are braver and can face topics that in real life we find overwhelming. A child who needs practice at interacting with sensory stimuli may feel more able to do so within the context of a story, and by repeating the story you build security. You can grade stimuli and increase the challenge when you revisit the tale. For

example, if a child finds a sticky-touch experience challenging, you can begin with touching water, then gradually make the substance stickier each time you tell the story. (Grace 2013)

The sensory story should not be restricted to the child with special educational needs. All children are special and deserve their school story time to be magical and exciting.

When I see a teacher sat reading a small book to a group of nursery children without any props or sensory elements, I think that the children are amazing for sustaining their attention. I also think an opportunity is being missed to truly engage, excite, reward and inspire them.

Sensory fairy tales
The Three Bears

- Make porridge so that children can experience the feel, taste, smell and temperatures.

- Have chairs with different textures, hard wood, soft cushions, etc.

- Have beds and bedding for children to experience and choose from.

- A long blonde wig or a doll with long blonde hair for children to link with the name 'Goldilocks'.

- Have bears and the texture of fur.

- Get the children to physically step with their feet when Goldilocks goes up the stairs and runs down the stairs.

The Three Pigs

- Have props for the straw, wood and bricks so that children can feel the textures.

- Wave the big book or a big piece of card to create wind when the wolf 'huffs and puffs'.

- Get the children to run with their feet when the pigs run from one house to the next.

- Have some bricks or boxes so the children can experience building.

- Have toys for the pigs and wolf.

The Gingerbread Man

- Make real gingerbread or gingerbread play dough so the children can experience the smell and feel of warm gingerbread before it is cooked.

- Have a real gingerbread man and puppets of the main characters.

- Have a water spray and a long piece of blue material for when the gingerbread man gets on the fox's head.

- Clap your hands for 'snap went the fox'.

Jack and the Beanstalk

- Have real beans so the children can experience handling them. Count them out.

- Grow real beanstalks and get children to experience watering them.

- Try to create a growing beanstalk with a length of green fabric and an assistant climbing a step ladder as it grows.

- Have puppets for the characters.

Three Billy Goats Gruff

- Cut up crepe paper to create long, green grass.

- Bring in freshly cut grass for the smell.

- Recreate a bridge using a low table or bench with a cardboard bridge painted on the front.

- Use coconut shells for the clip clop of the horses.

- Have a water spray or tray and make the big splash fun.

Red Riding Hood

- Have a basket of food for grandma.

- Have a red cape to place around the children.

- Have branches to recreate the feeling of the forest.

- Turn the lights out to make it dark.

- Have a puppet or soft toy for children to feel the eyes, nose and mouth.

- Cut a large axe out of cardboard so the children can experience chopping like the woodcutter.

More stories to try

We're Going on a Bear Hunt by Michael Rosen

I love this book! I will never tire of teaching it because it *always* gets the most fantastic reactions. Children go outside at playtime and want to walk through the story. There is something about it that captures them all.

You will most likely be familiar with the story, but for those who are not it takes you on a journey through long grass, dark forests and snow storms to eventually find a bear in a cave. The structure, the pace and the rhythm of the story add to the anticipation. Have fun with it. Gather story props. We use long-grass hula-hula skirts for the grass, a water spray for the river and wellies in a tray of squelchy mud; the children turn out the lights for the dark forest and close their eyes while we wave tree branches; and snow can be anything from white confetti to fake snow, but if you want to add a bit of fun squirt a large amount of shaving foam on one hand and clap them together to create the snow. Be warned, this can be messy! For the wind I tend to wave the big book to create the feeling of wind. The dark cave is a parachute over the children with a torch shining on pictures of the eyes, nose and ears. Let the bear be the shock of the story. If you can, get a member of staff in a bear onesie or else use a big bear toy. Then you backtrack quickly through the whole story until the children all end up under the blanket saying, 'We're not going on a bear hunt again.'

Figure 9.1 We're Going on a Bear Hunt *classroom display*

There is a lovely animated version of the story on YouTube which can be used as a reward at the end of the lesson. Videos can really help bring a story together for visual learners as they can take in the story without the distraction of a teacher.

Other sensory stories

- *The Very Hungry Caterpillar* by Eric Carle
- *Aliens Love Underpants* by Claire Freedman and Ben Cort
- *Walking Through the Jungle* by Debbie Harter
- *The Gruffalo* by Julia Donaldson
- *The Snail and the Whale* by Julia Donaldson
- *Farmer Duck* by Martin Waddell
- *One Snowy Night* by Nick Butterworth
- *What makes a Rainbow* by Don Freeman
- *The Tiger Who Came to Tea* by Judith Kerr

Displays

Have fun with displays. Make them wonderful and interactive. You do not have to be brilliant at art. I was able to use the *Aliens Love Underpants* display in Figure 9.2 to tell the story. The aliens came out of the rocket; the pants came off the washing line. The display also shows how you can print Makaton line drawings of signs which are a great visual reminder for the teacher telling a new story. Learn the new sign with the children. Don't be afraid to show the children that you are learning too. Rather than tell a child how to do something let them observe an adult get stuck and model how they work things out. This display in Figure 9.2 also shows how we work with the children, which can help any new support staff. They look at the display and see that, when you give a member of staff a colouring sheet, it is so that they can model colouring and help children problem solve by watching others rather than waiting for an adult to prompt them. When you do a story display see it as another visual teaching tool. Make it fun, visual and interactive. A display can really enthuse children about the story.

Figure 9.2 An interactive display with aliens and a working washing line

Story massage

> Story massage is a fun and interactive way of enjoying positive touch through story telling and simple massage strokes. Everyone can join in, whatever age or ability. (Story Massage website n.d.)

Story massage is a sequence of touches relating to the story you are using. It uses the power of touch to add another consistent sensory element to story time. Incorporating 'touch' into a story can help a child feel more secure and help engage them and sustain their attention. A massage can release endorphins, reduce pain linked to cramps or spasms, reduce anxiety and improve concentration.

Story massage can add interest to a story and is especially helpful for children developing their sense of proprioception (where their body is in space). Create a visual for massages linked with repetitive language so that the story massage is consistent. If your class are more able, perhaps they could make up their own massage sequence linked to the story.

We had school training on story massage, which was wonderful. If you can get training, do. Be aware of school policies, as you may need specific consent for story massage, but it can add a great new element to storytelling.[1]

Out and about
Signs everywhere

Look out for numbers, letters and words when you take a walk. They are everywhere and children will often enjoy spotting them with you. It's not a task, but a fun

---

1   More information is available from www.storymassage.co.uk.

activity. Relate it to the child: 'Oh look! A number 3. You are 3.' Or: 'I see a M for Matthew. Can you see it too?'

Libraries

Libraries are a wonderful place to take children. I'm sure that with busy lives many parents will forget. Libraries are laid out to attract children with sofas and cushions and low-level book storage that they can explore.

Libraries are free. Children can choose their own books and you can return them as interests change. Children can even have their own library cards. I love libraries, and I do hope people will continue to use them as they are such an amazing resource.

Book shops

If you do not have a local library visit a book shop. Again they should have a child-friendly layout and there is nothing to stop you staying a while and letting your child explore different books.

Charity shops and second hand sales

Charity shops are another wonderful place where children can explore books. Let children handle the books and look at them together.

Modelling
Model reading for a purpose (shopping lists)

Let children see you reading. Use shopping lists for the food shop. Draw little pictures above the words so that children can read them with you. This can be done in real life or role play. Play 'Can you spot…?' and point to the picture of bananas. See if they say 'bananas'. Involve the child in any activity like this you can think of.

Model enjoying reading (great excuse)

Settle down with a book and say, 'I love this book.'

There is no 'one system' for teaching children to read, but the starting point is to get them interested. They must associate reading with fun.

Children learn differently – they see differently, process differently and have different motivators.

Phonics

There are those who argue that phonics is the *only* way to teach a child to read. Phonics is a great system for teaching children to decode words, but it must be used in alignment with other natural reading strategies such as whole word recognition and prediction.

So what is phonics?

Phonics is a system based on learning to decode letters and sounds so that children learn to read by decoding words rather than by recognizing whole words.

Children begin by learning that letters (graphemes) represent single sounds (phonemes). Next they then learn to blend the sounds together to read simple words.

Children are taught about 40 different phonic sounds. Some of these sounds will be two, three or four letters long.

In 2011, Ofsted (who regulate and inspect English schools) published a report called *Removing Barriers to Literacy*. The report was clearly in favour of schools teaching reading through phonics:

> Schools should teach phonics systematically as part of reading and ensure that pupils' progress in developing the phonic knowledge and skills is regularly assessed. (Ofsted 2011, p.8)

As Ofsted regulate and inspect them, schools are very likely to follow the guidelines they provide.

There has been a huge government push in England, encouraging schools to embrace systematic synthetic phonics. Funding has been allocated as an added incentive. Screening tests have been introduced, which will then be used to assess a school's success in teaching reading. Teachers are focusing on phonics to push children through the controversial phonics screening test.

Phonics screening test

In 2012, a phonics screening test was introduced in England for children in Year 1. The test checks that children can decode 40 words by using phonics. As well as real words the test includes some 'made up' words. Children sound out each word using phonics. This test has been controversial with teachers and parents.

My concerns about the phonics screening test

Phonics is one of the strategies which can help children learn to read and I have used this system with great success with some children.

Children who are auditory-sequential learners learn phonics easily, can sound out spelling words, learn step by step and progress sequentially from easy to difficult material.

But we must also consider the visual-spatial learner, who learns whole words easily, must visualize words to spell them, is a whole-part learner and learns complex concepts easily, but struggles with easy skills.

What if a child does not get phonics? What if they process sounds differently like so many of the children in our special education classes? The phonics screening test would set these children up to fail because, even if they learnt all the words by memory, the test includes random 'nonsense' words. The time this would waste, the negative feeling it would give the child and their parents, who see a failed test at the age of six. What if the teacher then provides more intensive phonics instruction and the parents keep trying at home? More self esteem battering would follow.

I am certain this test will not stay in our system, but as I write this book it is still in use. Our own sons have brought home preparation for the test with lists of words and 'nonsense' or 'alien' words.

Researching the phonics test, I saw YouTube films designed to train teachers. The six-year-olds taking the phonics screening test look dulled and deflated. The teachers also seem defeated by having to tick ridiculous boxes when their instinct would be to teach the child to enjoy reading. I wanted to reach into the computer and free them (the teacher and the child). That test is a tool for assessment. It is not creating those sparks we hope to see fly. What about creating a love of reading and language? This test has not been thought of by a teacher wanting to move children on and see them succeed.

The literacy expert Professor Joan Freeman commented in an article in the *Independent*:

> It is beyond belief. Any psychologist would say this is crazy. Children should be taught to interpret meaning. Every word is connected to a meaning. Those who designed this test have no idea about what one does with a collection of letters on a page… This isn't the way to help children understand words in context. I'm more than horrified with the phonics screening test. (Quoted in Jackson 2012)

A parent interviewed in the same article said:

> This approach not only punishes the more able children, it demoralises them, and can create problems for children at every level. They are teaching children to pass the test, not to read and write correctly. (Quoted in Jackson 2012)

In an article for *SEN Magazine* David Maytham writes:

> We are working in an increasingly data-driven education system and, regardless of the way in which this data is gathered, this level of data collection looks set to persist or even increase in the future. (Maytham n.d.)

Initial sounds

The starting point with phonics is for the child to learn the initial sounds. They learn to associate the image of an 'a' with the sound 'a', as in 'act'.

The sounds are best taught in a general way, but also broken down into small groups so that children can achieve rather than feel overwhelmed. If you are teaching phonics, then Jolly Phonics is worth looking into. The addition of signs associated with the phonics can really help children learn. Do take care when introducing phonics to children with speech difficulties, who are also trying to learn communication with Makaton signs.

> Jolly Phonics is a fun and child centred approach to teaching literacy through synthetic phonics. With actions for each of the 42 letter sounds, the multi-sensory method is very motivating for children and teachers, who can see their students achieve. The letter sounds are split into seven groups. (Jolly Learning n.d.)

CBeebies' Fun with Phonics program and associated books, posters and DVDs are another great resource for motivating visual learners to learn initial letter sounds and blends (Wainwright 2008).

I think that phonics can be a fantastic way to introduce initial sounds to most children, even if once they move on to blends and sounds containing two or more letters it becomes problematic. Knowing how much phonic instruction occurs in mainstream schools, when we have a child at our SEN school who we believe could reintegrate to mainstream school, we begin by teaching letters phonetically. We do this to support inclusion back to mainstream.

CASE STUDY: Natty

Mum Hayley Goleniowska writes about teaching Natty, who has Down's Syndrome, her initial sounds through phonics.

When Natty was around two years old, a speech therapist from the charity Symbol UK visited our local area and told us she was ready for sound work. We were using Makaton and Natty was making some lovely sounds and simple words at that point. (It's hard to remember, but I think 'Daddy', 'cake', 'star' and 'biscuit' were among her first essential utterances.) We were also using the See and Learn materials from DownsEd which involved matching pictures in the early stages.[2]

She put two cards in front of Natty, one with an 'a' and one with an 'n'. She then held up an 'a' card and using Makaton she asked her to find the 'same'. Natty did this with her eyes. I remember watching her closely and seeing her look at the other 'a'. She had done it!

This was a very emotional moment for us all and there were a few tears. Why? Because we could have been doing this sooner, but had lacked the guidance. Because we were relieved to see the way forward. Because we wanted everyone to know what was possible for children with Down's Syndrome (DS). Because we knew a lot of hard work was going to be involved from now on…

We rushed out to buy various sets of flashcards with the letters written clearly on them. We kept a set in the bathroom at home and preschool (potty time seemed to work well for us as a time to work with sounds). Most usefully we bought two Jolly Phonics friezes, from Amazon, showing all the sounds and an accompanying action. For example, 'a' is a tapping motion going up the arm, signifying 'ants crawling up the arm'. We played a CD with catchy rhymes in the car.[3]

Children with DS are visual learners, so seeing a picture as well as doing/watching an action helps cement the sound they are hearing/producing (in the way that Makaton works wonders for language development). Natty's Daddy and I spent a week of evenings cutting pictures to size, laminating them and rounding the corners for safety. Time and money well spent, as we still use them. If you can beg, borrow or buy a laminator you will use it constantly.

Natty's mum also shares these great tips for teaching initial sounds:

- Focus on one sound/action at a time.

- Choose sounds your child can already make at first.

- Then show two different cards and ask them which one is 'a', for example. Looking at the right card counts as a correct answer, so your little one doesn't have to be able to point.

- Children who are able to walk love finding the letter sounds hidden around the house, or jumping on to the correct sound on the floor.

- With two sets you can play snap and other matching games.

---

2   For more information about the See and Learn materials see www.seeandlearn.org/en-gb.

3   Early literacy CDs are available from the ELC website at www.elc.co.uk.

Phonics, hearing and processing difficulties

Children with autism often have different ways of processing and heightened sensitivity to sound. A child might have a physical condition which affects their hearing. Children with DS often have hearing difficulties associated with their condition. Children with Cerebral Palsy may hear the sounds, but not be able to say them in the same way as their peers. Hearing and processing challenges could make learning through phonics virtually impossible for some children.

Unlearning

Some children will find learning the initial sounds through phonics works, but they struggle when it comes to blends. The individual sounds make sense, but the blends do not. It's like they are having to unlearn or relearn something they thought they already knew, which causes confusion and lack of trust.

Helping children who do not 'get' phonics

If phonics is the *only* approach being used and is causing feelings of confusion and frustration, then we are setting the child up to fail. We need to be building positive associations, linked with reading, and make the child want to learn to read.

What if a child cannot meet the 'standard' of the phonics screening test? The current guidance in England from the Standards and Testing Agency is:

> If children do not meet the expected standard, schools must determine the most appropriate support for these children to help them catch up. These children must be considered for a re-take of the phonics screening check in the June of Year 2. (Standards and Testing Agency 2014, p.1)

When a child does not 'get' phonics and struggles with these assessments, surely the answer is not more phonics. We must protect these children, because if they start to believe that they can't read, if their self esteem is damaged, then we teachers have failed them. There will always be government initiatives creating boxes to tick and assessments. It is up to us to find ways to protect children who do not learn in the same way as their classmates. Sometimes this will mean going against the tick boxes. We must always put the individual child first.

We must also ensure that the parents of children who have not made the grade in the phonics screening test do not take it upon themselves to get their child through the test in Year 2. These children are still learning to read, and concentrating teaching efforts on getting through the phonics screening test rather than developing a positive attitude to reading could have life-long implications. We do not want learning to read to become a seemingly impossible chore.

If a child is a visual learner who is struggling with phonics, but responding to visual-based methods, it may be that this assessment is not appropriate.

The Oxford Owl website advises:

> There is a process in place for reviewing children with special educational needs, so if your child's teacher thinks there are very special reasons related to your child and their needs that make them think the phonics screening check may not be appropriate, they will decide on appropriate action and discuss this with you. (Oxford Owl 2014)

Protecting self esteem and focusing on 'can dos' and differing learning styles would all be reasons to consider the test inappropriate. I don't think we should use this assessment if a child cannot decode words due to hearing or processing difficulties. We would be setting the child up to fail. We cannot afford to do this with any child, but when a child has a learning difficulty or autism spectrum condition (ASC), even more care must be taken.

In 2014 NATE (the National Association for Teaching English) asked for professional views from the classroom on phonics instruction and early reading (Hodgson *et al.* 2013). When asked to comment on 'Learning and individual differences', more than 16% were concerned that exclusive early instruction in systematic synthetic phonics disregards the different aptitudes and capabilities of different children.

Below is a selection of quotes from the survey:

> All children do not learn to read via phonics. It is setting children up to FAIL before they have really begun their education. (Chair of Governors of a Junior School)

> A former teacher of the deaf (as she describes herself), now a senior leader in a primary school, reports that she has had years of experience teaching deaf children to become good readers, 'despite the fact that they cannot hear many of the phonemes they are reading'.

> There is so much more to learn than phonics for an autistic student. (Private tutor)

> I have spent an inordinate amount of time this year on phonics as opposed to providing for the wide ranging needs of my Reception and Year 1 Class. (Senior infant teacher)

When asked to comment on teaching phonics to their own children, responses included:

I was teaching phonics as requested by my school without giving it too much thought until my own daughter began in reception this year!… I have taught her to read at home in the good old fashioned way as she does not understand the phonics. (Infant teacher)

A secondary head of department is dismayed that her daughter, who has 'excellent visual memory skills', is 'being forced to use another system of reading INSTEAD of supplementing her preferred technique'.

My eldest son (Level 5 in Year 5) was bored rigid by phonics. (Advisory teacher)
(All quotes from Hodgson *et al.* 2013, pp.1–11)

I could go on about how I feel about this phonics assessment and the negative effect it could potentially have on a child who cannot learn through phonics, but as this is a UK assessment, which will I hope in the future be altered or dropped, I will stop there.

Children who do 'get' phonics

There are many children who will successfully learn to decode and sound out words. There is a wealth of fabulous resources for teaching phonics (many are free). If a child is keeping up with phonics then that is great because it will enable them to be included with a mainstream group. Get them a motivating poster for the wall. There's a great one along with the *Fun with Phonics – Letters and Sounds* (book and DVD) by CBeebies. Don't start a completely different system if you believe what is already in place is helping a child learn to read.

Children who learn visually may be able to sound out and blend words. Many will be fine using this system. There are really positive elements. Many resources will directly appeal in a multisensory and visually appealing way. There's a host of computer games, YouTube videos of songs and countless Apps. Phonics is well resourced before you even begin to buy books. The school will also be set up and ready to get going, especially while they are screening progress with phonics 'checks'.

Strategies for teaching reading to visual learners

When teaching reading we must teach in a way that suits the individual child. In this chapter my focus is on the children who do not 'get' phonics, who require a different approach.

Using motivators

First, use words linked to motivators and things that are meaningful to the child. Get them to see that words have meaning. Label drawers with pictures and words to show the contents. The labels will show what is in the draw, but will also draw the child's eye to the words.

Have a set of drawers at the child's eye level. Photograph the contents. Use a program like Word or Paint to copy and paste the picture and then add a typed word below, creating a word with a picture above. Alternatively you could use a symbols program such as Symwriter or Communicate in print to create labels. Use a font with letters similar to handwriting. Comic Sans and Sasson Primary are favourites with teachers or you could use a dyslexia font. It may be helpful to print these on to pale blue or another favoured pastel colour, as black and white can cause letters to strobe, wobble or flip for some children with reading difficulties. It's useful if the drawers can be moved to create a learning opportunity, because the child will have to keep 'reading' rather than learning the positions of the drawers with their favoured or most-used contents. The drawers offer a reading opportunity, but will also increase independence and life skills, encouraging children to get things they need and also put them away.

Next think about what the child likes. Is there a particular cartoon, film, toy? Whatever it is, take it and use it. Take photographs or print pictures from the internet. Create matching or word-building activities. Anything that will motivate the child to start distinguishing individual letters and looking at words.

Names

A name is of course a great starting point and can be used in so many functional ways, as highlighted in Chapter 8. I will not repeat myself here, but if you are starting out with reading please read that chapter as well.

So we come to a point where the child knows to look at words and that they have separate meanings. We want to get them reading in a way that they can enjoy books, but the reading schemes seem too tricky. The ones with just pictures to talk about are not motivating as the content is not relevant to the child, but the next stage is too tricky. If a child wants to read these books alongside their peers then we can use a program such as Symwriter to print words with symbols or we could type words and draw little stick impressions (if art is a strong point).

Some teachers print off our Fairy Tales stories and laminate them. This is time consuming, but it does mean they have a book that uses simple language and includes the first 100 high frequency words with symbols above.

Get creative with books. If they are not working for the child then work to make them accessible.

Books with sounds

Books with sound buttons can be very motivating to the new generation of techie learners. They like to press the buttons and hear the sounds. This gets them lifting up a book and looking. If it gets their attention then use it. Whenever we start a new topic we look to see if there is a sound book version of our story. Often there is!

Photo message books

There are now some fantastic baby books on the market where you can add photos and record little messages. These are a great way to get a child to enjoy turning pages. This is a part of reading. Do they hold the book the right way up? Do they turn the pages or, if they cannot do this due to physical disability, do they indicate they want you to turn the pages? Wow!

Talking photo albums

These are another opportunity to record sound. Sometimes children are more motivated to hear a book read than to hear you read it to them. They may find the book recordings more predictable than a person reading (even though they are recordings of your voice). You could also get a favourite person to do the recording, but take care that this will not cause attachment issues. It's about knowing the child. You can add text to these books. They do not have to be for photographs. There are so many possibilities.

Recorded books

I recently found a lovely set of books where you can record the story being read. They are beautifully illustrated as well. Some people do not like the idea, believing that children should always be read to, but these books can be wonderfully motivating. We have a child who lights up when he hears his mother's voice. How amazing to be able to share a story read by her when she is not there!

Figure 9.3 *A child turns the page and hears her mother's voice reading*

Comic book Apps

As children get older, comic books can be a great way to spark interest in reading (particularly in boys). There are also amazing Apps like Pixton (see Figure 7.8 on page 119) where children can personalize comics by selecting details to create their own characters, scenery and props. This App has so much potential for our visual learners to create their own reading materials. A teacher can monitor the comics and decide when they are ready to be shared with classmates. Imagine the potential of a class of children creating their own books and sharing them.

This App could also be used to tailor stories explaining social situations, schedules and change. Wow!

What a difference a determined parent makes

Reading is not something to be left until a child starts school. The sooner the better! Bedtime is a lovely time to start building in the routine of sharing stories. We give out specially adapted bedtime stories on our home visits with new children. We incorporate signs and symbols so that children can link the words to meaning and so that parents can begin to use some signs to bring words to life. When parents back up what is being taught at school by sharing books and developing matching and sequencing skills, a child can progress so much faster.

I'm going to hand over to two lovely mums now, who have given their little ones an amazing head start, through investing their own time, research, creativity and determination. These mums are a great example and have kindly allowed me to share their journeys towards helping their children learn to read.

CASE STUDY: Teaching my child with autism to read

Claire Moss is a wonderful mum. I asked her to share with me how she got her son reading. She's kindly allowed me to include her little man Harley's journey so far.

Harley's big motivator was sweets, lollies, chocolate and milk. He would constantly take my hand grunting, pulling me to the kitchen cupboard where he knew these goodies were kept. I'd keep telling myself, 'He's doing great, this is a great form of communication.' If only he was picking one of his five a day! Not giving him a reward would result in the biggest meltdown ever. He would get cocky and have me trawling through my entire cupboard looking at everything it had to offer.

I couldn't go on like that and neither could his teeth. I emptied the entire cupboards and put a few of his favourite things in a few small Tupperware containers:

- Container 1. 5 × Haribo sweets – lid tightly shut with a Haribo label stuck on the front
- Container 2. 3 × small chocolate buttons – buttons wrapper stuck on the front.

I did this for crisps, Fruit Shoot (only juice he would drink) and raisins (which he hated). Raisins were going to be my control test. Next day Harley was in for a shock.

Little Man soon learnt that the label represented what was in the container, and when the container was empty what was in it was finished and gone until the next day. He didn't like it, but very soon accepted it.

From here I moved on to PECS (Picture exchange Communication System – see Chapter 11). Little picture visuals I stuck to the fridge door. I started with two – lolly and milk (both huge motivators for Harley). Every time he dragged me to the fridge for one of them I made him 'exchange'. For what seemed the longest time ever I persevered with this until one night (probably the early hours at this stage as Harley never slept) he brought me a PECS symbol of the lolly. I burst into tears and, although it was stupid o'clock, immediately rewarded him with his lolly.

From there we started the PECS program all the time – persevere, persevere, persevere would be my motto. All this time each PECS symbol had the printed word typed on.

Harley went to mainstream nursery against the recommendations of the special needs school. They did some of the See and Learn program with him and at the end of the year I introduced written text instead of the picture for his favourite things.

As he started reception and was still unable to vocalize I asked school if we could move away from phonics and start with the See and Learn program. After all we already knew Harley was fab at matching and was such a visual learner. I wasted no time going home printing and laminating.

I started with four pictures and words and went through four stages:

1. I would make sure that Harley understood what the picture was, e.g. I would ask 'Which is the cat?', and he would select it from the choice of four pictures.

2. Matching the visual to the text. I would give Harley the picture and he would match it to the correct word. (It was easier to match the visual to the text than the text to the visual for Harley.)

3. Matching the text to the visual. I would give Harley the word and he would match it to the correct visual.

4. Finally, I would remove the visuals and see if he could give me the right word. I would ask: 'Harley, which one is the cat?' Harley would give me the word requested.

I would then introduce four more words with that same process and then another four.

Next I introduced the words he learnt in a home-made book with a very simple sentence for each word or group of words. Harley would have to pick the correct word from an ever-increasing group of words.

This process was relatively quick. It took just over a few weeks. We are now moving on to creating and constructing new sentences.

I can't say for sure whether it's the latest approach that has got him reading or whether it's just been the whole two-year approach to visuals, PECS and now this. One thing's for sure, he's amazing us all with what he can do!

Update

We have had Harley's statement review and he has made amazing progress. He has even overtaken some of his peers with his reading. I was honoured to have the educational psychologist attend and we are all quite excited about what he may be capable of achieving. I had to stop myself from crying at hearing this. To think that two years ago I couldn't get him to even leave the house without screaming with anxiety. He's come so far. Very proud of him!!

CASE STUDY: How I taught my daughter with Down's Syndrome to read

Deepa Garwa is a teacher and a mum to two children. Her little girl has Down's Syndrome. She's kindly allowed me to share a post from her blog 'Parenting in Two Minutes'.

After a lot of research, I got to know some strategies that were being used to teach special needs children around the world and the research happening on it. Initially I was overwhelmed – there were so many different methodologies and varied information available that I had to tread carefully. After following it all up for a while I looked for people who were credible and had years of experience like Sue Buckley, Natalie Hale, NACD and other DS education associations who were researching in this field. I read about well-researched ways of teaching, ways to increase concentration, retention and other important things to get me started. I realized that the secret was not in buying as many books as I could. The secret was in understanding what will work best for my child. I met a few parents and therapists who told me flash cards wouldn't work or it was too early to start, but I wanted to give it a shot with all the faith I had in the things that I had researched for and the effort I was going to put into it. It was important to be consistent, creative and individualistic and I tried to be just that.

Natalie Hale's blog 'Special Reads' helped me immensely. I started by making some flash cards, personal books and modifying other available books for Aarshia. I followed her advice to the tee. I did all of this while she was still in her play school and the results were astonishing! In three months she was reading better than most of her peers in play school and the teachers were super impressed. I used the mix of sight words, phonics and personal books and mixed it with the things she was interested in and it all worked well for her.

Today, when I see her taking a book every day to the school and when her teacher tells me that she loves to read I feel proud of her because reading has given her immense confidence. I still remember the first book she ever read in her class and the amount of self belief it gave her. (Garwa 2014)

Using the internet, software or touch screens to teach reading

More and more parents are using program from the internet to teach their children to read. Schools also set homework for children to read on sites such as Bug Club where the teacher can add books and track progress.

SEN Assist software

In 2004 we began to develop ideas for new story software.

I began by breaking down stories into simple language with repeated use of the first 100 key words in the English language. We added symbols above the words and they were animated to draw the child's eye towards them as they were spoken. The animation and images were deliberately simple and uncluttered because we wanted the child's eye drawn to the words. The idea was that, by seeing those words more frequently, they would learn to read by recognizing their pattern. Please see Chapter 17 for more information about SEN Assist.

Dyslexia fonts

If a child is used to a dyslexia font, where letters are weighted to avoid them being moved around, it may be worth creating letters in this font to add to the resources.

More simple strategies
Overlays and coloured papers

Experiment with different-coloured acetate overlays, seeing if the child notices any benefits. These are not expensive and can make a huge difference. A child may be better able to read when worksheets and reading materials are printed on paper of a certain colour. We must keep tweaking and tailoring to meet the needs of the individual child.

Chapter 10

Teaching a Child to Read High Frequency Words
A Structured Approach

The man who moves a mountain begins by carrying away small stones.

Confucius (551BC–479BC)

You may hear reading specialists suggest teaching through mental orthographic images (teaching high frequency words as sight words). A child gradually builds a bank of high frequency words they can read by sight. They are taught through visual repetition. There are several fun, hands-on, visual ways to help students master the sight words.

The website Dyslexia Help suggests the following:

- Help students to visualize letter patterns by having them create colorful, meaning-based, word art. For example, in order to remember 'yacht' your student may draw a shape of a boat with the 'ht' leading up to the sail, and the 'y' leading down to an anchor. Ask the student to close her eyes and make a 'photograph' of how the word looks. If the student truly has a mental image of the whole word, she will be able to fluently spell it forwards or backwards.

- Play with the words in a card game of 'Go Fish', 'Old Maid', or 'Memory'. This is especially helpful for kinesthetic learners.

- Repeatedly practice a small set (no more than half a dozen) of sight words until they are mastered with 100% accuracy on several different days. Frequently recycle the words, so that they are not forgotten.

(Dyslexia Help 2015b)

CASE STUDY: Teaching Natty to read high frequency words

Once Hayley Goleniowska's daughter Natty had mastered initial sounds, they kept going with the phonics work (see Chapter 9), but also started to work on sight reading the high frequency words.

When Natty began school at four, she knew most of her phonic sounds by sight. However, she began reading using a *whole word* approach. There is evidence that children with Down's Syndrome (DS) are very able at this, recognizing whole words by shape alone. It's very useful for high frequency words that follow no logical sound pattern as well. So we:

- made flashcards with words on and stuck them around the house/on the fridge
- matched the mini flashcards to words that were the same within texts
- made simple games of snap/bingo with the words.

She then began reading simple texts (such as the Oxford Reading Tree) using these words, but we kept up the individual phonics work with a view to her learning to blend and write. After all, we all read using a combination of whole word recognition, blending and prediction based on understanding of what will come next.

New resources[1]

Children with learning difficulties will often learn best when an approach is linked to their high interest motivators, structured, broken down to an achievable task and repeated. I realized that we needed a way of teaching children to read the high frequency words. I wanted it to be motivating, hands-on, visual and based on strengths such as matching. So we grouped the high frequency words together into smaller sub-groups and taught the child six at a time. Once the first six were mastered we could move on to the next six.

Thinking (as always) of saving teachers' time too, I thought if we created a set of 'high frequency words' reading folders then they could be shared with other classes. Each folder would be colour-coded to link with the child's level. Children would master the words in the yellow folder and then move on to the orange folder. In a school the resources could be used again and again by many children.

I discussed the idea with our headteacher and another teacher and we decided to trial it with a small group of children (with consent from their parents). These

1   The resources referred to in this section are available to download from www.jkp.com/catalogue/book/9781849055987.

trials are still in the early stages and the resources are not presented as having been researched, but so far I have found the 1:1 reading sessions have really motivated the children involved and they are making progress. When the children see me come to class with my folder they jump up excited to leave class and work 1:1 on reading.

The set of resources we have developed will help teach the first 45 high frequency words as well as three additional words: 'off', 'want' and 'help' (to make up eight sets of six words). The three additional words are in the first, second and final set, so if teachers prefer to omit them they can.

The word groups are shown in Table 10.1.

Table 10.1 High frequency word groups

Yellow Level 1	Orange Level 2	Red Level 3	Pink Level 4	Purple Level 5	Blue Level 6	Green Level 7	Grey Level 8
I	in	get	look	and	am	was	going
up	can	it	went	cat	he	of	away
on	see	for	at	dog	is	like	this
go	a	me	day	dad	to	they	my
we	mum	she	no	the	play	you	help
off	want	said	yes	big	all	are	come

Baseline assessment

To begin ideally (for research or to demonstrate progression), you would create a baseline by getting a child to read through the high frequency word sets and write down any that they can read, but research ideals can diverge from what is ideal for the individual child. A child's self esteem and self confidence are paramount. If you know they cannot read any high frequency words, do not start them off with a series of fails. You will be setting up this whole process wrong because you want the child to feel happy when they see you with their coloured folder. They must anticipate 'fun' and praise rather than hard work. If you want to have a baseline for your records then say, 'Let's read these words together.' Read the words, but never allow a child to feel they are failing. You could say, 'Can you help me? I'm going to try to read these words.' Read each one, but do leave enough of a pause so that they can say the word or sound if they recognize it. If they read one, act amazed. Tell them how clever you think they are. Relate your own experiences of learning to read. Let them know you understand and admire their determination and willingness to 'have a go'. Inject positives at every opportunity.

Is the child attempting to sound out or break down the word using knowledge of phonics or letters? This system is a scaffold for children who may not use phonics to learn to read, so do look out for any natural tendency to sound out. There are many ways to learn spelling and develop reading skills.

If you want to assess all 48 words, split this between other activities. Do not make this a negative for the child. If you know after the first 15 words that the child will not read *any,* do not push it. The last thing you want to do is harm a child's self esteem. You could assess reading set by set, noting if they read any words at the start of the word set. For research a baseline is helpful, but if the focus is pure teaching there is no real harm in doing the assessment at the start of each word set as the child matches the words.

Recording

Record each session in the simple tick box recording sheet provided in the resources. This will give you an idea of speed of progression and emerging reading skills. If a child seems stuck on the first phase and shows no sign of recognizing any of the words, you may need to think of another method to teach them. No one system can work for every child. These resources are simply another idea and a strategy to try.

Abbreviations for recording

Time is short. We want to use it for teaching, so abbreviate any recording. These abbreviations are also noted on the sheets for consistency.

M: Modelling
HOH: Hand over hand
P/P: Physical prompt
V/P: Verbal prompt
I: Independent

MODELLING

Modelling in teacher talk does not involve catwalks or glossy magazines. It is showing a child how to do something by doing it rather than helping them or instructing them. This can be a great way to introduce new tasks to a child who struggles with verbal instructions or a child who becomes particularly anxious when demands are placed. Modelling can remove the verbal and remove the demand, which is a way in with some visual learners.

HAND OVER HAND

Hand-over-hand support is when you guide the child's hand. Make sure they are looking at the task and there must be cooperation. There is no point in taking a child's hand and doing things completely for them. Hand over hand should be a way of walking the child through the motions so that they learn the rhythms of the task and can eventually do it independently.

PHYSICAL PROMPT

A physical prompt might be a gentle direction such as pointing to the task, lifting a symbol and putting it in a child's hand to remind them to start a task. The child should then begin to complete the task independently.

VERBAL PROMPT

Maybe you say the child's name to prompt them to begin, or you instruct 'put with the same' for matching or give them the start of the word or first word in reading.

INDEPENDENT

Hooray! The child knows exactly what to do and completes the task with no prompting.

Is the child ready?

Before you begin teaching sight reading of the high frequency words, a child should have achieved building their own name and be able to select their name from a choice of six or more. They should be able to match some motivating words to words, and words to pictures. If they are not able to do this they will not be ready for this stage yet. Continue to work on their name as shown in Chapter 8 and word and picture matching discussed in Chapter 9.

Creating resources

What you will need

Ideally you will keep all the resources created in a box or file of a corresponding colour. So for the first resource set you will need yellow paper to mount each resource, laminating sheets, hard and soft sticky Velcro, a laminator and a guillotine (for speed).

Magnetic paper clips and a magnetic fishing rod will add fun to the fishing task. This task is described in more detail later in the chapter.

Include a motivating word matching task

Include a matching task with the resources so that they start out with something familiar. If they have been using the same old task for a while it would be worth creating a new motivating one. This will spark their interest and they will be happy with a task they know that they can do.

Figure 10.1 *This child loved dogs so the matching task was based on matching dog breeds*

Getting started

Approach the child at a good time. There is no point starting out on this when they are hungry, tired or engaged in something you will not be able to compete with (such as watching YouTube videos on the computer).

Be armed with your yellow file, but also a motivating soft toy or plastic cartoon character, linked with their high interest motivators. One of the students I worked with on this liked dogs, so when we started out I went to collect him with a couple of toy dogs and the first task was matching dogs and dog types. Always start with motivating matching and finish with fishing. This way the child has a clear idea of when the session is nearly finished.

Word matching

Help them achieve this even if they find it difficult or seem to lack motivation. Maybe start by getting a favourite character or toy to hold the words to get them looking at them, as shown in Figure 10.1. Read the words as you hold them, encourage them to look, but help them get it right. They are learning the task. You are not expecting them to complete it independently right away. If they do, then it's fantastic!

Modelling and using actions

Can they read any of the words? Model reading each word, pointing to it and reading slowly and clearly. The first set of words can be linked to actions to add to the visual. If a child is pre-verbal or non-verbal, their actions may indicate that they are able to read the words. Look out for this and make a note of it.

If a child uses Makaton or sign language then learn the signs for each word. This will get the child's attention. Our school have the Makaton symbol set attached to our Symwriter writing with symbols program. Using this I printed the signs and symbols for each word, adding another visual layer (see Figure 10.2 on page 156). This proved a great way to provide a child with a quick hint when they were trying to read. If you are not using Makaton signs then there are some ideas below for adding another visual layer by associating set actions with the words in the Level 1 words.

- I – Hold up your pointer finger so it takes the shape of the 'I'. Comment on this, then point to yourself.

- up – Point upwards or stand up. Talk about the 'p' being stuck in the mud to give another visual cue.

- on – Make an 'o' shape with your finger and thumb so that the child sees it. Say 'o' as a single sound, then seperate the fingers so that they form more of an 'n' shape and place them on something.

- off – Make the 'o' shape again, sitting your 'o' wherever you placed your 'on', and then dive with two of your fingers in an 'f' swoop.

- go – Gesture away and say very sternly 'go'.

- we – Point to the child and point to yourself. If the child mirrors actions, you could hold up a hand with the fingers spread out in a 'w' pattern. Touch palms and say 'we'.

Only do these things if they are motivating the child. A child with autism may prefer to get on and match without all this interaction and language to process.

Introduce one word set at a time so that the child learns to read these words by sight without images to prompt.

Figure 10.2 *High frequency word matching set with Makaton line drawings to show signs*

Fishing resources

The fishing resources can be used to create a simple fishing game. Use the same words from the high frequency word set you are working on. There will be six fish. Each one will have a different word. Take it in turns with the child (or if you are working with more than one child, support them taking turns with each other). Place the fish (word side down) on a blue piece of paper cut into a pool shape. Add lily pads (if you are feeling creative). For my tank I use a large upside-down drum (as we work in our music room). Use what you have. A hula hoop from the sports cupboard can also make a good pond.

Put paperclips on the fish head or tails and use a magnetic rod to go fishing. The fish can be used for other activities as well. Fishing games are a great way to spark interest and get the child looking at the words.

Finish with fishing

I always finish with fishing when working through a word set. This way, no matter how many tasks are included in between, the child knows that when they see the fish they are nearly finished. This is particularly useful with children who become anxious or restless when they do not know the exact expectations, for example those with autism or ADHD. Children tend to see the fishing activity as 'easy' (it's a game). You can use this to your advantage. Different children will cope with different demands. If you sense them getting anxious or losing focus, you might want to say 'One more, then fishing' or 'Fishing next'. As they learn the structure, they will realize that the fish are a visual which signifies that they are nearly finished.

Coding through fish size and colour

There are long fish for longer words and shorter fish for the shorter words. Fish are coloured to correlate with the colours of the ground, grass and sky, which may help a child with positioning letters and holding the word the right way up. This will help show a child which way up to hold the fish to read the word.

If you want to, you can colour code the fish by backing them with coloured paper and cutting around them. Use the same coloured paper as the word set that you are working on. This can provide an extra hint for children as you build on the number of fish in the tank.

Including motivators on the fish

You could add a little motivating high-interest picture to the back of some of the words. If you Velcro the motivators then you can keep sets of motivators and change them for different children rather than remaking the resource for each child.

Take turns ensuring the child gets their motivating fish. Act disappointed when you don't get a motivator. This will appeal and amuse some children, spurring them on to 'win' the motivating fish.

The fishing resource can be used in many ways. You may be able to get hold of a rod with a magnet at the end. You can add paperclips or little strips of magnetic tape to the fish.

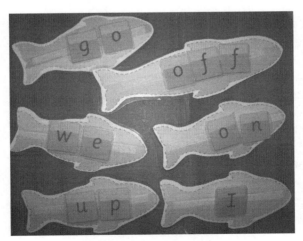

Figure 10.3 Fishing resource

Begin with having whole words on the fish, but in time you may want to fish to build words (first one to build the word wins). Get creative with this resource. Anything that gets the child looking at the words and letters will help.

Word reading, building and writing tasks

Next they complete a word reading, building and, if they would be willing, writing task from the set of six 'yellow' reading, word building and writing tasks.

You are using the same words each time until they are mastered. All the time this helps the child to learn them. Having six words to learn seems achievable. Without breaking it down, the child just sees a sea of different words and it may be difficult to process this jumble and imagine ever being able to read. It must seem possible and achievable so that the child does not become overwhelmed.

How many tasks should a child complete at the start?

This will entirely depend upon the child and their concentration, motivation and independence skills. Some children will whizz through this and want another folder. Explain they have done great and get the next folder when they can read the six 'yellow' words. This may be another motivator to learn.

Once you have assessed how many tasks a child is likely to complete, it will help if you tell the child how many tasks are left. Knowing expectations can greatly help a child who learns visually to stay on task.

Take care with writing

Remember that the focus here is reading. If you've got a willing writer then this is a great opportunity to build those skills. Some children are more than happy to practise handwriting. The more they practise, the better they will get.

If they do not yet write and are resistant, they may trace over the word.

If you know that seeing that writing symbol will be a trigger and cause a child huge anxiety, then chop this bit off the task and tackle writing another time. Similarly, if you are working with a child who is still at a mark-making stage, you could cover it with a bit of paper for them to do this or again remove the task.

Or perhaps writing skills are more advanced and a child would be able to copy the word without tracing. If this is the case, cover the tracing letters and allow them to write. Do keep an eye on letter formation, though. It is difficult to unlearn once a child gets into the habit of moving around a letter in the wrong direction. The focus here is reading, so if in any doubt leave handwriting as a separate task for another time.

Figure 10.4 A child builds the word, then writes the word

Starting to read words together and creating meaning

Finally they have two simple texts to read to show that their learning has meaning. All of these resources are available to download from www.jkp.com/catalogue/book/9781849055987.

One word set at a time, but do revise

Complete one colour band at a time until a child has mastered matching and reading words from the set, then move them on. Occasionally swap back to a mastered set to check that those words can still be read. If a child uses tray tasks then you could include a mastered word building task in with their independent work.

Give praise if the child can recall the previous words. This indicates that they will progress with reading the high frequency words. Some people learn in such a way that they cram information and then when it is no longer needed they forget it. If you do not revisit mastered words a child could choose to do this. They must know that word lists will reappear.

Always set the amount of work to what the child will be willing to do. Push gently and add extra work if your instinct says he'll manage. As the child gets more familiar with the words and the structure of these tasks, he will get quicker. These sessions should be short and motivating.

Ideally tasks should be done once a day (ideally in the morning or when a child is most alert and happy to learn). They can be stored in folders along with a set of stickers to reward the child on successful completion. Make this time really happy and positive with plenty of praise for any achievement. Include individual motivators in the box or use whatever is motivating the child that day. If a penguin toy has the child's attention, get the penguin to hold the words and direct the child. Make it fun and make the child smile. You cannot expect a child to show you his best work if your teaching style is half hearted. Become a motivator. Make it so that the child associates seeing you and his yellow folder with a fun part of the day.

Make a huge fuss when a child moves on a level. Print a certificate and tell the parents so that the child knows you are really pleased. In time, as the routine is established and more tasks are being completed, you could record a session for the parent to see. The child will soon make progress if this is taught at home, but it's important to be consistent. The last thing you want is for a child to start seeing the tasks in a negative light. Know your individual child, their parents and your staff and use instinct to decide if these activities are best kept at school or sent home.

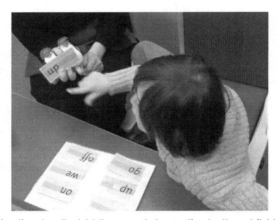

Figure 10.5 A motivating toy 'holds' the words to motivate the child to look and match

Figure 10.6 Level 1, yellow word set – matching task

Figure 10.7 Building a simple sentence with Level 1 words – 'I go up'

Saving time for busy teachers

In time you will have built a bank of eight coloured folders filled with resources for each phase. These can be pulled out by teachers for different students. All they will need to make is the motivating tasks tailored to the child's high interest. Encourage them to add these to another file so that in time you can also have a bank of motivating tasks, which will save even more time. As these grow, add file dividers for quick reference. Interests repeat – dinosaurs, wild animals, sports or Disney princesses. No matter how bizarre the interest seems, it's worth keeping the resources once they've been made. They may even provide ideas for a teacher to follow a resource structure. Keep these resources together and some day they will make a busy teacher smile.

Ten tips for getting started with the word set resources to teach a child to read the high frequency words without symbols

- Try to make this a motivating and fun activity. Inject a huge amount of enthusiasm and praise. 'Jenny is soooooo clever!', 'Good girl', etc.

- Have a reward or motivator for when the activity is finished.

- Let the child see the work in the folder so they know your expectations before you begin.

- Set the amount of work to what you think the child will cope with. Maybe just start with matching.

- Get a motivating toy to 'hold' the words and ask the child to read.

- Work in a distraction-free area (if the child is happy with this).

- Introduce other people to work with the child once the first word set is mastered.

- Record progress on simple chart and make notes after.

- Add stickers to the child's home contact book and share progress with parents.

- If you are making good progress, film how you work with the child so that there is a consistent approach when others start.

Possible modifications for fine motor difficulties

You may find that the letters are too small and fiddly for children with problems with fine motor skills. If you have a colour photocopier in school you could enlarge and print the resources A3 size.

Another helpful trick if fine motor is an issue is to thicken the letter with a bit of smaller card glued centrally on the back. This will raise up the symbol and make them easier to lift.

Chapter 11

Visuals for Communication

An Introduction to the Picture
Exchange Communication System
and Going Beyond 'I Want...'[1]

As Walt Disney once said, 'Of all of our inventions for mass communication, pictures still speak the most universally understood language.' Pictures communicate when we need to get important information across fast. Think of swimming pool safety signs, road signs and warning signs. Children will find meaning in pictures long before they learn to read words. For a child with communication difficulties, pictures can allow them to make requests, communicate feelings and comment. They can also help the child feel included and be active in group discussions, increasing learning opportunities and raising their self esteem.

Temple Grandin, who is a well-known and much admired adult with autism, and author of numerous books including *Thinking in Pictures,* states:

> It's very important for the parents of young autistic children to encourage them to talk, or for those that don't talk, to give them a way of communicating, like a picture board, where they can point to a glass of milk, or a jacket if they're cold, or the bathroom. If they want something, then they need to learn to request that thing. (Grandin 2006b)

Andrew S. Bondy and Lori Frost developed the Picture Exchange Communication System (PECS) in 1985:

> PECS begins by teaching an individual to give a picture of a desired item to a 'communicative partner' who immediately honors the exchange as a request. The system goes on to teach discrimination of pictures and how to put them together in sentences. In the more advanced phases, individuals are taught to answer questions and to comment. (PECS n.d.)

---

1 I would like to acknowledge Donna Banzhof, MEd, BCBA, of Pyramid Educational Consultants, who has helped with this chapter.

I have seen so many children learn to communicate effectively through PECS. When a child makes progress it is the most exhilarating feeling. I would compare it to the feeling which sky divers must get each time they take that first leap out of a plane. This never changes, never dulls… It is one of the amazing buzzes of special needs teaching.

If you are a parent or teacher working with a child with significant communication difficulties and can possibly get to a Level 1 two-day basic PECS training course, it will be worthwhile and empowering. This chapter offers a glimpse into ways I have used my PECS training to improve communication. The case studies and classroom practices I give in this chapter are examples of how PECS can be put to use in school, but they are no substitute for proper training. PECS courses are currently run by certified Pyramid Educational Consultants. The PECS website is the best place to find more information about PECS courses and resources.[2]

Creating a Picture Exchange Communication System may sound like a lot of work to set up, but it is well worth the effort. If you are starting out with PECS, try to ensure that pictures are available to the child in all settings – school, home, respite or Gran and Grandpa's house. This will make so much difference to the child's progress. Once they are using pictures to communicate, the child should have access to this wherever they are. Be consistent and grab each opportunity, because the more practice a child has, the faster they will make progress.

A child using PECS progresses through six phases. They should master each phase consistently before moving on to the next.

The six phases as listed on the PECS website are:

PHASE I
How to Communicate

Students learn to exchange single pictures for items or activities they really want.

PHASE II
Distance and Persistence

Still using single pictures, students learn to generalize this new skill by using it in different places, with different people and across distances. They are also taught to be more persistent communicators.

---

2   See www.pecs.com.

PHASE III
Picture Discrimination

Students learn to select from two or more pictures to ask for their favorite things. These are placed in a communication book – a ring binder with Velcro strips where pictures are stored and easily removed for communication.

PHASE IV
Sentence Structure

Students learn to construct simple sentences on a detachable Sentence Strip using an 'I want' picture followed by a picture of the item being requested.

Attributes and Language Expansion

Students learn to expand their sentences by adding adjectives, verbs and prepositions.

PHASE V
Answering Questions

Students learn to use PECS to answer the question, 'What do you want?'

PHASE VI
Commenting

Now students are taught to comment in response to questions such as, 'What do you see?', 'What do you hear?' and 'What is it? They learn to make up sentences starting with 'I see', 'I hear', 'I feel', 'It is a', etc.[3]

Getting started

Our first priority is to discover a child's motivator, which may be anything – their bottle of milk, a squeaky toy, a tickle or even a twig. Whatever it is (as long as you can supervise and ensure it is safe), then that is the best starting point. Print a photograph or symbol for whatever the motivator is. Ideally you will laminate the picture as this will help it to last longer. (The symbol will be handled many times so a paper one will not last.) If you are not ready to invest in a laminator you could use sticky-back plastic or even cover it in sticky tape. PECS symbols are usually laminated with Velcro stuck to the back of them. This means they can be added to a communication binder or to a PECS board when a child progresses to making choices.

---

3   Copyright © 1992–2014 Pyramid Educational Consultants, Inc. All rights reserved.

We have a rule in our special school to remind us of which type of Velcro to use. The mantra is 'soft to symbol and hard to the card', so the soft Velcro goes on the back of the symbols and the hard Velcro goes on the 'card' (board or book page).

Sticky Velcro, laminators and laminating pouches are all available to buy online and worth the investment if you plan to use PECS. There are also companies that ready-make symbol sets to save busy parents time. If a child is already using PECS at school then ask if you can have copies of symbols which they are using.

The six phases
Phase I: How to communicate

Once you have the symbol for your child's motivator, display this symbol somewhere prominent within the child's eye-line and immediate reach, such as on a table in front of the child.

When a child is first learning Phase I it is important to have two people so that one person can support the child in making the exchange and the other person can accept the symbol, model language by labelling the motivator and then give it to the child. The person supporting can silently guide the child to lift the symbol and hand it over, as shown in Figure 11.1.

Repetition will help the child learn the process of taking the symbol and handing it over in exchange for their motivator. The exchange gets them what they want. Assistance should fade over time so that the child is independent and will instigate PECS exchanges.

Figure 11.1 Phase I of PECS. A child being supported to hand over a symbol

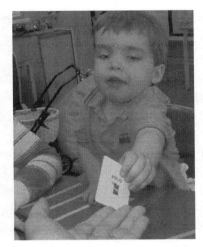

Figure 11.2 A child lifting the symbol independently and making the exchange

Only have one PECS symbol in front of the child at a time. When a child hands you the symbol spontaneously, without assistance, their reward must be instant.

Phase II: Distance and persistence

This is an exciting stage because you really see that the child has understood that they can get what they want through exchanging symbols. The child has already consistently mastered handing over a picture in exchange for their motivator. Now you teach them to travel across the room and get your attention in order to get what they want. When a child masters this phase, we celebrate because we know they are going to make great progress communicating with people. This phase is also reintroduced after each of the next phases to ensure that the child remains a persistent communicator.

Figure 11.3 A child travels across the room to make a PECS exchange

Phase III: Picture discrimination

At this phase the child selects the picture of what they want from two or more pictures which are on a communication board or in a folder or book. You continue to use whatever you have discovered motivates the child. This phase begins by pairing a picture of a motivator and a picture of an item they do not like. Once discrimination is evident, then two pictures of their motivators are paired together. More symbols are added, and children learn to open their communication book and flip through the pages to find the symbol of their motivator.

Ensure language is consistent. If there is any chance that staff would use a different label for a motivating item, then add the label you want used to the symbol. The idea is that each time the child makes the exchange they hear the correct label. If language is inconsistent, this could cause confusion. All the time we are building scaffolds for communication.

Snack time

If a child has been using PECS to get food or drink, then snack time is a great time to move them on to selecting a favoured picture.

It can be helpful to label snacks and bottles of drink with the same symbols that you are expecting the child to discriminate between. This can help the child make a connection between the snack and the symbols.

Remember that the point is to get as many exchanges in as possible, so do not be overly generous. For example, do not give them a whole packet of crisps for one exchange – only give two or three. At this stage a child should be making multiple exchanges.

It may help to create a PECS folder for snack time, which can be used by children and staff who do not have PECS books. Children who have advanced further can become models by exchanging symbols to request snacks.

Figure 11.4 *A child opens their folder and selects their choice of snack*

Don't get stuck on snack time

Snack time is often a great starting point for teaching communication (if food or drink are motivators), but children should be taught early that pictures can also be used for communication during choice time, lessons, lunch and at playtime (*all* times).

Choice times

For PECS choices, photograph toys in a cupboard or in a box. Lock cupboards and store boxes out of reach so that the child has to ask. If a child likes specific books, DVDs or music, then create a visual choice board. Use whatever motivates the child to communicate.

Playtime

Take a look at your play area. If a child wanted a ball or a bike, but could not communicate this through speech or signs, how would they ask? Are the symbols set up ready on a board or do the children take their PECS books out to the playground? What if a child needs the toilet or hurts himself? All of these things must be taken into consideration if you have children with communication difficulties accessing the playground. Never miss an opportunity! It is time consuming and it can be frustrating as symbols disappear or get ruined, but it is vital to keep on top of it. This job can be delegated. Maybe a playtime supervisor would be willing to take this on if you explained how important it is. Get them excited about the opportunities for communication. Explain the progress that a child can make and get them thinking about how they would feel without the means to communicate. Do not be afraid to ask other people for help, because it is impossible to take on responsibility for making every symbol and keeping an inventory of which ones need to be replaced.

Never be put off by comments like 'We've tried that before' or 'The symbols will all get lost.' It is up to you to inject the enthusiasm and get tired-out staff determined to stay on top of those symbols and try things again. Reply with 'But we know how important it is.' Or 'I know *you* can get people keeping on top of this' and 'You are giving the child a voice – how amazing that is!' Do not accept excuses, because right now *you* are a child's best chance of having a voice.

Lunch

Lunch is another great opportunity for communication. Ideally a child will be able to select their choice of food by using symbols, but if this seems too daunting then you can colour band choices so a child chooses red, green or white. The different foods are placed in areas highlighted by colours so that a child who does not have the specific food symbol could select the 'red choice' and get the food that they want. Ideally they will have the right food symbols to make their selection.

At the table there is another opportunity not to miss. Symbols such as 'knife', 'fork', 'spoon' and 'plate' should be available.

At my school we also use colour-coded symbols for 'more', 'finished', 'toilet' and 'help' everywhere, including lunch times. It is so important to teach children how they can communicate these basic needs.

Figure 11.5 Using PECS at lunch time

Phase IV: Sentence structure

During this phase a child is taught to construct a sentence, such as 'I want ball'. A sentence strip is introduced along with an 'I want' picture to the child's communication book. At this stage they learn to first take the symbol and place it on the sentence strip next to the 'I want' picture. The child then lifts the sentence strip and hands it over. The next step is for the child to learn to place the 'I want' picture on the sentence strip and the reinforcer picture. They are then taught to point to 'I want' and then the picture. Once a child can point to the pictures, a pause is then inserted when reading the sentence to the child. Always leave a pause when labelling to allow the child to try to make a sound or say the word themselves. The pause shows that the expectation is that they should be doing the speaking. You are modelling what they should be saying. If they do start making sounds, use your instinct and hold back while they make their best sound. There may be no physical reason why a child is not speaking. PECS can provide them with the right structures and supports to develop use of functional language quicker when they start speaking.

CASE STUDY: Isaac (age 7)

Diagnosis: Down's Syndrome

Isaac had made fantastic progress with PECS and had reached Phase IV. He was able to get his PECS book and request things he needed to complete tasks in lessons. We wanted to build on his communication opportunities, and as food was a motivator we decided lunch was a key time.

My amazing teaching assistant took on the responsibility of making symbols for every possible dinner choice and then each day she would check the school menu and ensure he had the right symbols in his PECS book to request what he wanted.

We also included symbols for cutlery, help and the type of help – cutting, pouring, peeling, etc.

Isaac made fantastic progress and was able to go to the dinner hatch and ask the dinner lady for what he wanted using symbols and speech. His speech improved and seemed to become clearer by the day, and his ability to recognize and read symbols increased as there were so many opportunities. He also learnt to use his PECS to form the sentence 'I want help cutting'.

There are so many opportunities to develop communication during lunch time. I'm thankful that I had such a devoted teaching assistant willing to put in extra time to move this boy on. The reward was to see the incredible progress he made with using his PECS and how clear his speech was getting.

Attributes and language expansion

Once the child has mastered using a sentence strip we want to get them to expand their sentences by adding adjectives, verbs and prepositions. This can be introduced at any activity in the day where a child has a strong preference about some aspect of their motivator. For example, during snack time: 'I want short breadstick', 'I want long breadstick' or 'I want jam on toast'.

CASE STUDY: Breakfast club

My new class were arriving from their long journey to school flustered and unsettled. I knew that it would be unfair (okay, impossible) to expect them to start 'working' right away. Some of them had had long journeys, which involved having to sit still for a long time, and prior to this they had experienced the school run bundle that can happen in busy families. I was also aware that some of them might not have managed to have any breakfast. I did not want to start them off on the wrong foot. Children should enter a classroom and feel at home and secure. If you are battling rumbling tummies and anxiety, then children will not be in the right frame of mind to focus and learn.

I decided to start a breakfast club. As the children came into class they would smell the homey aroma of toast. I wanted to use the toast as an opportunity to start the day off with multiple PECS exchanges. Once the toast was ready I would put it on a plate in front of me and cut it up into small pieces. The idea behind this was to get as many communication exchanges in as we could. As well as the toast I had a knife, plates, butter and a variety of spreads. I kept these all together out of reach of the students. We had a great horseshoe-shaped table which was ideal for this type of session. The shape of the table made it clear which adult was in charge of the toast, as they would be sitting at the centre. We changed the person leading the session so that the children got used to communicating with whoever was leading. The staff enjoyed leading the session and it was a great opportunity to develop their skills.

Most of the children had PECS books, and I put the symbols in their books so they could create a sentence to ask for what they wanted. I made a communication board with all the symbols and an 'I want...' PECS strip set up for those without PECS books. The support staff were great at modelling making sentences. 'I want toast, butter and honey on toast please.' They were really motivated by this new start to our school day too.

These sessions were an amazing success. We saw students move on quickly from handing over a big 'toast' picture to making the sentence 'I want toast', to creating more complex sentences like 'I want butter and jam on white toast'.

The support staff were great models and the children learnt from each other. Another key to motivating the students was that they soon realized that the toast would run out. If they wanted to get some they needed to communicate. The children not only made great progress with their communication skills, but the day started on a really positive note. Breakfast club did not take up much time, but meant that the children started the day happy and communicating to the best of their ability, which would impact their ability to learn when lessons began.

Lessons

Colours can be a great starting point to getting a child using their PECS. I often begin a literacy session with a selection of coloured boxes containing motivating toys so that the children need to request a box by colour (see Chapter 5 for more details).

Figure 11.6 Image showing PECS strip:
'I want yellow box please'

Phase V: Answering questions

At this phase the child is taught to use PECS to answer the question, 'What do you want?' Set up opportunities in the day, such as a cutting activity without any scissors, colouring without any pencils or a shut door that they will have to ask you to open. I get support staff to model answering questions with PECS.

Never miss an opportunity! In addition to asking questions, it is important to encourage spontaneous requesting. Set up the classroom or home environment with symbols at the ready for childen to be spontaneous and as when *they* need to. In the classroom shown in Figure 11.7 the pens, pencils and scissors were all kept just out of the children's reach so that they needed to ask for them. The more opportunities the child has to communicate, the faster they will progress.

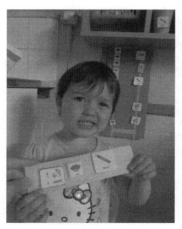

Figure 11.7 Using PECS to request a pink pencil

Phase VI: Commenting

Set up opportunities for a child to comment on a story. Let's take the example of the classic *We're Going on a Bear Hunt* by Michael Rosen. Ask the children 'What do you see?' and have a PECS board or individual PECS books set up so they can answer 'I see green grass', etc. Reward the child for commenting with praise. If praise is not very motivating for the child, try to add elements of fun suited to the individual. Maybe they would enjoy hearing the rustle of grass or getting a chance to use a water spray. Reaching Phase VI and having a child comment should be hugely celebrated because the child has gone beyond the functional 'wants' and is communicating their understanding and/or point of view.

At Phase VI we hope the child will start to communicate by commenting on what they see, feel and hear. Ideally a child will have reached a stage where they enjoy communicating and want to make comments.

Using tokens to motivate

If a child does not seem motivated to comment it may be that we still need to use a reward system. Maybe they could have a token board and get a token each time they answer a question. A token board gives the child a clear visual reward system. The child needs to answer a set amount of questions to get their reward. In time this could build, so the questions and answers are worth one token towards the reward.

Where to start? I choose 'I see...'

Structuring commenting opportunities can be a daunting task. With the best intentions there are always constraints on preparation time. How can we have a symbol ready for a child to answer every question?

The starting point is to select a sentence starter for comments. The sentence starter you choose should be interesting to the student. I usually begin with 'I see...' and create a set of symbols linked to our story. *Brown Bear, Brown Bear* by Eric Carle is an excellent one to use as you can prepare symbols for colours and animals.

Figure 11.8 PECS symbols board for Brown Bear, Brown Bear

A teaching assistant can help support a child to answer questions within a group by sitting alongside them with a PECS board and sentence strip.

How *all* visual learners benefit from PECS structures

Visual learners without any speech difficulties can also benefit from this structure. They may not have the social understanding as to why the children all have their hands up. They copy the action, but do not know the answer when asked, or they may know the answer, but get distracted while they wait and forget what it was. By having the answer in their hand they have a visual prompt. This helps the teacher to know whether they knew the answer or not.

The visual structure can also help smooth over gaps in speech. Pronouns are so often a sticking point, and practising answering 'he', 'she', 'they' or 'it' questions with a PECS sentence strip structure can really help with this.

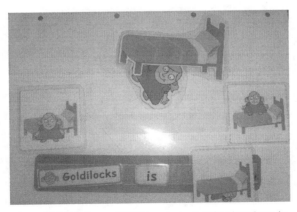

Figure 11.9 Using a PECS sentence strip structure to comment on prepositions – 'Goldilocks is under'

The Fairy Tales resources

When we created our SEN Assist Fairy Tales software I wanted resources made ready for PECS Phase VI. I wanted the structures we use in our special school literacy sessions to be available to children in *all* settings. Resources had to be quick to prepare and easy to use. Once made, the resource could be used again and again. Having a PECS board prepared will help sustain a child's focus and ability to participate during a literacy session.

If teaching a lesson about Goldilocks and the Three Bears, the teacher could quickly assess a child's knowledge of prepositions by asking, 'Where is Goldilocks?' With the initial support of an assistant the child could use a PECS board to create a sentence, 'Goldilocks is on...' The child answering could use a picture or the word with a symbol, depending on reading ability. The support staff could teach the child to hold up their answer. This creates a stepping stone towards understanding the structure of putting up a hand to answer questions in a group. The sooner we can put these structures in place and create an understanding of what fellow students are doing, the better for the child. With the right structures in place there is so much children with communication difficulties can achieve. Seeing what children can do will inspire staff to create more opportunities for a child to extend their communication throughout the day.

Chapter 12

Augmentative and Alternative Communication (AAC)

Switches, Buttons, Android, Eye Gaze and iPad Apps

Treat people as if they were what they ought to be and you help them become what they are capable of becoming.

Johann Wolfgang von Goethe (1749–1832)

Augmentative and Alternative Communication (AAC) is often associated with high tech devices, but the term covers anything that is used to facilitate communication. This might be pictures, a letter board, a book, a switch, a computer or a tablet. AAC has been a passion of mine since I was a child and I love being in a special school where I can constantly learn more.

CASE STUDY: My cousin Louise

Diagnosis: Cerebral Palsy

When I was a child we lived in a big old house which had been separated into three different parts. At one end was my family and at the other end lived my aunt and uncle with my cousins. My cousin Louise is five years older than me. She has been profoundly physically disabled by Cerebral Palsy since birth. She is not able to speak and communicates with facial expressions and by saying 'UMM' for 'Yes' and 'NNNN' for 'No'.

Louise was always included in our play and we learnt how to phrase our conversations, incorporating her 'yes' and 'no' answers so that she could communicate. We also learnt to read her eyes and expressions.

My aunt and uncle fought for Louise to access every possible innovation, so when they learnt about AACs, which could provide an electronic voice, Louise had to have one. Louise was physically disabled apart from being able to move her head, so the device was specially made so that she could operate it by pressing switches, which were placed below her chin. Louise would navigate through categories on a visual board by pressing the chin switch. She would track little lights highlighting symbols, until she got to the one she wanted. She would stop on the right one, raise her chin and it would say what she wanted. It was time consuming at first, but fascinating, and Louise was so determined to master the device. She very quickly became absolutely brilliant at it. The communication board did have limitations and looked prehistoric compared to what is now available, but it was amazing to us that Louise, who previously could only communicate with the people who really knew her, could say what she wanted in a group. As well as the usual functional comments, the device was loaded with comments, which allowed Louise to demonstrate her great sense of humour. I remember how she made us all laugh by asking 'Can I have a Babycham?' or she would say, 'Goodbye' when someone arrived at the house or simply comment 'Bloody hell' in the middle of lunch.

Seeing Louise use that communication board was such an inspiration. I never thought that the time I spent with Louise was training for my future job as a special needs teacher. It was wonderful to have experienced first hand how an AAC helped someone so close to me. That was the 1980s, and so many advances have been made since, which are giving so many people like Louise the chance to have a voice.

Responsibilities go beyond school

The strategies which allow us to facilitate communication are continuously being built on. It is frustrating to think of the adults who are still living in care homes and not accessing the means they need to communicate. Care home managers have responsibility to their residents. If they know someone could communicate and they had the opportunity, they must help them.

If a person cannot use their legs to walk they would be provided with a wheelchair. If a person cannot use their voice to communicate then they *must* be given the means to do so. For people without functional speech, access to AACs is a human right.

CASE STUDY: Frustration!

Many years ago, after returning from working with adults with learning difficulties in America, I decided that I wanted to be a care worker. I took a job in a home in Manchester. My husband Quentin took on the role of 'Activities Coordinator'.

In that care home there was a man who was physically disabled and had no speech. He made a lot of frustrated noise. The staff and other residents seemed annoyed by his noise, but I could see he was trying to communicate. As a child my cousin Louise had taught me to understand non-verbal communication – to read feelings using instinct and empathy.

I could see that this man needed to communicate. That was the reason for his disruptive roars.

I went about the home trying to find some paper and a pen because I believed if I created a grid with letters he might be able to spell out what he wanted and express the frustration so that I could help him. It took a ridiculously long while to find a pen and paper. I made a big grid of letters as he did not have the coordination to finger point. I sat beside him with the board and asked him, 'What do you want?' His fist immediately lifted and he hit 'f', 'a' and 'g'. 'You want a cigarette?' I asked. (Fag is English slang for cigarette.) The man's eyes lit up and his fist hit 'y', 'e' and 's'.

I went and asked the other staff if the man smoked. The answer was he did but they kept his cigarettes away or he would smoke one after the other. And when did he get them? I got a blank look. Is that why he chain smoked when he got them? He never knew when he would get another. He usually had no way to ask, but to roar. I got the man his cigarette and he smoked it happily. We formed a bond. After that cigarette he started to spell more words.

We had lasted in that care home job for two weeks. It was frustrating to see so much wrong and not be able to right it. We knew that it was not run in the way it should be and we could not change it, which was heartbreaking. I realized I was not going to be a care worker. I loved being in the company of the residents with physical disabilities and learning difficulties, but I did not have the same mentality as the other staff. I was too curious about the 'Can dos' and communication possibilities.

The manager came to say 'Goodbye' and saw the letter board I'd been using. Quentin told him about the man communicating and the manager said that the man 'used to do that years ago,' when he first came to the home. I was so shocked. How could he know the man could communicate and not provide him with such a basic means to do so? No wonder he had been making so much frustrated noise.

CASE STUDY: Introducing AAC

Martin Pistorius, author of Ghost Boy

Ghost Boy is a book that everyone should read. Pistorius tells the story of his experiences spending years trapped in an unresponsive body. He explains how he saw and how he felt, and helps show how important it is that people with physical disabilities can access whatever AAC will help them communicate.

Martin Pistorius relates the first time he was assessed for AAC and his reaction to being given the opportunity to communicate through a switch:

> Soon Shakila goes to a large cupboard and pulls out a small rectangular dial. It has more symbols on it and a large red pointer in the middle. Shakila sets it on the table in front of me before plugging it in to the end of a flexible stand. (Pistorius 2011, p.26)

Yasmin the speech therapist explains:

> 'This is a dial scan and head switch,' Yasmin explains. 'You can use the yellow switch to control the pointer on the scan as it goes around and stop it to identify the symbol you want.' (Pistorius 2011, p.26)

Martin is asked to stop the pointer when it gets to the symbol for 'tap':

> The red pointer starts to inch around the dial. It goes so slowly that I wonder if it will ever reach the picture of the tap. Slowly it drags its way around the dial and I watch until it nears the tap. I jerk my head against the switch. The pointer stops at the right place on the dial.
>
> 'Good Martin,' a voice tells me.
>
> Amazement fills me. I've never controlled anything before. I've never made another object do what I wanted it to. I've fantasised about it again and again, but I've never raised a fork, drunk from a cup or changed TV channels. I can't do up my shoes, kick a ball or ride a bike. Stopping the pointer on the dial makes me feel triumphant. (Pistorius 2011, pp.26–27)

Adults may not have had access to the amazing AACs available now, but being able to communicate makes such a huge difference, as a 2014 article in *SEN Magazine* explains:

> Rachel Monk, a 31-year-old from Dumfries and Galloway, uses AAC because of her cerebral palsy. Rachel feels that her communication aid has made a huge difference to her quality of life. 'It allows me to convey my thoughts, feelings and opinions,' she says. 'I can voice concerns, make choices, tell jokes, and chat with friends, like anybody should be able to do.' (Nicholls 2014)

CASE STUDY: Starting out with switches

Lola (age 4)

Lola is a little girl with an ability to win all hearts. She has been severely disabled since birth. She has not yet developed much functional speech. She is able to vocalize 'Mamamamama' when happy and she can make a lot of noise when she is hungry – so she does communicate. Lola is very aware and will opt out when she does not want to do something. We recently discovered that she pretends to sleep when she knows she is going in her standing frame.

Lola is able to indicate a preference by looking in the direction of what she wants when she is motivated by the choices. She is also able to use her smile purposefully to say 'Yes'.

As Lola has some control over her hands she is able to press a switch, and we wanted to develop her ability to do this as it would extend Lola's functional communication.

Food is a big motivator for Lola. She has been known to make a lot of noise if we are late getting her lunch ready. I currently job share with a very lovely and proactive teacher, who shares my passion for improving communication. She saw the opportunity for using switches with Lola at dinner time. She set up two switches – one switch had a 'food' symbol attached and the other had the symbol for 'drink'. When Lola pressed the switch she could hear the pre-recorded message – 'food' or 'drink'. This meant the words were modelled again and again. Lola soon showed that she understood the cause and effect of using the switches and seemed to enjoy having some control at lunch time.

Lola takes the switches home so she can get more use out of them. This is the starting point, and we will gradually increase her use of switches as appropriate.

One day recently I was giving her lunch. When we got to the end the switch landed on the floor. Was she indicating that she knew it was finished? This child also uses the switches at home, and her mum says she will press it constantly when in the kitchen to be 'cheeky'. Switches can be a great way to get a child interacting, getting reactions and seeing that they can communicate.

Quick tips for using Big Macks and switches

- Pre-record messages or responses in the Big Mack switch – a large switch a child can press to play a short pre-recorded message or sound. These can be sent back and forth between home and school.

- Add symbols and pre-record messages to allow children to make choices.

- A child can activate singing and dancing toys with have been adapted for switch use.

- Link a switch to the computer or interactive white board to activate switch games or books.

- Activate equipment, for example blending a drink, a hairdryer or electric fan.

CASE STUDY: Proving he can

Peter (age 5) Diagnosis: Cerebral Palsy

Peter did not seem very motivated to show it, but I knew instinctively that he was a bright little boy capable of so much if given the opportunity. Peter had no speech at all and was not motivated to do any of the usual tasks. He did not try to communicate when presented with pictures and we had not yet found anything motivating enough to make him want to exchange a symbol. The one thing that seemed to spark his interest was the computer. Observing his reactions to computer programs made me think that he could communicate with the right tool.

I spoke to our speech therapist about the possibility of trying Peter with an assistive communication device. This was over ten years ago, before iPads and Apps, which would now be much more accessible. I was told that to even get a device to try I would first need to prove that Peter had the ability to use one. It seemed ridiculous. However, rather than be put off, I was determined that I would prove Peter's ability and get him the communication device he needed.

After many requests I had got an interactive white board installed in our classroom. Peter loved this, but I had found that many of the programs I wanted to use were not designed with the interactive white board in mind. Buttons were too high up; answers which needed to be clicked and then dragged caused frustration; and even adults struggled with not getting in the way of the projector.

I knew that Quentin was able to make programs, which would not include all these problems. He was able to make a simple game where Peter could click the letters of his name in the right order and when it was done his face would appear on the screen. Peter's reaction to this was fantastic and we quickly progressed him to answering a whole series of questions in this way. He could tell us the day of the week, the weather, the number of children in the class… All these things would have got a non-response with symbols, but he was so motivated by the computer.

When our speech therapist, ICT technician and headteacher observed what Peter could do, they agreed that it was essential to get him the assistive communication device.

Peter is now 16 and communicates brilliantly at home and at school using an iPad.

Apps

There are now so many Apps for communication. It's wonderful that tablet technology has so quickly been put to such amazing use for AAC. These Apps are particularly wonderful for children who have got to the stage with PECS where they can communicate wants and understand categories, but have reached a point where they need a never-ending supply of symbols. An AAC App can provide this.

CASE STUDY: Proloquo2go

Shay (age 8). Diagnosis: Autism

Some children are *amazing* at communicating using the Picture Exchange Communication Systems (PECS). I have seen this system help so many children learn to communicate. When I first taught Shay he had already fully mastered the use of symbols to communicate. He would search the classroom for the right symbol. If it wasn't in his PECS book he would look in other children's books. I knew that we needed to try and get Shay using a communication App so that he could have access to a larger bank of symbols. I was also keen to try this with Shay because, as well as being diagnosed with autism, he was known to have pica (he would put anything in his mouth and swallow it). For this reason he needed to be closely watched at all times and I was reluctant to give him access to smaller, laminated symbols. At this time iPads were new and very expensive. The communication App I wanted to trial was also expensive, but I was convinced that Shay needed to have access to it. He was brilliant with PECS and liked to communicate, but at that time did not use any words at all. He could get extremely frustrated when he could not communicate or get his point across. I felt that he needed this App in the same way as another child with limited mobility might need a walker.

With Shay's Grandmother also fighting his case I knew we would somehow be able to get him an iPad.

I convinced our school to purchase the Proloquo2go App for the school iPad (at that time there was just one iPad to share between classes). Shay picked it up immediately and was so motivated. He would go straight into the program and soon understood the categories. He was even able to use the App on a smaller iPhone. Sometimes he would go into the colour category and repeatedly press 'brown, brown, brown, brown, brown', but this was not due to lack of understanding. I could tell it amused him and wondered if it was due to brown looking like a chocolate button. The reason I knew that Shay was having a joke was that when it came to wanting something he was straight in there – he could go into the colour category and select 'green' and then into 'foods' and find 'crisps', so he was saying 'I want green crisps'. Green crisps were a favourite request when he used PECS (he knew the bag for his favourite crisp flavour was green).

We took photos and videos, and when it came to updating his IEP (Individual Education Programme) targets we made sure to highlight his need to develop use of the App.

In a short space of time (with some gentle persuasion) our school agreed that our class needed our own iPad, and Shay's Grandmother started to look into charities who might fund him having a personal iPad. I'll never forget how happy I felt when his Grandmother phoned me at school to say that a charity was not only going to provide him with an iPad, but also the App and the tough case he needed to protect the expensive bit of equipment. Shay got his iPad and his App and has since made the most amazing progress.

Eye Gaze technology

Eye Gaze is an incredibly exciting advance in AAC because it means that people with no control of their body at all may still access communication using their eyes. The Eye Gaze bar is stuck to the computer. The person then needs to calibrate their eyes with the computer by looking at a series of dots. Eye Gaze technology is probably the most exciting development during my time as a special needs teacher. We are all still learning about it and finding ways to truly use it to its full potential.

The other exciting thing about Eye Gaze is that, with an internet connection, it opens a door to the world. A person can communicate with those who are with them in the room, but they could also potentially send emails or interact on social networks. They could learn, they could share, they could teach the teachers and they could even write books.

Eye Gaze has the potential to literally transform a person's life – imagine the difference it could make to mental health and resilience; what must it do for self esteem? A child could potentially feel properly included for the first time, be able to express fears, frustrations or physical pain, their wants and desires and their sense of humour. Advances such as Eye Gaze show how essential it is that education does not stop when a child hits a certain age. The next case study is fictional, but I hope that it demonstrates why we must all speak up for those adults who have been left without ever having access to these wonderful, freeing advances in technology.

Timmy's Time Machine (a fictional case study)

Timmy was born in 1960 with severe physical disabilities associated with Cerebral Palsy. He could not control any part of his body and could only make a few indistinguishable sounds, but was able to show his emotions through facial expressions and sounds. His sense of humour was evident early. He would often laugh and smile and really enjoyed being amidst other children.

Timmy is now living in a care home. He spends a large amount of time sat in front of the TV. He loves nothing more than a visit and a change to the usual routines. He still has an active brain, but he is only able to make simple choices. He cannot communicate his brilliant thoughts or explain the more complex reasons behind his expressions.

What if we were to travel back in time to the day Timmy was born and allow him to start life in 2015?

Timmy is still born with Cerebral Palsy and the same limiting physical disabilities.

Timmy's first teacher realises that Timmy is able to control his eyes. She works with Timmy to develop his ability to make choices with his eyes. Does Timmy want to watch *Thomas the Tank Engine* or *Snow White*? Timmy learns to eye point to the right picture. A speech therapist suggests using Eye Gaze software. Timmy loves this. He is able to play games with his eyes. He can burst balloons on the screen! Timmy loves these sessions. He smiles and laughs a lot. Timmy's whole family enjoy seeing Timmy able to show off his new skills. Timmy can play with other children – he has to learn about turn taking, waiting and when other children come to play they need to learn to use the Eye Gaze software. Timmy is the best by far! This does wonders for his self esteem.

As Timmy's skills develop he learns to use a communication grid. He starts off by making simple choices about wants, but soon learns to say how he feels: 'I feel sad'; 'I want my Mum'; 'I feel thirsty'; 'I want orange juice.'

Timmy goes to school. He is now able to use his Eye Gaze communication on the move. He is also able to operate an electric wheel chair. He is very popular. The other children love chatting with him. They think he is amazing. He shares jokes and makes them laugh.

While the other children learn to handwrite Timmy learns to type using his eyes. His teacher uses the Snaptype App to take pictures of worksheets and Timmy completes them.

Timmy continues to learn. He takes exams. He gets a degree. He gets a job. He has a good life and uses his brilliant brain.

But what if we had left little Timmy back in the 60s? What if we went to visit him now? What if we gave the older Timmy access to all this new technology? Could Timmy still learn? It may take longer, but yes he could. My question is: Why doesn't Timmy, who was born in the 60s access this?

As technology improves and Eye Gaze technology develops we must ensure that the children who can benefit have access to it. If we do not have funding we must find all ways to get it.

We must also speak up for the education of those adults, who missed out on this amazing technology at school. There are so many adults with physical disabilities who could possibly use Eye Gaze to communicate, interact and learn. It is our responsibility to speak up for these adults, who could use Eye Gaze software. They must not be written off and forgotten. They have stories to tell, discoveries to make and most importantly the basic human right to communicate their way.

Eye Gaze at playtimes

In an article titled 'Successful individuals with disabilities and disability awareness for all of us', Valeska Gioia makes a wonderful observation of students' interactions with a child using Eye Gaze technology to communicate:

> When we include students with disabilities in the general education classroom with accommodations and modifications, you can see the difference of the comfort levels of all the students!! I've seen students fight to hang out with a child at recess who was non-verbal and in a wheelchair, but was able to communicate with her peers using an electronic eye gaze device. This is what we need to see more of in our schools. (Gioia n.d.)

Chapter 13

Actions Speak Louder!

Gaining Attention, Adding Meaning and Improving Communication Through Facial Expressions, Signing and Movement[1]

I am not imposed upon by fine words; I can see what actions mean.

George Eliot (1819–1880)

What if you were lost in a foreign country? You knew that you needed to get a number 2 bus to the airport to catch a plane. The only way you could find the information to get you there was to ask a passer by, but the passer by had no understanding of your language and you had no comprehension of theirs. There are no pens and paper, no mobile phones – just two people who need to communicate.

Maybe you would invent some gestures to indicate you are looking for a bus to get a plane. You may already be thinking what these would be. Your signs create a made-up language and you find some mutual ground. You communicate beyond spoken language. As you do so you will also naturally speak, but speech will be simplified to necessary words only. Maybe some of your language will be familiar? Hold this situation in your mind. Maybe your student's first language is the same as yours, but maybe they process your speech in such a way that it comes out as an incomprehensible verbal jumble. How can you help? Simplify language and use visuals to communicate – drawings, actions and signs.

Acting out or signing can be a great way to communicate meaning when the language is foreign. These can also be a great visual scaffold when trying to illustrate the spoken word to children who find it difficult to hear or process or comprehend language.

Way, way back before humans developed the complex and diverse spoken language we know today, how would they have communicated? They would have used signs and sounds to communicate. As these developed so the human race made advances, because communication allows ideas to be shared, suggestions to be made, change to happen and progress to be made. Without developing communication skills, would we still be living in caves?

---

1   I would like to acknowledge Margaret Walton from The Makaton Charity, who has helped with this chapter.

Moving on through history, one of the earliest written records is in Plato's play *Cratylus*, from the fifth century BC, where Socrates says: 'If we hadn't a voice or a tongue, and wanted to express things to one another, wouldn't we try to make signs by moving our hands, head, and the rest of our body, just as dumb people do at present?' (Bauman 2008, p.50).

There are many, many versions of sign language, which are fascinating, but for the purpose of this book I will focus on Makaton, which is the main sign and symbol set used in special needs schools. It is also the one which is most likely to be familiar to non-deaf visual children as they may have seen it on CBeebies' *Something Special*.

Makaton

The Makaton Charity website defines Makaton as 'a language program using signs and symbols to help people to communicate. It is designed to support spoken language and the signs and symbols are used with speech, in spoken word order'. They further state: 'With Makaton, children and adults can communicate straight away using signs and symbols. Many people then drop the signs or symbols naturally at their own pace, as they develop speech' (The Makaton Charity 2015).

Malcolm Wright, Managing Director of ITV SignPost, which produces British Sign Language-translated television programs and Apps for sign language stories[2] explains that

> sign language is decoded by a different part of the brain to verbal communication. So for those who struggle with words – deaf children, children with autism and children with dyslexia, for example – this visual language can provide an alternative route. It's not necessarily a route which will always lead to success, but it's a route worth exploring. (Wright 2014, p.43)

Interaction and confidence

Using signs with children gives them an additional scaffold to comprehend what someone is saying. Children can begin to communicate their ideas and feel like they are part of the conversation. When they can communicate their ideas they will be more likely to show interest in other people's.

Wright further states:

> Using sign language brings confidence to those who lack communication skills. It is a natural outlet for expression. It helps build bonds in the family and the school

---

2   See www.signedstories.com.

room. And while sign languages around the world differ, there is a large core of iconic signs, which we instinctively understand. (Wright 2014, p.43)

CASE STUDY: A child with autism in a mainstream assembly

I remember observing a little boy with autism sitting on the floor in a mainstream assembly. He was wriggly and squiggly and his attention visibly wandered. He would sometimes distract the other children by taking their space. He was fascinated by the girls' hair and sometimes forgot himself and reached out to touch it. He might wriggle over and accidentally push a child to the side of him, which all had a knock-on, distracting effect. He was a child who wanted to please and he was not doing this on purpose. I'd been told he didn't like assemblies, and I could see why. During the assembly each time he forgot himself he would get a reminder – 'Stop doing this or that...' He clearly felt bad, but within a minute he was doing it again.

I knew he needed some visuals to help with this difficult time of day. At the front of the assembly hall I printed out a poster, which said:

Look with your eyes.

Listen with your ears.

Sit still.

Figure 13.1 *Poster showing Rules for Listening*

I stuck the poster at his sitting level so it would be exactly in his line of focus. I was sure the poster would help other children remember what they were supposed to be doing as well. I also made some visual prompt cards so that if he did get wriggly, rather than a teaching assistant having to say his name and then tell him what was expected of him, such as 'good sitting', they could point to the prompt card and show him. This not only avoided too much distracting language, but helped him know exactly what he needed to focus on. I noticed some of the other children were also using these visuals. One boy in particular, who struggled with behaviour and learning, was drawn to sitting near me, and I would use the visual cards to help him stay on track.

Observing the assembly I also noticed that it was often times when a teacher was addressing all the children that attention would wander. Assembly is a distracting time, and the child was so focused on not squiggling and looking as though he was listening attentively that he was not taking in what was being said. Children with learning difficulties can find it easier to decode a more simple way of using language. I recall one little girl with autism returning from mainstream inclusion and explaining that 'the teacher spoke too complicatey.'

I saw that when the teacher happened to gesture with her hands the boy's eyes returned to her in an instant. This made me think how easily she could get the boy's attention, keep him focused and allow him to get some content from her speech if she were to use some Makaton signs.

Using Makaton in a special needs school

Special needs teachers use signs because a lot of children respond really well to them. Children with Down's Syndrome are often brilliant at signing, and I have seen so many times how this helps them develop speech. Some children will not use the signs themselves, but seeing the teacher use them may grab their attention and help illustrate what she is saying.

Sign of the day

Every morning our school has a whole school meeting, and a part of this is 'sign of the day'. Everyone will copy the sign and say the associated word. It is so important to say the word because this models the language for the children. Doing this all together gives staff confidence and reminds them that Makaton is an important strategy which all staff should be using.

Signs on displays

I like to incorporate the visual signs on to displays to help remind staff to use them. I also use the posters of songs from the *Something Special* magazine, which are wonderfully visual.

Figure 13.2 *Makaton line drawings of signs on a story display*

CBeebies' *Something Special*

When I first saw *Something Special* I was so excited. Finally a television program that would perfectly suit our children with learning difficulties! The program has a central character called 'Mr Tumble' who uses Makaton. Each program has a topic-linked theme. It is so clear and so visual and a really fantastic teaching tool for *all* children. I've seen children with special educational needs (SEN) standing in front of this and teaching themselves the signs. It's wonderful for language development and reading! I also love that this program uses children with SEN and is a favourite with all children.

The *Something Special* magazine is also a fantastic resource to use with children. I especially like the way that they display the Makaton signs with photos of Mr Tumble doing them. These can be more appealing to children than line drawings and seem easier to follow.

Parents using Makaton

Teaching in Early Years, we are lucky to be the first contact with new parents. We are finding that more and more parents are not waiting until school to get their child accessing supports. They are finding ways to help their children through their own extensive research. Gone are the days of waiting weeks to borrow that one specialist book from the library. The internet and social networks are making parental research quicker and more efficient. Parents can access current professional dialogue and support from other parents who have been there, done that.

So as we do our home visits we are meeting children whose parents are already wonderfully clued up. They've already got the laminator and made a load of symbols. They know about strategies before we introduce something. We are always thrilled when we visit a home and find that a child is already accessing so many supports. This gives them a huge push in the right direction and makes the transition to school so much smoother.

CASE STUDY: Jay (age 4)

When we went to visit Jay for the first time it soon became clear that his home was very well set up to encourage him to communicate. There were symbols on drawers so Jay could use them. He was able to happily engage in an activity matching toys to photos and symbols. He was also signing. His mum said she had already been on a Makaton course. This was fantastic. We saw the communication between them and were thrilled. With all this home support and structure in place we were going to see great things from this little man. During Jay's first week at school we noticed that sometimes he would sign and staff would not know his meaning. This may have been due to him having his own version of some signs, which we needed to become familiar with. It may have been that he had such a huge bank of signs that he was using ones that staff did not know. We were keen to support Jay and encourage his signing. The first thing we did was to start looking out for any areas where he might sign. We wanted to ensure that staff were consistent and Jay had a visual for our signs. We added the Makaton visuals for signs in areas where he would regularly see them – e.g. toilet, open the door, help, more, finished. We added topic signs and symbols to displays. We also asked all other school staff to be aware that Jay might use a sign they were not familiar with, but to show that they knew he was trying to communicate and persevere. We also asked his mum to list signs Jay regularly used so that we could learn what he was telling us. If a child begins school already trying to communicate it is so important that, even if you do not understand, you try your best and you show without doubt that you know they are communicating. Next step is asking home for help, because the last thing you want is for the child to think there is no point in trying.

Helping children who do not process language well

In special schools we address groups of children with simple language and will also use Makaton signs to help illustrate and highlight certain words. A child who is not processing all the language may pick out a sign such as 'look' or 'cat'. Even if they do not get the whole sentence they can pick up some direction and meaning. This is not only helpful to children with learning difficulties and autism, but can also help children with English as a second language. Makaton signs often create a visual picture, which allows the child to make a connection. The actions also get the child's attention focused on the speaker.

My ten tips for encouraging use of Makaton signing in school

- Print out the Makaton line drawings of signs and include them on displays so that staff and children can learn signs linked to stories.

- Display Makaton line drawings of signs for likely language in specific areas – e.g. the school office. Display signs for 'register', 'good morning', 'good afternoon', 'hello', 'copy', 'pen', 'envelope', 'post a letter', 'phone', etc.

- Include books containing Makaton line drawings of signs in the book corner.

- Open school Makaton training courses up to parents and carers.

- Repeatedly use specific Makaton signs at set times of the day so that they become familiar.

- Look at episodes of *Something Special*. (There's probably even one that links with your topic.)

- Find songs by 'Singing Hands' on YouTube.

- Include Makaton signing when reading stories and singing songs.[3]

- Incorporate Makaton signing into assemblies and school plays.

- Speak to The Makaton Charity if you need advice for good practice or are stuck interpreting a particular sign.

CASE STUDY: Mathew and Makaton

Jill M – M was so impressed with the way that Makaton improved communication for her son Mathew that she wrote a case study for the Makaton website. She has kindly allowed me to reproduce it here.

My little boy Mathew has autism spectrum disorder (ASD). He's five-and-a-half years old and you can't shut him up, especially when he wants to talk about his favourite obsession (currently McDonald's and Subway). It wasn't always like that though.

Mathew didn't babble as a baby; at the age of two he was still almost completely silent (apart from when he giggled) and we were referred for speech therapy. By age three he was still non-verbal but had at least progressed to making noises in the back of his throat. By three-and-a-half

---

3   See the Singing Hands website: www.singinghands.co.uk.

he still had no words, was just starting preschool, and our speech therapist was saying she thought he might have verbal dyspraxia.

I did some reading up, and a lot of sources said that using signing alongside speech can really help, so I enrolled for the beginner's Makaton course with our local tutor, Helen. I mentioned casually at a meeting with the Special Educational Needs Coordinator (SENCO) at school that I was going, and she immediately suggested that Mathew's teacher and teaching assistant should train too. In the end my husband went as well, and we all started to use some basic signing and also symbols with Mathew.

At first he didn't seem to engage with it at all, he didn't seem interested and got quite upset when we tried to get him to sign back. Gradually, however, he started to show an interest in the symbols. School made him some visual aids based on the symbols, and he loved them. I started going through the vocabulary in the course handouts with him and signing the words to him, and after a while he started signing back. We also based all his visual aids at home on Makaton symbols. After a few months, words emerged; at first only a few, and then more and more, until by his fourth birthday he was stringing three or four together to make sentences. Around this time we were referred for the assessment for autism and also the school began the process of getting him a statement of special educational needs. Part of that process involved an assessment by the educational psychologist, where his language and communication was assessed as being at the level of a two-year-old.

Since then Mathew's progress has been remarkable.

He was awarded his statement and was diagnosed with ASD earlier this year. He now attends a school for children with SEN. His speech is still delayed and his pronunciation is odd sometimes and dyspraxia is still being queried, but the progress he has made is remarkable and he now rarely signs because he can speak the words instead. We do still use the symbols for all his visual aids at home, and he still likes to go through the vocabulary books now and then. He also enjoys signing along to his Singing Hands DVD and to *Something Special*.

Whenever I get irritated by his constant barrage of questions about 'What world is this Subway in?' and 'Is this Subway in Manchester – yes or no?', etc., I remind myself about the years and years I waited to hear him say 'Mummy' and 'I love you' and I'm thankful that we managed to break through the barriers and show him that communicating with us was worthwhile.

I'm positive we have Makaton to thank for that!

Baby signing

As a special needs teacher it was natural for me to use Makaton with our three children when they were babies. All of them took to this and were able to sign before they developed speech. Signing is great for babies, as the muscles in babies' hands generally grow and develop so that the child can make a hand gesture to communicate before they have recognisable speech.

Someone once expressed a concern that our son would continue to use the signs and not learn to speak. Of course, having seen so many children sign, speak and then drop the signs, I knew that this would not be an issue. There is one sign that all of my children still know. Whenever they need a gentle prompt to use their manners I put my palm up to my chin and they will remember to say 'please' and 'thank you'. It is a really useful little prompt as children get embarrassed when asked to say 'please' or 'thank you' in front of people. This way is much more subtle and saves them from feeling any embarrassment.

Body language

As well as considering introducing Makaton signs to our visual learners, it is important to be aware of the effect body language can have on children. Our body language can have a huge impact on certain children. Teachers need to be aware that they should give children enough space and adopt a friendly 'next to', rather than an intimidating 'right in front of', approach.

If a child is mid-meltdown, rather than approach the child upfront, go and sit down somewhere nearby with a symbol. We keep wipe-clean boards around the school so that staff can grab them and quickly draw some symbols to communicate meaning without too much language.

So much of communication is non-verbal. A child who is able to process verbal information when calm may not be able to do so when anxious. At this point they will look for visual reassurance. When decoding language becomes difficult, a child may look for body language and become adept at reading people. They may also become more empathic and pick up on the feelings of those around them.

Facial expressions

Exaggerated facial expressions can help children who find expressions confusing to learn to read them. They see you are happy because you have a great big smile and have signed and said 'happy'. They know when you are talking about a character in a story who is 'sad' because you point to the character as you read their name: 'Billy is sad.' They see your sad face as you sign and say 'sad'.

Including everyone with Makaton signs in songs

Using Makaton shows that you are thinking about *all* children and willing them to do their best. Teach your other children to sign songs together. This is a great way for them to learn (just like an action song, but more meaningful). It is also truly touching for the parent of that SEN child to watch when you come to do an assembly or Christmas play. Instead of feeling like their child stands out as the one who isn't getting it quite right, it shows that the children are being taught to adapt and include. It sends out a very positive message that you are a SEN-friendly, thoughtful setting where *every* child can be included. A little Makaton goes a long way…

Chapter 14

Listening and Gaining Attention

Becoming a Good Listener, Tutorials, Intensive Interaction and Attention Autism

There's a lot of difference between listening and hearing.

G. K. Chesterton (1874–1936)

Some people seem to thoroughly enjoy the sound of their own voice. I expect you are thinking of someone like that right now. These people may be great at talking the talk, but the most gifted speakers, the ones who really get their message across, listen first. And not only do they tune into what people say, they tune into how people feel. The sense of listening is not necessarily with the ears, but can be led by intuition, by feelings, by the heart…

Teachers do a lot of talking, but sometimes it's those quiet times when they sit and listen that both the children and teacher learn the most.

Adults spend an average of 70% of their time engaged in some sort of communication…of this an average of 45% is spent listening compared to 30% speaking, 16% reading and 9% writing. (Adler, Rosenfeld and Proctor 2001).

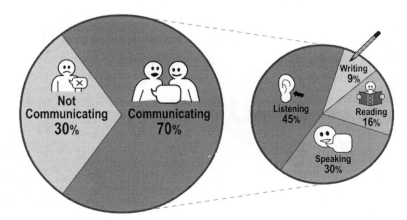

Figure 14.1 *Visual representation of time spent communicating in different ways (according to the research of Adler et al.)*

CASE STUDY: Sam's research

Age 9 Diagnosis: Autism

Sam is a brilliant boy with an amazing mind. Sam knows more about the military than many soldiers. I've witnessed a conversation between Sam and a soldier. Sam's exhaustive knowledge completely blew that soldier's mind. 'That kid knows so much more than me about the military and weapons,' he said.

One day I suggested to Sam we read a book together. It was not high-interest military, but was about the planets, which I knew was another topic that appealed. 'I'm not reading the book with you,' said Sam. 'It's pointless.' He turned back towards the computer. I was not going to give up. You see, Sam, despite his brilliant brain and extensive knowledge, could not read. I knew that each time we read together he was looking at those words I pointed to. Sometimes he filled ones in. 'Sam, this book's about the planet Mars. It's an interesting book,' I said.

'I'm not going to read it because the computer is more up to date. That book was written too long ago.'

I was blown away. What a brilliant boy and how right he was. Information on the planets changes all the time and the book was not new. 'You're right, Sam. You are so clever!'

It was nearly playtime and I knew Sam would need time to process and drag himself away from the computer. 'Sam, playtime is in five minutes.'

'I'm not going out to play. I'm researching.'

'You can research after playtime. Playtime is important, Sam. It's when you get exercise, which keeps you healthy. It's when you learn other important skills.' I saw Sam thinking about this and left him to process it. I placed a five-minute egg timer nearby. He clocked it, but said nothing.

Shortly after the sand ran out Sam asked if I would come out to play with him. I had a zillion things to do, but didn't hesitate. 'If you are quick,' I said. He got up and we went out to play.

Sam is in a school for children with severe learning difficulties. Sam is a brilliant boy, but due to anxieties he is only just starting to read and write.

I listen to Sam a lot. He has taught me a lot.

Developing listening skills

So how do we develop our personal listening skills? We practise being quiet. We ask questions. We leave gaps beyond gaps. We wait. We set up times for individual tutorials when we can sit 1:1 with our students in an atmosphere that is in their comfort zone. They may be engaged with Lego® play or a train set. We do not try to engage directly, but play alongside them, mirroring the way they play, attempting to gain their interest in a non-intimidating way. They may not be making any sounds, but they are making ripples. They pick up a car. We pick up a car. They examine the wheels. We examine the wheels. They make a 'Ssss' sound. We echo it exactly. As we do this they begin to notice us. We are listening to them. Our actions and our sounds are non-threatening and familiar. We are creating the starting point of communication. We are using 'Intensive Interaction'.

Intensive Interaction

Intensive Interaction is an important first step towards communication. It involves a lot of observing, listening, following and mirroring.

Intensive Interaction is exciting to see in action and amazing to feel working. If you are teaching children with severe learning difficulties and communication difficulties, it is worth going on an Intensive Interaction course. If that is not possible, Dave Hewett PhD and Melanie Nind PhD, who were teachers at Harperbury School, and carried out Intensive Interaction research projects at the school as part of the development work, have published three books on the approach.

The Intensive Interaction approach was developed during the 1980s by the team of staff working at Harperbury Hospital School in Hertfordshire. This was a school for young people with severe learning difficulties. The developments followed the work of the late Geraint Ephraim PhD, a psychologist who worked in Hertfordshire's long-stay hospitals.

The Intensive Interaction website defines it as

an approach to teaching the pre-speech fundamentals of communication to children and adults who have severe learning difficulties and/or autism and who are still at an early stage of communication development. (Intensive Interaction 2015)

Think of how a parent interacts with a newborn baby – the way they mirror expressions and sounds. This interaction comes quite naturally and forms the basis for communication. It lays a foundation, and so for children who have severe learning difficulties it can be a fantastic starting point. Compare it to a little crack in a fragile door letting in light. The more we can gently ease the door open, the brighter the room will get. We cannot just push the door open because it will break and the door *must* stay intact. The process is gradual.

Nind and Hewett (2005) reflect on the time they started exploring Intensive Interaction techniques at Harperbury Hospital School:

We began to incorporate interactive play into our daily routines in school. Dressing situations, for example, changed from being a non-personal and stressful routine in which skills were prompted and reinforced, into the context for a peek-a-boo game where we were playful, offered warm physical contact, and gently narrated the action. In escorting students to other parts of the building we nagged less, and instead blended our walking rhythm with that of the student, building some mutuality based on shared timing of movement. (Nind and Hewett 2005, p.6)

They state that the introduction of Intensive Interaction 'had a spiralling effect of positive change' at the school (Nind and Hewett 2005, p.6). It helped with communication, behaviour and also staff morale. What an exciting, enlightening time it must have been for those staff.

Intensive Interaction begins when the teacher gets within the child's comfort zone. They get to the child's level, mirror their body language and copy any sounds they are making. Their play is based on how the child plays. The adult follows the child's lead. An example might be a child lying on their back examining the wheels of a car. The teacher takes a similar car and lies down nearby examining the wheels in the same way. The child turns the car around. The teacher does the same. The child makes a 'b' sound and the teacher makes the same sound.

Intensive Interaction is never the same and changes with every child and teacher. Nind and Hewett do suggest games, which may provide a useful start, but the teacher must use instinct and intuition because there is no set structure:

- Peek-a-boo

- I'm going to get you

- Round and Round the Garden

- Rocking in unison

- Swinging arms as you walk

- Taking turns to hum

- Blowing raspberries

- Rough and tumble.

(Nind and Hewett 2005, p.8)

A teacher must also trust their instinct to know when a session is finished. A child may walk off or they may begin to disengage.

I love this approach and the effect I see it have on children. It seems so obvious, but until support staff and parents are told about it they don't know what a positive change it can make.

Music therapy

I have supported children through so many music therapy sessions and am always uplifted and inspired to see children with learning difficulties and high anxiety begin to engage, relax and interact. Seeing our music therapist work her magic has inspired me to trial musical cues and comments with some harder-to-reach students. I would love every child who comes through our Early Years class to access music therapy.

A music therapist is an allied health professional who will have completed an approved music therapy programme. They are trained to use music in a multisensory way to improve communication, social interaction or physical or mental health.

Music can be a great way to engage children and create a platform to bridge communication. Babies respond to music before they can communicate or decipher language. We use music to settle and comfort young children. Music is used to create atmosphere and influence mood and feelings in theatre and film. A child who tunes into music might listen and respond to musical cues in the same way. Music may relax the anxious child into being able to engage or explore in ways they usually would not.

This links in with Intensive Interaction and the parent–child relationship. When parents share sounds and songs with their children, they are enriching them with new vocabulary, rhythms, sequences and connections, which develop their communication.

The British Association for Music Therapy have a wonderful explanation on their website:

> Music plays an important role in our everyday lives. It can be exciting or calming, joyful or poignant, can stir memories and powerfully resonate with our feelings, helping us to express them and to communicate with others.
>
> Music therapy uses these qualities and the musical components of rhythm, melody and tonality to provide a means of relating within a therapeutic relationship. In music therapy, people work with a wide range of accessible instruments and their voices to create a musical language which reflects their emotional and physical condition; this enables them to build connections with their inner selves and with others around them. (British Association for Music Theraphy 2012)

CASE STUDY: Finn (age 4)

A child in our Early Years class would often come in as grumpy as can be. He would make a lot of noise and sometimes bang his head in temper. He seemed more cross than sad – like he had just woken from a nap and was somewhere he really didn't want to be. He had learnt to use the

Picture Exchange Communication System (PECS) to ask for 'outside'. While this was excellent in terms of communication, it was right in the middle of winter. Outside was freezing. Even if outside made him happy, we could not have him out there all the time.

On Wednesday mornings our grumpy Finn would have music therapy. This was where the transformation happened. As soon as Finn entered the music therapy room his mood completely changed. He would explore the instruments while our music therapist, Jenny, sang about what he was doing. He would stay in this good mood for the entire session and then return to class the same. After music therapy he was able to take part in our story time; we got more interaction and engagement in our lessons.

I spoke to our music therapist Jenny. What was it that he loved? What could we do in class to see a happier Finn? She said he liked exploring the instruments and her commenting on it by singing. It was all led by him. We started to get out the same big musical instruments in the morning and tried to mirror the approach. It did not always work. I think saying goodbye to his mum, going to school and getting on and off the bus were not favoured activities and made him grumpy, but at least he could see that once at school we were trying to meet him halfway and greet him with the instruments and atmosphere we knew helped create his calmer, happier moods.

What a difference those music therapy sessions made to us and Finn.

Magical music therapy

I would love to see every Early Years child with a communication difficulty access music therapy. Time and again I have seen our wonderful music therapist Jenny work her magic. These sessions can make such a difference to a child's engagement and enjoyment in other sessions.

Attention Autism

I've never known a course to get experienced special needs teachers more excited than Attention Autism, delivered by specialist speech therapist Gina Davies. This approach is not only amazingly successful with children with autism, but children with other learning difficulties are completely engaged by it as well. Davies suggests that 'we could think about the autism learning strengths rather than the things that are going wrong. These children are fantastically visual and this gives us a way forward and they have the most amazing memories...' (Davies 2014).

In a YouTube video on the Gina Davies Autism Centre website, Davies explains that children coming into therapy are usually there because they are not doing something that is asked of them or they are doing something they should not be doing: 'We are asking them to take the risk of learning something new and probably that's going to be difficult, so what I try to do is look at my activities first and ask, is my activity absolutely irresistible?' (Davies 2011).

Davies doesn't ask the child to join her – she does something visual that attracts their attention and engages them. She doesn't behave like a 'normal' grown up. The child wants to know what she will do next.

Attention Autism sessions are so exciting and can be used with children of all different abilities. Children love the visual structure of these sessions. We tell them at the start what we are going to do by making pictorial representations on a white board. We cross things off as they are finished.

We start off with a box or a bucket full of tricks and a song which becomes familiar. The box is a treasure chest of exciting light-up toys, wind-up toys and battery-operated dancing toys. The teacher takes out one thing at a time, playing and exploring. Staff model excitement and engagement. The session builds up with a set structure, which might include making a big, colourful volcano or making play dough. There are so many wonderful, exciting ways to get children's interest.[1]

The session can also include a turn-taking activity, such as being rolled in a blanket or making a rocket take off, and as the children's ability to sustain attention develops, they reach the stage when they are ready to include a task.

These tasks, or 'mini makes' as one of my lovely groups called them, must be made up in little kits beforehand. There will be a kit for each child, one for the teacher to model and one or two for staff to model with.

Play dough can be a very adaptive part of the kit (as long as you do not have a play dough eater in your group). Let's take an example of using the kit to make cupcakes. Each kit has a cupcake case, some play dough and a candle. The teacher takes the play dough, rolls it into a ball and places it in the cupcake case. She then puts the candle on the top and transfers the cupcake on to a baking tray. Next the teacher hands out kits to individual children and the staff models. The staff model will sit with the children and speak about what she is doing. The idea is she models for children who get stuck. They learn to look to her rather than seek an adult prompt. When all the cupcakes are on the tray the session is finished.

These sessions take some time to set up. They take some thought and creativity, but do not be put off. When you see how engaged the children can be, how much cooperation your group can achieve and how their thinking skills develop, you will be completely sold.

If you can get on an Attention Autism course it is so worthwhile and will inject new energy, new ideas and positivity into your teaching. If you cannot get on a course there are YouTube videos and Gina Davies' website to explore.

---

1   See the Gina Davies website: ginadavies.co.uk for ideas.

Chapter 15

Functional Communication

Within School and Out and About

It had long since come to my attention that people of accomplishment rarely sat back and let things happen to them. They went out and happened to things.

Leonardo da Vinci (1452–1519)

Communication at school

There are so many opportunities to build communication skills in school. It is up to teachers to ensure that these are not missed. The more children use their skills, the more motivated they will be to develop them.

Opportunities can be set up around the school in all areas. Have pictures or photographs so that children can ask for things. Label drawers and cupboards with visuals to promote independence. All the things you do so well in the classroom should spread out around the school.

The office

Office staff will usually really embrace the opportunity to support children with learning differences if they are given some support.

Provide visuals so that a child who uses pictures to communicate can ask for what they need – an envelope, a register or petty cash. A motivating poster explaining the phases of the Picture Exchange Communication System (PECS) may also be helpful.

You may also add a poster with a set of common Makaton line drawings of signs so that office staff can gain confidence using and understanding them.

One of our students delivers our registers around the school. She collects the registers from the school office, then knocks on each class door and hands over the register. Our class doors are painted in colours to link to the colours on the registers, meaning that students who cannot yet read class names may still be able to do this task by matching colours.

At each door she is greeted by a student or teacher and they will speak with her. Even if it is just a smile and a 'Thank you', it's communication. The daily task not only builds her confidence and self esteem, but shows ways to interact with different people in a safe environment.

The library

The library could be a great area for work experience for older students in school, and with a little creativity can be set up so that more children can gain independence through checking in and out books and putting them away in the correct place.

Again, have pictures to enable *all* children to communicate likely 'wants'. This could also be a good opportunity to incorporate ICT with a cataloguing system on an iPad or computer.

Again, posters of PECS phases, library rules and some basic Makaton line drawings of signs will help get everyone communicating in a way to promote progress.

The computer room

Here's a room where the children have a big motivator, and a big motivator equals a chance to get them communicating. But when we have a big motivator we must also tread carefully because we do not want to create battles or prompt meltdowns. Timers can be a useful way to communicate that a session is coming to an end, but do be aware that we cannot simply show five minutes and then turn computers off. If a child is mid-activity, look at what they are doing and say, 'At the end of this game/YouTube video, computer is finished.' Try to avoid open-ended activities. Display turn-taking visuals, but also visuals so that children can select what they want to choose to do once the lesson is finished.

It is also important that a child has a visual way of asking for help and asking to go to the toilet. A waiting symbol can be very useful if the computers are to be shared.

Computers and tablets are a huge motivator for many students, so the computer room is full of opportunities.

The playground

Is there a shed full of bikes and toys? This is a great way to increase opportunity with a lot of motivators. Photograph the things in that shed so that students can ask for them.

The playground is also a good place for a 'buddy bench' where a child can go if they want a friend to be with.

Get playtime supervisors on board. This is not a time to stand and chat with each other. This is a great big learning opportunity and is not to be missed.

Reception

Display symbols for greetings, school behaviour rules and information about the different ways students might communicate in school. If classes create books, then put them in reception so parents can sit and look through them while they wait. This will show parents some of the things that happen in school and give them ideas for home.

Corridors

Display expectations on the walls of corridors. Also label doors and display simple maps so that students can navigate their way. Have a visual map with photographs a child can lift off to ask for help if they get lost.

Some children can find transitioning extremely difficult. This may be due to physical disability or anxiety linked to conditions such as autism. Displaying positive visuals and messages showing expectations along the way may help a child understand the 'rules' of transition. I once taught a child with autism who would get 'stuck' transitioning, but liked puzzles, so they carried a board showing the room they were transitioning to, for example the multisensory room. As they went along the corridor they found puzzle pieces to match until they arrived at the room and the puzzle was complete.

Toilets and changing rooms

Display visual schedules for washing hands, dressing and undressing so that a child can learn the order and link words to pictures. Have a 'Have you washed your hands?' with 'yes' and 'no' options visual on the exit.

Staff toilets

Don't let the staff off. One brilliant speech therapist came up with the idea of sticking up the phases of PECS on the inside of the staff toilet doors. She added motivating pictures for staff of film stars, etc. This meant staff were learning while they were on the loo. Why miss an opportunity?

Art room

There are so many opportunities in the art room for children to communicate – colours, materials, techniques and feelings. Get the art room set up so that no opportunity is missed. It's a great place to learn Makaton signs. You could have a display showing the Makaton line drawings of signs for colours and other typical language:

- painting

- sticking

- printing

- tearing

- scrunching

- choosing

- drawing

- cutting

- folding

- cleaning.

If you have children who use switches it can be really good to pre-record them with the names of colours as it will give them an opportunity to practise using the switches. You hold up two bottles of paint – 'red' and 'yellow'. The child has two corresponding symbols and you ask them, 'What colour do you want?'. They press the switch and it says 'Yellow', so they get yellow paint. Switches are incredibly easy to use and they can make a massive difference to a child.

School council

I am a great believer in pupil voice and have led school council at both the special schools I have taught at. School council is a fantastic opportunity to get children involved and they can have a big impact on things. It should not only be about the children present. These children are representatives of their class or year groups. It is important to allow them to collect ideas and feedback.

School council can be an opportune time for children who are not enjoying aspects of school to voice this. It also means that other children can put their ideas to a vote and get an idea of how outlandish they are. Do not restrict children from speaking up. School council is their chance.

One of the lovely things for me about our school council is that I get a chance to catch up with students, now almost adults, who I taught when they first came to school. I always enjoy typing up the minutes of these meetings and smiling at some of our more quirky ideas. If you get a chance to lead school council, don't shy away. Grab it and make sure it really does become the pupil voice.

Letters

Writing letters can be a really good way to help a child present their thoughts and feelings. The child does not have to be able to write. They could dictate a letter. Ideally a teacher would type the letter using a writing with symbols program so that the child sees the symbols linked to their words. While they are looking they are gaining skills for reading, making a connection between the printed words and the symbols.

A pre-verbal child could choose from pictures of emotions. How do they feel? Then they could select pictures to go in the letter to increase meaning.

The act of putting thoughts to paper and physically posting it can really help if a child feels there has been an injustice, a dreadful change to the schedule or they just do not want to be at school.

Home – choosing DVDs, music, books, food

Children can get lazy when at home because they have learnt to communicate with those close to them with little effort. Mum knows that when Johnny looks to the kitchen cupboard he fancies a biscuit, that he will *always* want to watch *Peppa Pig* and his bedtime story is *The Hungry Caterpillar*.

People at home need to get out of these habits because they are missing opportunities to move a child on in their comfort zone. The assumptions can also be incorrect. Johnny might just choose something else in time, but how can he without being given the opportunity? It's up to us to get into the home and reveal these opportunities. Parents will get on board once we explain and support them in getting started. When a child develops communication skills at home their progress can be remarkable. Collaboration and mutual support are hugely beneficial.

Community

It is up to us to go out into the local community and educate shops, cafes and the general public about ways to communicate with our students. Maybe start with a local newsagent, cafe or fruit shop. Create visuals for outings such as choosing boards for the cafe. Going to a cafe is a great opportunity for pre-verbal students to use their PECS books. Show the people in these places that make accommodations for your students that you appreciate their support. It doesn't take much – a 'thank you' note or even a spoken 'thank you' will mean a lot and help staff forgive the occasional time your students slip up with behaviour. We can make a huge difference to our students' future by educating the local community, who will one day be a part of their support system. A huge task it is, but if we *all* start doing it what a difference we could make.

If outings are difficult

If regular outings are not possible, then setting up role play situations in class or in the school can create a great communication opportunity. At our school we have a Curriculum Day once a term. We will often decide to transform our classrooms to provide experiences and create memories linked to our topic. For example, classrooms may each become a different country, with the school hall being an airport. They go to the airport and go through customs, then get on a pretend plane. They even have little passports, which get stamped as they travel. Another time classrooms might be rooms around the home with linked activities or shops or emergency services. I love how excited the teachers get and how much love and additional effort they put in to making these days brilliant. These days are safely staged in school, but provide a host of new experiences and communication opportunities. They also encourage reflective conversations about what the children liked and disliked.

When teachers really put their hearts into getting creative and going that extra mile, the children's excited expressions will so reward them.

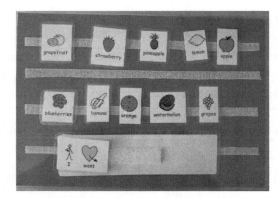

Figure 15.1 *PECS board for the fruit and vegetable store created with the Symwriter symbols*

Chapter 16

Organization, Order and Visual Structure

Symbols, Schedules, Tick Lists, 'To do' Lists, Diaries, Calendars, Wall Charts and TEACCH

Symbols
Symbols in special schools

Symbols are usually seen everywhere in special schools. We use symbols for the timetable, for individual schedules, for personal care schedules and to show behaviour expectations. Special school support staff and teachers even wear key rings with symbols attached, which show 'walking', 'sitting' and 'standing in a line'. We use these symbols because they make such a huge, huge difference to the children we support.

Perfecting the symbols

I spent three years teaching at an autism-specific school, and it was while I was there that I realized that the symbols gave children a much better understanding of expectations, and when they understood they could process those expectations and make an informed decision about whether the expectation was reasonable or not.

Knowing this made me examine the symbols more closely. I realized that many of them could be confusing. Our horse riding symbol showed a stick person on a horse without a helmet. The child would get on the bus and look at the horse riding symbol, and then when we got to horse riding they would be asked to wear a helmet, but that had not been a part of the plan as far as the literal, visual child with ASC was concerned. Putting on a helmet might be a *huge* issue and the symbol was not accurate. Once I saw this, I realized that we would need to completely redesign the symbols we used and make each and every one as near perfect as I could get it. This task was taken on by my husband, Quentin, and the new symbol set were all on the CD Rom that went with my first book, *Colour Coding for Learners with Autism*.

Figure 16.1 *These horse riding symbols will look very different to a literal and visual child*

Symbol use in mainstream schools

When symbols are used in mainstream schools it is usually with one or just a few children. The symbols are put in place to meet the needs of individual children. Those using the symbols may not have had training about why the symbols could work or how to make them most effective. There can be confusion between symbols for communication and symbols for schedules, and if the adults are unsure then they will not be able to get the most effective use from using symbols. The symbols may not be correctly used. They may be pulled out for observations and otherwise get very little use. But symbols are *so* beneficial and not only to the children who have had specialist input. Symbols can show the anxious child, who finds change difficult, what is going to happen in the day; they can help children who process slowly or have hearing difficulties, the children who do not speak the language, the children who struggle with organization, the children with attention issues and the children who do not like being told what to do. Symbols can improve independence and self confidence.

Symbols for EVERY child

Symbols should be used in every learning environment. The current system is wrong, with children arriving at a school not set up to meet their needs. Weeks may follow or even months before someone advises the use of symbols and support strategies for that one child. These are weeks where the child's first impressions of education are made (precious weeks when the child is being completely failed). And what about the children who would so benefit from visual symbols, but do not have any diagnosis? The children who just have a more visual learning style or slightly slower processing than the rest? If these children are not educated alongside a child who does access support, they will never, ever benefit from symbols.

Exciting innovations in Scotland

Sandra Miller, Principal Teacher at Fife Assessment Centre for Communication and Technology, explains in an 'Autism Toolbox' YouTube video titled *Why Use Symbols?* that there have been some fantastic developments in Scotland.

Miller took part in a project aimed at getting symbols into all mainstream schools in Fife – 'Symbolising the Environment: A Whole School Approach'. A support for learning tutor noted that, in a class where symbols were introduced in a more generic way, all children benefited from their use in a variety of ways, therefore challenging the previously held perception that they were only for those pupils with a recognized additional support need (Miller 2013).

The symbols helped children with attention difficulties, those who needed structure, those who struggled with change and those who struggled with new concepts and vocabulary. They helped the children to self monitor and become more independent. Children looked at the written text and were able to learn the shapes of the words linked with the symbols, helping them to develop reading skills.

Altogether 146 schools became involved in the Fife pilot project. Schools were supported and guided and needed to have a teacher take on the coordinator role. *All* staff needed to be trained to understand why they were now using symbols as a whole school, where they would be used and how they would be used.

When I first saw Sandra Miller talking about getting the symbols into all these schools in Fife I felt like jumping for joy. If 146 schools in Fife have taken this on board and seen the positive effects, then surely it is only a matter of time before other mainstream schools follow suit. Mainstream schools are needing to support more and more children who benefit from visual supports. These supports need to be a part of the school's structure. Once mainstream teachers start using them and see their power, they will begin to incorporate them into lesson structure. What a huge difference this will make to so many children's experience of school.

Symbols in ALL learning environments

I was absolutely thrilled to learn of the pioneering symbols project in Fife. Now that this has shown that having visual supports helps all children learn, it needs to be put into place in *all* learning environments. This would make such a huge, huge difference to the academic success, emotional well being and confidence of so many, many children. I will continue to speak about this until visuals become as commonplace in mainstream schools as they are in special schools because so many more children could then stay in mainstream schools and have a better chance of achieving their potential.

Schedules

Having a schedule is so incredibly important to a visual learner. It allows a child to see what you have planned for the day. If there are any changes then they can process them and prepare for them. If they do not like the changes they may be able to question them. Have a visual schedule. Talk through the schedule at the start of the day.

If something has to change on the schedule then alert the children to this as soon as you can. You can use a 'whoops' symbol to show that something is different and then show the replacement activity. If a child is looking forward to an activity and it has to be cancelled, then try to replace the activity with another activity they will like; for example, if a child loves football, but it is raining and football is cancelled, try to think of another activity they will enjoy. Do not replace the football symbol with maths (unless of course maths is their favourite subject).

Figure 16.2 *A visual schedule with a whoops symbol*
Symbols from Colour Coding for Learners with Autism (Devine 2014)

Individual schedules

Individual schedules can break information down even more. You could, for example, show the structure of your literacy lesson. The children will start on the beanbags for a story, followed by free time (toys) and then do some work at the red table. The child can take the symbol off the schedule and match it to a transition board. They see the symbols on the schedule reducing as they get towards an activity they enjoy. This visual system can particularly help children with autism spectrum conditions (ASCs), attention deficit hyperactivity disorder (ADHD) and Down's Syndrome. Being able to see breaks really helps.

The reason that this is so helpful is that it allows a child to count down through activities they do not like. For some children, just being away from home and having any demands feels like a physical pain. Think of a woman giving birth. The pain is so extreme, but she knows it will end, and when it does end she will hold her baby. If the woman thought that the pain was going to be eternal and there would be no reward, she would not be able to cope. The schedule can help a child cope.

Tick lists and 'to do' lists

Some of our visual learners will benefit massively from having things to do written down. This could be a 'to do' list, the order of events (like a schedule) or preparing for something different that will happen. In a recent interview on BBC Radio 4, John Harris, of the *Guardian*, spoke to Penny Andrews, a university researcher, who, after a difficult childhood and adolescence, was finally diagnosed as autistic in her early thirties. Speaking about learning visually, she explained that she does not see in pictures, but she remembers words in a visual way. She has a tick chart of ideas for work colleagues, and one of the accommodations she requests is 'Don't just tell me something. Write it down.'

Writing things down can help with organization, but it can also make tasks seem far more achievable and less confusing. Words are said and then gone. They could be misinterpreted or have hidden context or missed bits. When something is written down it can be referenced and checked.

'To do' lists can be written on a writing with symbols program which will help to show meaning for visual children who are not yet reading. The pictures will show the words have meaning and some may be read.

Niall Greene reflects on his school experiences with organization before he was diagnosed with ADHD:

> As a child having no organisation skills meant lost or forgotten homework assignments and inadequate, to say the very least, planning for exams. I was in a constant state of worry knowing that at some stage I was going to be scolded for not doing my homework and once I was scolded I couldn't concentrate because I had been once again humiliated in front of the whole class by the teacher who was perceiving my difficulties as me being lazy. The impact of the teacher's negative, uncompassionate and intolerant communication would spread like wildfire throughout the classroom. 'MISS, Niall is copying me,' a classmate would complain. I'd whisper *'Please, I don't know what to do'* which was usually followed by *'MISS, Niall is talking to me again.'* **'NIALL GET UP HERE TO THE FRONT OF THE CLASS SO I CAN KEEP AN EYE ON YOU,'** the teacher would roar. There I would sit for the rest of the class with my head down, red faced, angry and frustrated at myself for being so stupid. I can see now that if some time had have been put into helping me build the organisational skills that I was clearly lacking, things could have been somewhat different. (Greene 2015d, para.3)

Diaries, calendars and wall charts

Home/school diaries

We use diaries as home/school books at our school. They work so well because we can write in up-coming events for parents. I add little photos to the diary of what the children have done in the day, which the parents can share with their child. When a child does not yet speak, a photo can prompt a lot more conversation than 'Jack had a good PE session'. Photos showing Jack on the balance beams, climbing the wall bars and bouncing on the trampoline give a parent lots more to talk about.

Homework diaries

Children in mainstream schools get to an age when they are expected to take responsibility for writing down their homework, but some children need to be taught this as a skill. It's no good thinking a child is 'lazy' because they do not do their homework. Check what they wrote down. Talk to them about it. Try to understand and put in some strategies to help. Keep checking these are working. Praise the child when they do remember. Tell them you know it's hard. Tell a story about when you forgot to write down an important date. Be a person. Do anything you can to make that child feel great about themselves. Learn to love their little quirks when they don't quite get it right. Never, ever belittle, judge or put a child down.

Calendars and wall charts

Try to write down events in a visual way and get a child to refer to them and take ownership of remembering things. A great place for these charts is opposite the toilet. Again, if a child does not read, you can cross off days and use simple pictures to highlight what the dates are. Tell the child what they represent. You could even get the child to suggest what image could represent an event. Something as simple as a wall chart can make a huge difference to a child.

It is good to establish the habit of writing things down or finding a way of setting reminders when the child is young because they will need to be able to do this if they are going to be independent.

TEACCH

Division TEACCH was set up in 1966 at the University of North Carolina as a research project focused on children with autism and their families. TEACCH is a fantastic approach and the training is amazing and well worth attending if you possibly can. I can only touch the surface of the TEACCH approach, but I hope to provide a starting point and a signpost towards some amazingly effective visual structures and supports. TEACCH can completely transform the education experience for the child who needs visual explanations and maximize their chances of success.

My ten most favourite things about using TEACCH

- *Respect and relationships* – The TEACCH approach is centred around understanding the individual, finding out all about their needs and building a respectful, loving relationship with them.

- *Building trust* – A child may start school having had some dreadful past experiences. We must build a child's trust before we can teach them. We do this by making expectations very clear and introducing demands at a pace which enables them to succeed.

- *Motivators* – We investigate and find out what motivates the individual child and use those motivators to get them to want to cooperate and learn. If a child likes tractors we will have tractors on their schedules and token boards and base tasks around tractors. This is amazingly powerful!

- *Structured environment* – We look at the physical environment and arrange it in such a way that a child knows where to go for different activities. When space is limited this can be done with simple changes such as adding lunch mats to a table at lunch time. We find ways to make it very clear where a child should be and what the expectations might be in that area. In time they will learn to follow a schedule and transition between areas independently.

- *Visual information* – TEACCH is a very visual approach. We use objects, photographs or symbols (whatever the child can understand on their worst day).

- *Breaking information down visually* – We show the child a schedule for the day. We break this down further, showing the structure of a session, the structure of an individual task in a lesson, how many tasks there will be or steps to an activity. such as getting dressed.

- *Making expectations clear* – The more clear we make our expectations through visuals and schedules, the more confident the child will feel that they can have a go.

- *Quiet and calm* – When information is being presented visually and staff understand the anxiety that noise can cause some children, the classroom becomes more quiet and calm. This reduces anxiety and helps the child feel safe and more able to learn.

- *Independence* – One of our main aims is to improve independence and reduce a child's reliance on prompts. We do this by structuring things so that there is a time to learn new tasks 'with the teacher' and then a time (once they are mastered) to complete tasks independently. Building towards independence in all areas is a huge focus.

- *Focus on futures* – The aim is that in the future the child will be able to live independently and have a job. We know that this will lead to future happiness and fulfilment for both child and parents.

Structured work area

Visit a special needs school and you will most likely see a workstation set up. There may be another storage unit on wheels with a series of trays. You can see an example of a motivating TEACCH work system set up in Figure 16.3 (on page 219). The work to complete is always on the left. The child takes a folder or tray of work and when they complete the task they stack it or leave it in a tray to their left. The workstation may have a screen around it to avoid students being distracted.

This workstation probably came into being after a teacher from the school attended a TEACCH course.

The Principles of Structured TEACCHING:

- Understanding the culture of autism

- Developing an individualized person- and family-centered plan for each client or student, rather than using a standard curriculum

- Structuring the physical environment

- Using visual supports to make the sequence of daily activities predictable and understandable

- Using visual supports to make individual tasks understandable.

(TEACCH 2015)

TEACCH – Where to start?

The TEACCH structure is so effective. Just under a decade ago I was job sharing a class with another teacher. After attending the five-day TEACCH course we decided to completely rethink the way our class worked. We moved everything, creating designated areas for 'work', 'independent work' and 'play'. We created visual schedules for our students.

There were a few raised eyebrows from support staff, but we persuaded them that we were convinced that this would work. The class was quite unruly and we were in need of structure.

We decided to begin with numeracy lessons and created a very set structure for these sessions. First we set up individual schedules for each child with their photograph at the top. The children would start at the red table choosing a number song such as five little ducks or ten green bottles. We would use props to go with the story to make it more visual. The children all sat around our red horseshoe-shaped table and enjoyed this start. After this the children would be given their photos to match to their schedules. Four children would go to the play area, two would go to the independent workstations and one would 'work with teacher'. When an activity was 'finished' the child would be given their photo, which they would take and match to their schedule. The schedule would show what they were going to be doing next.

At the start the structure was quite difficult to manage, with children needing a lot of support as they learnt to use the visual schedules. The play area was also a bit of a distraction, particularly as all the children were drawn to the computer. We brought in a huge screen to block off the play area. We quickly realized that the play area had the potential for linked learning, so we put in equipment and activities linked to our lesson focus – number, shapes, measures, etc.

It didn't take long before we had the sessions running really well. The staff, who had initially been sceptical, appreciated the new system. Everyone knew what they were supposed to be doing and where. Staff really got behind it and took on the jobs of changing tasks and setting up the play area. Numeracy had become a great lesson. The 'work with teacher' table also worked fantastically well, allowing 1:1 teacher time to move children on to new tasks. Having this teacher time built into the lesson meant children were getting more academic stretch and tasks could change over faster, which kept them motivated.

TEACCH in a literacy lesson

This system was working so well we decided to use it in our literacy sessions too. Again we followed a set structure. We'd begin with a sensory story, then split for 'work with teacher', 'play' and 'workstations'. The play area was again themed to the lesson, with dressing up, small world puppets and a doll's house to encourage communication. Our tray tasks for literacy were different and linked to developing letter recognition, reading and filling in gaps in communication.

We were very structured and rather proud of our model TEACCH class. It was amazing to see how the children moved on academically and how much better behaved they all were.

So I was well and truly sold on TEACCH, but I was convinced there was more we could be doing. What if we could add another layer to this lesson? What if we could get these effective TEACCH structures on to our class computer? Chapter 17 looks at how we did this in more detail.

Using TEACCH with children with other learning differences

TEACCH was developed for and researched with people with autism, but it is highly visual and sequential, which can be fantastic for other children who benefit from visual structures.

TEACCH structures can be particularly effective with children with Down's Syndrome who respond well to motivating personalized tasks and a clear visual structure.

TEACCH systems can also help children who find it difficult to organize, prioritize or stay on task.

Children with autism can have difficulty processing language, they may have highly sensitive hearing and they often like to know exact expectations before they begin a task. TEACCH structures reduce the need for so much language and the familiar routine can reduce anxiety.

The system was developed and researched for autism, but as many of the strategies and ideas are visual, motivating and provide a clear structure, they also work for other visual learners.

Why teachers often love TEACCH

TEACCH is so much more than the workstation, but seeing one set up is a sign that a school is aware of how visual structure, having things broken down into manageable parts, using individual motivators and reducing distractions can improve a child's capacity to complete tasks.

Once special needs teachers realize the power of this structured way of teaching, they incorporate it into the day. I've seen the most challenging classes of students with autism suddenly sit and settle to their work. The class goes quiet; they are all content. Staff get to know exactly what they are doing and know not to talk. This time is a relief to both the children and the staff. Tasks are tailored so that they are achievable and motivating. Demands seem to be off for a while.

If a whole class are following TEACCH structures, this is the time when the teacher can work 1:1 with students, moving them on to new tasks.

The tasks the children complete should be highly motivating. For example, if they are into cars, they will be moving cars into garages, copying a picture to create a car from building bricks, completing an aquadraw mat based on Disney's *Cars* and doing a cars puzzle.

The child will have a work system to follow. They will have a schedule of motivating pictures to match to the same pictures in the same order on task trays or in folders. See an example of this in Figure 16.3.

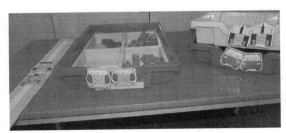

Figure 16.3 Transport themed work system using SEN Assist motivators

TEACCH structures at home

These systems can be set up at home. There is no need to go out and invest in expensive new furniture for home or school. All you need are a table and chair, a makeshift screen (if distraction is an issue), another small table for tasks ready to be completed and a box or washing basket for finished tasks. Teach the child to always work left to right. Tasks to be completed are on their left. Once completed they move them to their right.

I recall showing a child, who was overwhelmed by homework tasks this structure. We put all the homework that he needed to do on the left and then placed each assignment in a finished tray on his right as he completed them. This little bit of structure was such a relief to this boy.

Developing this sort of structure at home can be really helpful with getting homework done (if this needs to be built into the day).

Beyond tray tasks

TEACCH is not only about tray tasks. It's about creating structure, which helps people with autism become more independent. These structures can be following a schedule, using a tick list or knowing where to stand in a sports lesson. Examples are extensive, and the best way to find out about all of them is to go on a TEACCH course.

Chapter 17

SEN Assist

Teaching Literacy Through the Class Computer

The inventor…looks upon the world and is not contented with things as they are. He wants to improve whatever he sees, he wants to benefit the world; he is haunted by an idea.

Alexander Graham Bell (1847–1922)

The computer is a big motivator. The interactive white board or plasma screen can grab the attention of a group of children who are engaged in other activities and can bring them all together like magic.

Children are drawn by the white board. Playing a YouTube video or song is a great way to get their attention at the start of a session or bring them all together at the end.

But in my classroom there were frustrations as the children could not always reach the buttons (they were often placed at the top). The touch screen was not accurate, and clicking and dragging was difficult for even the teacher to master, as you had to be aware of the shadow cast by your arm and how it could interfere with the projector.

I thought that there must be ways around these things. I discussed it with my husband, Quentin, who is an animator and multimedia designer. He came up with a series of activities that my class could do. We began with a name sorting task. The letters would be jumbled up and the child would click a button to drop a letter into a box to spell their name. When they completed the activity their photo would appear on the screen and it would say 'Well done'. The children were so motivated by this. I wanted more…

TEACCH structures (see the previous chapter) were working in our lessons and I started to formulate an idea for incorporating the computer into our structured sessions. What if we could get TEACCH structures on to the computer? The more I thought about it, the more it made sense. TEACCH was developed for people with autism, but we were using it effectively with a class of children with varying diagnoses. We had children with Down's Syndrome, a child with Cerebral Palsy, a child with Global Delay and children diagnosed with autism. We were also differentiating for a wide range of abilities, from children with severe learning difficulties to one child who was on an academic par with children his age in mainstream school.

Looking to the future

Something that is quite striking in young people with severe learning difficulties is their contrasting abilities when it comes to ICT. I had children who struggled with sequencing story cards, but were able to navigate their way on the computer. I recall watching transfixed as one child created an animation using PowerPoint. On paper this child had a severe learning difficulty and seeing her classwork you would not question it, but on the computer she was displaying signs of brilliance. These skills were self taught. What else could she learn to do if it was on the computer?

I would watch with a mixture of admiration and frustration as a child who seemed unable to do simple class tasks was able to click start, find the internet button and go to 'favourites' and then select what they wanted to do.

There had to be a way to tap into this. This was an employable skill and the potential was being missed.

The computer is such a huge motivator and something our visual learners can really excel at. The IT skills of children diagnosed with learning difficulties can be better than same-age peers. These computer skills (and I am particularly thinking of children with autism here) do not measure up against the rest of their academic profile. But because their computer skills were not correctly channelled, the children would become stuck. How much more could they do with proper structure? How much could they learn?

I could see that more and more children were going to have access to touch screen devices in the future. Would these be a way in to getting more children from different socioeconomic backgrounds reading? Could this get more techie boys reading? Could this get more children with SEN reading?

Current use of touch screens for reading at home and in Early Years settings

Children are accessing stories through touch screen devices as well as books, and these devices are a great way in with some learners. They are particularly useful for getting boys to enjoy reading stories. They are also being used by more and more parents at home. In December 2014 the National Literacy Trust published results of a survey called *Children's Early Literacy Practices at Home and in Early Years Settings*. The survey found that:

Almost all children have access to books at home (99.7%) and 91.4% have access to a touchscreen at home. A quarter (28.2%) of children look at or read stories on a touchscreen at least once in a typical week. (Formby 2014, p.8)

The survey also highlights the increased access children have to touch screens at home, stating that a 2014 Ofcom survey showed that tablet use by children (aged 5–15) at home had increased from 42 per cent to 62 per cent between 2013 and 2014 (Ofcom 2014).

More and more Early Years settings have touch screen devices which children can access. The National Literacy Trust survey found that: 'All practitioners say that children have access to books (100%) and 2 in 5 (43.1%) practitioners say children have access to a touchscreen, in their setting, which is double the number in 2013' (Formby 2014, p.10).

More and more children have access to these devices every year and they are now very much a part of life. We might prefer books, but that should not stop us exploiting the touch screen device as a teaching tool.

Careers

Our TEACCH trays of independent work were based on factory-type tasks. The idea was that our children could one day achieve independence working in factories, but we now have access to so much technology. Times have changed. The type of careers young people with special educational needs (SEN) can aspire to have changed. I could see that there was a new area of employment opening up and growing every day. The information technology (IT) industry was somewhere I could really see some of our children, who may still have communication differences or social interaction differences, succeeding if we could just teach them how to structure their computer time and use it for learning instead of playing. The computer was in itself a motivator, but was often being used for play, which was led by the child's personal agenda.

I could see a wasted opportunity. We needed to support children in learning what a computer could do and get excited about learning or coding before they got into the repetitive playing of YouTube videos or one of the many, many other addictive game sites, where they repeat rather than learn. I look at adults who are completely addicted to playing games like 'Candy Crush' or 'Patience'. They repeat and repeat. Are they relaxing or stimming?

Niall Greene recalls, 'Unfortunately Technology can easily be a distraction from daily tasks. *I was on level 108 of Candy Crush when it dawned on me that I had actually wasted days of my life playing that pointless game*' (2015d).

We need to be giving today's children the skills to not get 'stuck' in pointless computer games because this could reduce their motivation to gain skills for employment. They might believe they are happier playing in the Candy Crush world, but that is not really living.

Why IT instead of a factory?

- IT is often a natural motivator. It's something the person enjoys and feels comfortable with.

- IT constantly advances. It is an industry that needs creative, innovative, divergent thinkers with new ideas.

- Being brilliant in IT does not require an amazing ability to do social chit chat. In fact the more a person can zone in, focus and pay attention to details, the better.

- IT relies on email communication, so those who struggle with handwriting or do not have clear speech can communicate effectively.

- There is a clear structure and tasks will be achievable. The person can even excel and have a great career.

- There is less of a dress code. I recall my husband Quentin going for an interview with a new media company in jeans. I questioned this, but he got the job.

SEN Assist
What if?

- What if we could get our lessons on to the computer?

- What if we could get those tray tasks and speech therapy activities presented on the computer or touch screen?

- What if there could be a program which incorporated a child's personal motivators and then taught them at their exact level?

- What if there was a clear start and finish and a work system so that a child knew how much they needed to do?

I'm sure many special needs teachers have had these ideas and asked these questions. The difference was I knew that Quentin would be able to make this a reality. I could see two things that the children responded to in our classrooms when it came to working independently – TEACCH visual structures and the computer. What if we could combine the structures with their greatest motivator? What if we could teach children to use their IT skills so that they could eventually gain employment and achieve future independence and fulfilment?

I knew we were contemplating something mammoth. I did not realize how all-consuming it would be. I did not anticipate the long uphill climb to getting others to be aware of our vision. I knew it would work. I knew it had to be done and I knew we were the people to do it. We did not look ahead, work out budgets or focus on any of the practicalities. We were a problem solving, creative couple and we knew that our idea was brilliant. It needed to become a reality.

An idea was born

I started to search the internet for anything like the software I needed, but there was nothing. Quentin and I would spend our evenings talking about it. I knew these children had so much potential and I knew that their IT skills could be the hidden key.

Together we came up with the idea of creating software that incorporated my specialist training. We would make it all incredibly simple. A teacher or parent should be able to turn it on and see it working. The motivators, the structure, the symbols and the tasks that I knew would engage children with learning differences would all be there ready so that the child could show how clever they really were. Our vision was to create this software for every subject and follow children through education with familiar structures.

I wanted to give teachers the tools they needed to really move the children on, but also save them time and lessen their workload.

How does SEN Assist support children with autism?

1. SEN Assist incorporates work systems based on classroom structures with a set number of tasks and a clear start and finish.

2. Activities are kept short and achievable with visual token boards. Ticks and crosses are included to help build tolerance to marking systems.

3. Forty-eight individual motivators, rewards and personal certificates are included. The motivators can also be printed for work systems, pegs, etc.

4. Structure and purpose for learning to typing names.

5. Individual levels raise self esteem (even includes a switch option).

6. Animated writing with symbols is ideal for visual learners.

7. Speech therapy activities including prepositions and pronouns.

8. Uncluttered backgrounds with clear areas of focus to avoid distraction.

9. Has just the right level of stimulation to keep the child on task, and click and click buttons to avoid the frustration of click and drag.

10. Includes a host of printable resources to support pre-verbal children in learning to comment and answer questions.

(Devine 2012)

The Fairy Tales

There's a story I love about Einstein. A mother, who had great ambitions for her young son, went and asked Einstein what her son should be reading if he was to be a great scientist. The story goes that Einstein told the mother to read her son 'fairy tales and more fairy tales'.

We chose to start with Fairy Tales for a number of reasons:

- They were always taught in nursery schools.

- They were on the Key Stage One National Curriculum.

- They linked with many topics.

- The repetitive language helped build familiarity.

- Repetitive language helped with role play.

- The predictable story lines were familiar.

- The dramatic elements of the stories appealed.

- They have stood the test of time.

- They could link to other areas of the curriculum.

- We loved that Albert Einstein story.

How SEN Assist works

Typing

To begin a child will type their name (with support as needed). Take the opportunity to encourage the child to look at the keyboard and build independence with typing. They will be learning to discriminate, to look and to read the letters of their name. It may help to write the letters on bits of paper and hold them above where the letter is on the keyboard. It is important that the child learns that the typing is a part of the exercise. Next select level 1. In time they may do all of this independently.

Motivators

In special education we know that using a child's individual motivator sparks their interest and makes them willing to try. We tailor resources to link with these interests. The same applies to TEACCH. If a child likes Disney princesses, use those princesses to make the learning seem more like fun. Incorporate the princess into everything as a little motivator, a cheerleader helping to inspire the child to want to follow their set schedule.

So the first thing I needed our new software to do was motivate the individual child. To do this we brainstormed and researched the different things which motivate children. We created four categories to help the child choose – animals, vehicles, fantasy and people. All together there were 48 individual motivating characters.

The child would then select their individual motivator. The child's motivator would stay at the side of the screen throughout, and each time the child completed a set of activities the little motivator would 'roar' or say 'yay', cheering the child on. This feedback was designed to not over stimulate. It was to be just enough to motivate the child and spur them on.

The story

Special needs teachers spend hours and hours adapting stories because we know the children benefit from simplified language. We retype text using programs like Symwriter to put symbols above the words because we know that the symbols get the children looking and show that the words have meaning. Because the white board or plasma screen are such a draw, we may scan the book to tell the story from the screen. All this takes a lot of work. The saving grace is that we use the same story over a number of sessions because children with learning difficulties benefit from repetition.

I knew that creating a story with the language already simplified and adding the symbols above the words would save teachers so much time. It would also ensure that children whose parents or teachers did not know about using symbols could also benefit.

Not to miss an opportunity, the language was taken from the first 100 high frequency words and, as the words were spoken, the writing was animated, creating another link for children who learn to read through recognizing words rather than through phonics.

Structure

The story was to be followed by six activities. Each activity would have four possible levels, which could be changed by a teacher using controls at the top. It is so important to be able to adapt our questioning and differentiate quickly when teaching children, but particularly children with autism who can get very anxious at not being able to get something right. At the same time these children will get bored if the activity is too easy. The activities were shown at the side in a work system so a child would know how many they had left to complete.

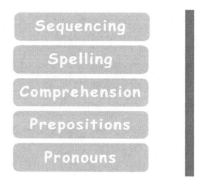

Figure 17.1 *SEN Assist work system*

MATCHING

The first activity is based on matching:

- Level 1 – Match a colour picture selecting 'the same' from a choice of three.

- Level 2 – Match a black and white symbol from a choice of three.

- Level 3 – Match a word from the story from a choice of three.

- Level 4 – Match words to create a sentence from the story, clicking in the correct order.

SEQUENCING

Sequencing is an important skill for speech. Children need to be able to sequence a series of events if they are going to talk about them. They need to sequence words to form a sentence.

- Level 1 – Matching three pictures in the correct sequence.

- Level 2 – Recall the order to match one picture and sequence the next two pictures.

- Level 3 – Match six pictures in the correct sequence.

- Level 4 – Match one picture and sequence the next five pictures.

COMPREHENSION

Comprehension is the most varied of the activities. Activities link with the story and are similarly stepped, but allow assessment and discussion relating to feelings, answering questions and story recall.

SPELLING

- Level 1 – Match a letter from a choice of three.

- Level 2 – Match an initial letter from a choice of three.

- Level 3 – Match letters correctly to spell a word.

- Level 4 – Copy a sequence to spell a word.

PREPOSITIONS

- Level 1 – Match a picture showing two prepositions: 'on' and 'under'.

- Level 2 – Select the correct preposition from the choice of three words with symbols: 'in', 'on' and 'under'.

- Level 3 – Select the correct preposition from the choice of three words with symbols: 'in front', 'behind' and 'around'.

- Level 4 – Select the correct preposition from the choice of six words with symbols.

PRONOUNS

- Level 1 – Match a male or female story character to a 'he' and 'she' symbol and word. This level includes a blue and pink colour code around picture and symbol.

- Level 2 – Select the correct pronoun from the choice of three words with symbols: 'he', 'she' and 'they' (no colour codes).

- Level 3 – Select the correct pronoun from the choice of four words with symbols: 'he', 'she' and 'they' or 'it' (no colour codes).

- Level 4 – Select the correct pronoun from the choice of three words with symbols ('he', 'she' and 'they') and the correct verb from a choice of three words with symbols to put two words together, e.g. 'they ran'.

Clear visual structure with a start and finish

The child will learn to complete the six activities independently on the computer, and the work system at the side will show how many tasks they have left to complete. Activities are designed to be quick to avoid frustration.

To get through each level the child must get between three and six ticks. The use of ticks and crosses was deliberate to prepare children for marking systems. A child will accept a cross from a computer. It is quite different to a cross from a teacher.

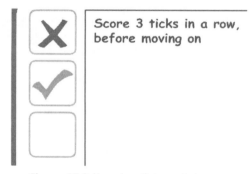

Figure 17.2 Showing ticks as tokens

The finish

At the end of the sixth activity the child sees a certificate, which shows their motivator, name and the level they have achieved. We only print the certificate if the child has completed the six activities independently.

Speech therapy

Activities are based on language activities used by speech therapists, including pronouns, prepositions, sequencing and comprehension. Developing communication is a priority throughout the programs. Even the praise is varied to extend the vocabulary.

The resources are based on PECS, allowing non-verbal children to comment and answer questions while learning the correct sentence structures. The resources allow a teacher to stretch children who may be more able, but do not have the language skills to show this. Using a sentence strip will keep a child on task and allow them to demonstrate what they know. Correct sentence structure can be modelled, and processing time can be allowed.

The simple act of putting a hand up to answer a question can be extremely difficult to teach and frustrating to the child. Using a sentence strip, a teacher can quickly assess a child's understanding and raise the child's self esteem.

Inclusion

SEN Assist was designed to include *all* children in the literacy hour. The switch-accessible software means a child can navigate the story with a switch or space bar. They can get a certificate for being able to press the switch six times independently (for many children this can be a huge achievement).

Figure 17.3 *Switch software can be activated by pressing the switch on the touch screen or by pressing a switch*

Figure 17.4 *Goldilocks comprehension worksheet from resource sheet*

Differentiation

Using the levels at the top of the screen, a teacher can easily differentiate questioning as appropriate for the individual child. For example, they can quickly skip from level one, matching character pictures, to matching all the words in a sentence at level four.

This raises the self esteem of the less able and keeps the more able stretched.

The resources are also designed to be quickly adjusted to meet the needs of the individual.

Lesson structure: Using the software with a special needs class over a half term[1]

In special needs schools the children benefit from clear structure and repetition. SEN Assist software can be used to teach one literacy lesson a week over the course of a year. The way to do this is to begin to structure lessons in line with the activities.

Week 1: Focus on reading

Focus	Activity description	Note
Story	Introduce the story on the computer.	Some children may be better starting off 1:1 on the computer.
Group activity	Model play with the puppet theatre. Make it fun so that the children want to be involved.	Children can make their own puppet (if able).
Worksheet	Print out the black and white masks and copy them to A3 size on a photocopier (if possible). Colour using pens, paint or tissue paper.	Sticking coloured tissue may be better for children with anxiety linked to sensory issues or anxiety linked to needing perfection.
Play	Puppet theatre in the play area.	Puppet theatre can be made from a cardboard box.
Independent work (trays or folders)	Introduce tray tasks linked with the story (these can be printed from the resources).	See Figure 17.4 for an example of a worksheet and 17.6 for an example of a matching tray task. Use free printable worksheets for more able children.
Computer work	1:1 computer time with support leading to independent work.	Try to keep the structure: story, activities, then finish.
Plenary	Look at the masks. Name characters.	Give praise and rewards at the end of the session.

---

1   The resources referred to in this section are available to download from www.jkp.com/ catalogue/book/9781849055987. This software is available from www.senassist.com.

Outcomes

All children will experience the story in different mediums.

Most children will show recognition of familiar characters and react to events.

Some children will remember character names and key events.

Additional ideas

Assess the ability levels of individual students through 'work with teacher' time. This can be task based or 1:1 time at the computer. Do not let the children feel they are failing. Make things motivating. Use rewards and praise.

Add sensory elements to the story.

Masks can be laminated or stuck to card for role play in future lessons.

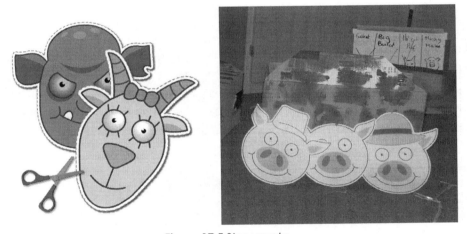

Figure 17.5 *Story masks*

Week 2: Play – Pairs or Snap

Focus	Activity description	Note
Story	Read the story on the computer.	Turns reading 1:1 during this time.
Group activity	Matching activities. Matching questions.	Use props and matching resources.
Worksheet	Matching resource. Differentiate to individual ability.	Match pictures to pictures and pictures to symbols or words.
Play	Puppet theatre in the play area. Pairs.	Print out the matching resources to make pair games.

Focus	Activity description	Note
Independent work (trays or folders)	Tray tasks linked with the story (these can be printed from the resources).	See Figure 17.6 for examples. Use free printable worksheets for some.
Computer work	1:1 computer time with support leading to independent work.	Try to keep the structure: story, activities, then finish.
Plenary	Drama – role play the story.	Give praise and rewards at the end of the session.

Outcomes

All children will match characters in different mediums.

Most children will match symbols, words and turn take with support.

Some children will write character names and predict their actions.

Additional ideas

Worksheet – Photocopy matching resources. Children to match pictures, symbols, words to words or words to pictures according to ability. For speed you could photocopy the matching tray task. You may need to cut out the answers for the child to stick (depending on ability). More able children could write character profiles. There are many worksheets online linking with Fairy Tales for more able students.

Figure 17.6 *Matching tray task: The Gingerbread Man*

Week 3: Focus on sequencing

Focus	Activity description	Note
Story	Read the story on the computer.	Turns reading 1:1 during this time.
Group activity	Sequencing activities and questions.	Use big story board for predicting what's next.
Worksheet	Sequencing resource. Cut out the pictures and stick them to coloured paper.	Repeat language 'first' and 'next'. Place words correctly.
Play	Puppet theatre in the play area. Pairs.	Use the pairs cards from the previous week.
Independent work (trays or folders)	Tray tasks linked with the story (these can be printed from the resources).	See Figure 17.7 for examples. Use free printable worksheets for some.
Computer work	1:1 computer time with support leading to independent work.	Try to keep the structure: story, activities, then finish.
Plenary	Drama – role play the story. Have a director.	Give praise and rewards at the end of the session.

Outcomes

All children will show awareness of the story sequence, anticipating events.

Most children will sequence six pictures from memory.

Some children will create a story map with pictures and key events in order.

Additional ideas

Get a teaching assistant to play out the story with puppets in the play area, but miss or change a key event in the story.

Figure 17.7 *Sequencing tray task: Red Riding Hood*

Week 4: Focus on spelling

Focus	Activity description	Note
Story	Read the story on the computer.	Turns reading 1:1 during this time.
Group activity	Spelling activities and questions.	Use big story board for spelling key words.
Worksheet	Visit www.senassist.com/resources.html. Children choose a motivator and create name labels for pegs. Print motivator and copy name.	Some will try to spell label for motivator.
Play	Puppet theatre in the play area. Pairs. Making labels on the laminator and adding them to pegs. Letters in play dough.	Use the pairs cards from the previous week.
Independent work (trays or folders)	Tray tasks linked with the story (these can be printed from the resources).	See Figure 17.8 for examples. Use free printable worksheets for some.
Computer work	1:1 computer time with support leading to independent work.	Try to keep the structure: story, activities, then finish.
Plenary	Drama – role play the story. Have a director.	Give praise and rewards at the end of the session.

Outcomes

All children will show awareness that their name labels are different.

Most children select their name and copy it using cut-out letters.

Some children attempt to write new labels using their knowledge of language.

Additional ideas

The pairs game will have been rotating. If it is working it is worth continuing. If not, you could adapt to a different game linking with the Fairy Tales.

Figure 17.8 *Spelling tray task using farm motivators*

Week 5: Focus on comprehension

Focus	Activity description	Note
Story	Read the story on the computer.	Turns reading 1:1 during this time.
Group activity	Comprehension activities and questions.	Use big story board. Use PECS boards for questions.
Worksheet	These vary according to the story. Print and structure according to ability.	Start to get children more independent (see ideas).
Play	Puppet theatre in the play area. Pairs. Making labels on the laminator and adding them to pegs. Letters in play dough.	Roll out play dough faces or names.
Independent work (trays or folders)	Tray tasks linked with the story (these can be printed from the resources).	See Figure 17.9 for examples. Use free printable worksheets for some.
Computer work	1:1 computer time with support leading to independent work.	Try to keep the structure: story, activities, then finish.
Plenary	Drama – role play the story. Have a director.	Give praise and rewards at the end of the session.

Outcomes

All children will experience repetitive story language.

Most children answer questions using pictures on switches, PECS boards or words.

Some children speak about their ideas relating to the story.

Additional ideas

These activities vary according to the story. Start getting the children to be more independent and develop thinking skills by not providing all the things they need, for example make sure they need to go and get their own scissors for cutting.

Figure 17.9 *Comprehension PECS boards: The Gingerbread Man*

Week 6: Focus on prepositions

Focus	Activity description	Note
Story	Read the story on the computer.	Turns reading 1:1 during this time.
Group activity	Preposition activities and questions.	Use big story board. Use PECS boards for questions.
Worksheet	Preposition activities using puppets and doll's house furniture.	Get their attention by physically going on, under, etc.
Play	Puppet theatre in the play area. Charades game with cards.	Extend prepositions if these are already familiar.
Independent work (trays or folders)	Tray tasks linked with the story (these can be printed from the resources).	See Figure 17.10 for examples. Use free printable worksheets for some.
Computer work	1:1 computer time with support leading to independent work.	Try to keep the structure: story, activities, then finish.
Plenary	Drama – role play the story. Have a director.	Give praise and rewards at the end of the session.

Outcomes

All children will explore and experience different prepositions.

Most children will answer questions using pictures on switches, PECS boards or words showing they can match prepositions.

Some children will develop language linked to prepositions and think of ones which are not in the story.

Additional ideas

Have fun with prepositions. Children will really enjoy the PECS activities and you can quickly assess ability by having all answer options on the back of the board.

Figure 17.10 *Prepositions worksheet and prepositions PECS*

Week 7: Focus on pronouns

Focus	Activity description	Note
Story	Read the story on the computer.	Turns reading 1:1 during this time.
Group activity	Pronoun activities and questions. Sort male and female characters on to coloured paper – pink for 'she' and blue for 'he'.	Use big story board. Use PECS boards for questions.
Worksheet	Children to do their own 'he' and 'she' worksheets.	Use children's magazines linked to interests.
Play	Puppet theatre in the play area. Dress up – male/female characters. Dress up dolls and toys.	Extend pronouns if already familiar. See ideas.
Independent work (trays or folders)	Tray tasks linked with the story (these can be printed from the resources).	See Figure 17.11 for examples. Use free printable worksheets for some.
Computer work	1:1 computer time with support leading to independent work.	Try to keep the structure: story, activities, then finish.
Plenary	Drama – role play the story. Have a director.	Give praise and rewards at the end of the session.

Outcomes

All children will experience sorting male and female characters into categories.

Most children will be able to sort 'he' and 'she' characters.

Some children will compare different versions of the same story and how characters/events are different.

Additional ideas

Pronouns are one of the most difficult things for a child to get right as they develop language, so do not be surprised by gaps. It's a good time to spot them. Introducing other versions of the same story widens the horizons of more able children.

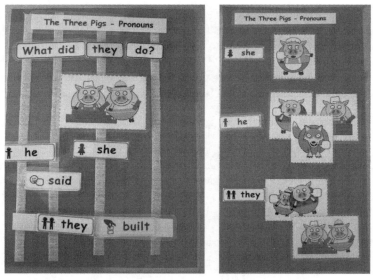

Figure 17.11 Pronouns PECS board and pronouns sorting tray task

CASE STUDY: Jimmy (age 9)

Jimmy was on 'an individual 1:1 program' and his behaviour was challenging. He would throw the classroom furniture at staff on a daily basis. Why?

'Jimmy will write his name independently'. Jimmy *hated* this Individualized Education Programme (IEP) target with a passion. It made him so cross that people kept asking him to write his name because it was something he saw as pointless and impossible to get right. He couldn't object verbally, so he threw things. When a child shows this level of frustration it's vital that we reassess what we are asking of them. Is it important, achievable or fair? Just because convention and curriculum suggest children do handwriting, should we stick by it or should we give the resistant writer a chance with a truly 'individual' education programme?

Was Jimmy ever happy? Let him on the computer and he would navigate his way to YouTube and spend as long as he could clicking/ stimming between favourite videos. Was this educating him ? Not at all. Was trying to get him to write his name 'educating' him? We needed to find some middle ground fast to break a very negative pattern of behaviour.

We only changed one word in his IEP: the target 'write' became 'type'. We stopped the writing all together. Clearly we needed to build trust and start again on his terms. Of course I had a hidden agenda – I was his teacher.

I taught Jimmy that he had to type his name to access the computer. He then had to complete a short set of structured tasks. He knew how many tasks because there was a clear work system at the side. I already had SEN Assist up my sleeve with a work system that mirrored his familiar structured tray tasks.

I helped him – hand over hand at first. I knew he'd learn to do things independently and I gradually withdrew my support.

Day by day we built on these skills and we built up trust and there was a significant change. No more flying furniture and no more frustration. In all areas there was a much happier Jimmy, who was willing to compromise and able to start using his high interest in the computer to learn. Within a term, Jimmy had moved back into the classroom – there was no need for an individual 1:1 program. We had met Jimmy half way with what he understood and trusted – the computer – and broken a destructive cycle. (Devine 2012)

Teaching children to turn take and share the class computer (they can)

The computer can be the most amazing teaching tool, but it also has the power to become an almighty distraction (if handled in the wrong way). Take care! You are the teacher. You must establish control of the computer and set rules from the outset.

You may be working with children already accustomed to ruling the computer – children who have discovered YouTube and have previously been allowed to sit (perhaps for several hours) doing exactly what they want on the computer again and again. It may seem an impossible task to break this habit.

CASE STUDY: Locking up the computer

I went to teach in one classroom and the computer was inside a purpose-built metal desk that was locked shut with padlocks. The previous teacher had never used the computer while the children were in the room because it would result in a bundle. The children were never allowed on the computer either because it resulted in tussles, anxiety, noise and meltdowns. I said to the teaching assistant that we would have to change this. The class needed to learn not to all bundle when they see a computer. If children have a clear visual structure showing whose turn it is and how long they have, they will cope much better. These children were *never,* ever allowed on the class computer. They were missing out on learning through the computer, but they were also missing the chance to learn some very important social skills.

'What if we went to a shop with a computer?' I asked the teaching assistant. 'We risk assess, and if there's a computer in view we would choose somewhere else,' I was told to my dismay. I was disheartened because I knew that by not allowing them the opportunity to learn the right way to behave on the computer these children were being set up to fail when out in the community. If children cannot share IT equipment then it is our responsibility to teach them how to in the classroom.

So, to add structure, I made visuals with the Symwriter program. I had a set of children and staff photos and would stick the visual to the corner of the computer. It would say: 'Fiona's turn on the computer.' I also made visuals to show who was next: 'Billy is next on the computer.' Rather than use a visual timer that might bleep at the wrong time, we used visuals showing: 'Fiona has 5 minutes left.' This was replaced by: 'Fiona has 4 minutes left.' The children soon learnt this structure and we were able to have the computer on without the bundle.

Once the children were able to share our class computer we used Social Stories and role play to show the children how to turn take on the class computer and how to behave around computers that belonged to other people. We went to real shops with real computers and so overcame the issue.

Figure 17.12 *Screenshot from The Three Pigs story*

Figure 17.13 *Small child using the space bar to operate the computer*

Possibilities

My aim was to put together story software which any parent or teacher could switch on and instantly engage a group of children, catering for a variety of abilities so that all children would have a chance to succeed at their own level. I believed that if I could create the framework and show how well it worked then others may follow. People asked if I was worried that what we were doing would be copied, but I hoped it would be copied. With the right structures and supports there is so much more that children with visual learning styles can achieve.

Chapter 18

Dance, Drama and a Sprinkle of Shakespeare

Sparking Creativity and Bringing Stories to Life Using Costume, Masks, Puppets and Props

Tell me and I forget, teach me and I may remember, involve me and I learn.

Benjamin Franklin (1706–1790)

Dance

In his speech 'Do schools kill creativity?', Sir Ken Robinson (2006) tells a childhood story about Dame Gillian Lynne (the amazing choreographer behind Andrew Lloyd Webber's incredibly successful *Cats* and *Phantom of the Opera*). Gillian's mother took her to see a doctor because the teacher had said that she was very fidgety in lessons. The doctor said that he would speak to the mother privately and left Gillian in the office with the radio on. The doctor asked Gillian's mother to look through the office window. Gillian was dancing. 'There is nothing wrong with your daughter. She is a dancer,' he said. Gillian's mother took her to a dance school, and from there she went to the Royal Ballet, became a ballerina and then went into choreography, making an amazing career for herself.

The point Robinson makes is that if Gillian had gone to a different doctor she could have been put on medication and sent back to school to do 'good sitting'. She may never have found the things she was passionate about, the things which would become an incredible career.

CASE STUDY: Darcy (age 3)

First ballet lesson

Our three-year-old daughter started to show a love of dancing. Maybe she would take after her Nana, who went to the Royal Ballet School. I found a local ballet school and took her along for a taster lesson. I watched the lesson and tried hard not to judge, but immediately there were little alarm bells ringing. The way the children were spoken to, the way they were not really listened to... The way the lesson just followed a CD. At the end of the lesson the teacher gave out big teddy stickers, but not to all the children. Children doing a taster lesson, who had not signed up to the 'certificate program', were not included. This lesson was followed by a tap dancing class in the same room, which was carpeted. The children were still expected to wear tap shoes. We left the class and I asked Darcy what she thought about ballet. 'I didn't get a teddy sticker' was her reply. She is only three. We are not taking dance seriously, but I take making lessons 'fun' and sparking creativity very seriously. I knew we needed a different dance school.

Darcy's second ballet lesson

We found another class and I observed Darcy joining in a lesson. As I watched, the lovely teacher transformed all the children into mermaids. They travelled around the room and the teacher explained where they were going. She had placed pictures on the wall for children who needed a visual to help paint a picture in their minds. I was transported back to the 'Creative Dance' lessons my mother used to do, when we were children. I'd forgotten how she would lead us all on a journey, imagining we were on magic carpets or inside bubbles.

Next the children were sorting through imaginary jewellery and delighting in choosing an imaginary colour for their long mermaid hair.

At the end of the lesson each child was given a tiny silver star sticker. Every child came out feeling happy. You could really see the sparkle in their eyes.

What a brilliant foundation these children were getting for creative writing, creative thinking and self confidence. This was so much more than dancing.

We must listen to our children, watch their reactions and be prepared to take action if things are not right. Children are best placed to judge a teacher. Watch them, ask them and listen to them, and if things do not seem right then follow your instincts.

When I was at primary school we did dancing. It was one of the most loved lessons. One of my primary school friends now teaches dancing. She absolutely loves it. She discovered this love when she was at school.

Not all parents take their children to lessons outside of school. It is vital that we bring these experiences in. I wonder if my early creative dance lessons were the thing that freed me up to think creatively and helped me use my imagination in lessons and have the confidence to share new ideas. Dance and drama are so important and must be incorporated into primary teaching, ideally introduced by specialist teachers.

Drama

Teachers sometimes shy away from drama, but role playing a story can be the most brilliant way to bring it to life for a child. Words and pictures on a page become real and the child is part of the action.

Many years ago, before I qualified as a teacher, I taught a drama class for children with learning difficulties. I remember agreeing to take the class. I thought it would be an amazing experience. But when it came to reality – the day I was going to first teach – I was suddenly terrified. I wished that I had not committed to teaching the class, but once I had got past that initial fear and met my little troop I loved every magical minute. It was wonderful to see their confidence improve and to feel that I was making a difference to their lives. I'm really proud that the drama group (Centre Act) is still going because I think it's absolutely fantastic for children with learning difficulties to access drama and also to socialize with other children and teachers outside their school circle.

Warm-up drama games to include ALL *visual learners*

When I think of drama warm-ups the first one that springs to mind is 'hot seating'. The children take turns to get into character and field questions from the group. This is much used in mainstream drama, but children with learning difficulties need a more stepped, less language-reliant approach.

Mirrors

Emotions – The children look in mirrors and copy pictures showing different emotions. Next get the children together in pairs. One shows an emotion and the other copies it like a mirror. Are they the same?

Routines – Children look in a mirror and pretend they are brushing their teeth, using mouth wash and getting ready for bed. Again try mirroring and guessing what the other child is doing.

Animals – Children imagine they are different animals while another child copies. When you say 'freeze' they can stop and guess. Have pictures of animals as prompts for those who can't think of an animal. These pictures will also be good communication aids for pre-verbal children.

Balls

Name game – A ball game to help remember names. See Chapter 8 for details.

Simple throw and catch – Keep it simple. Throwing and catching with a partner is great for cooperation, team work and awareness of self and other people.

Roll the ball – Not all children will be able to throw and catch. Roll the ball. As it arrives say, 'Katy has the ball. Who will Katy pass it to?' Encourage others to join in if they want to.

Imaginary journeys

When I was a child my mother taught a creative dance class. She was always taking us on exciting journeys. She would put on some music and lead us off on an adventure. Maybe we were going to space – maybe we were on magic carpets, in hot air balloons or inside bubbles floating in the air. These journeys were amazing for sparking our imaginations. I'm sure they must have helped us to write stories later on at school. Maybe without that early injection of creativity I would not be writing this book.

Children with learning differences and disabilities can benefit so much from this type of imaginary journey. For our visual learners, add some pictures and maybe some props. It doesn't have to be anything on a grand scale. Certainly not a presentation, but including pictures will help get the children started, especially the children who cannot process all your words. Keep language simple and have pauses they can fill with pictures.

If a child does not seem to be on the journey, support them a little more by modelling actions and expressions. Do not tell them how to act, but model for them.

Let the drama begin!

Sometimes role play can seem too ambiguous or distant for a literal child. This is where costumes and masks can really help. Masks are particularly effective, as a child with clothing sensitivities does not need to encounter that distracting anxiety.

I incorporate a lot of drama into our literacy sessions. The children are able to act out stories having seen them. I will play our SEN Assist software whilst the children act the story so that they have a visual prompt and can see exactly where they are supposed to be, and by linking their mask they can see who they are supposed to be. This is amazingly effective. It doesn't matter how the drama looks to the audience when incorporated into a lesson. The important thing is that the child experiences stepping outside of themselves into someone else's shoes. That is incredibly freeing both emotionally and creatively.

When it comes to scenery and props, keep things simple. For example, when recreating the Three Billy Goats story, a bench will do for the bridge, with some green material on one side for the green grass, brown on the other end for mud and blue in the middle for water. The troll becomes the troll because they have a mask. They do not have to hold it in front of their face. Drama in the classroom should be free. Even if they cannot hold the mask, others will understand that they are the troll because they saw you give out the masks. Handing out masks makes immediate sense to the visual learner. They might not take in a list of names linked to characters, but when they see you hand Joey the troll mask they *know* Joey is the troll. It just makes sense.

'Dr Drama'

I grew up hearing the term 'Dr Drama' from my parents, who were both actors and drama teachers, and from Lesley Hendy, who lived next door to us and co-founded Surrey Heath Young Actors Company (SHYAC) with my parents. Lesley has worked in education for 40 years. She is a former Senior Lecturer in Drama and Education at the Faculty of Education, University of Cambridge. So why 'Dr Drama'? Simply because time and again they have seen how drama can transform lives.

SHYAC was an all-inclusive group. Over the years they included children with all different types of special educational needs (SEN). They were always willing for children to come and try out SHYAC. They helped children with stammers, children with other speech difficulties, children who lacked confidence, children who needed rehabilitation following trauma, children with autism and children with learning difficulties. They never said 'No'.

A child does not have to be a future actor to be able to benefit from 'Dr Drama'. I saw first hand how SHYAC helped many children develop into confident, creative, happy people. Some of these children did go into the arts either as actors or dancers, or behind the scenes, but this was never the main aim. What Lesley and my parents made absolutely sure of was that *every* child was supported, encouraged and built up so that whatever they went on to do they were kinder, more confident and less afraid to have a go.

I would listen to Lesley, her late husband Mike and my parents enthusing for hours about the children in SHYAC, and the ones they talked about the most were those who had the stammers, the difficult behaviours and the mental health issues. They loved the brilliant actors, the naturals, but it was the children who most needed access to 'Dr Drama' that gave them the real buzz as they saw them achieve their best. They knew that their weekly drama was changing futures and they didn't fear taking risks. They once cast a Puck with a stammer, who somehow lost it by the time the performance came around. My mother recalls holding her breath sitting in the audience next to a mother of a child with autism waiting to see if he would come on stage and say his line. That mother was over the moon. She never thought she'd see her son do that. And not only did that boy gain confidence he won a group of friends for life. Lesley, Mike and my amazing non-conformist, creative parents are the sort of people *all* children need to access. These are the sort of people who use their passion (which happens to be drama) to transform children's lives.

The Oscar-winning actor Jeremy Irons recalled in an interview with Kate Bohdanowicz that he was 'a dullard at school'. He explained, 'I always seemed to be sitting at the back of the class, where I could hear little and understand less. Something would be explained and I'd think, "I don't really get that." But not wanting to draw attention to myself, I kept quiet. So I was always dropping down the ability streams' (Jeremy Irons, quoted in Bohdanowicz 2014).

But there was one English teacher called Robert Glen, who inspired him with his love of learning and who took time out to tutor him and a group of friends in play readings. Mr Glen was casting the school play and chose Jeremy Irons to play the lead.

After failing his A Levels Irons didn't know what he should do and ended up doing social work in London and busking. Then he saw an advert for a job in the theatre in Canterbury, got the job and loved it.

Mr Glen may not have got Jeremy Irons through his A Levels, but he opened the door to a happy future career. Teachers must think about what children *can* do and inspire them to go out and find what they love. Education is not just about grades. The children who fail the exams can be the ones who go on to have great lives (as long as teachers protect their self esteem and show them that they are capable).

Jeremy Irons concluded his interview with these wonderful words: 'I shall always be grateful to [Mr Glen] for giving me the opportunity to discover this place of storytelling that I've been luxuriating in ever since. He taught me that there really is a Neverland' (quoted in Bohdanowicz 2014).

I'm sure that Jeremy Irons had Mr Glen in mind when he agreed to become an ambassador for the Prince's Teaching Institute, which aims to inspire teachers through their love of their subject.

Next stop Shakespeare (how *every* child can learn to love the words)

What is it about Shakespeare? Why is he the only compulsory author on the English National Curriculum? Why is Shakespeare taught in over half the world's schools? Why am I so keen that *every* child should access Shakespeare?

Michael Boyd, Artistic Director of the Royal Shakespeare Company (RSC), explains:

> Shakespeare wrote plays and young children are geniuses at playing. Ask them to comment on a great work of literature and they will shrink away. Give a child the part of Bottom, Tybalt, Lady Macbeth or Viola and watch them unlock their

imagination, self esteem and a treasure trove of insight into what it's like to be alive that will feed them for a lifetime. Shakespeare remains the world's favourite artist because his living dilemmas of love, mortality, power and citizenship remain unresolved, vivid and urgent today. (Quoted in Royal Shakespeare Company n.d.)

In 2008 the RSC launched their 'Stand Up for Shakespeare' campaign. The RSC suggest children learn about Shakespeare by:

- doing it on their feet

- seeing it live

- starting it earlier.

Introducing Shakespeare

How were you taught Shakespeare at school? So many adults groan when asked this question. They talk of teachers reading aloud from texts, or worse still they recall the agony of listening to other students taking turns to read aloud from dusty books. Imagine how this would feel for a child with dyslexia, waiting for their turn to read a line – the unnecessary anxiety this may have caused.

We owe it to the current generation to rethink the way we introduce the Bard.

When I was a baby and couldn't sleep, my father, who is an actor and spent three seasons with the RSC, would walk around lulling me to sleep, reciting speech after speech.

As a teenager, I was cast as Helena in *A Midsummer Night's Dream*. I found it so easy to learn the lines. The rhythm and the structure of the prose were embedded. I did not just know my part, but every line in the play. Over 20 years have passed, but the words are all still there. If I had to perform the play again tomorrow, without a script, I probably could.

Shakespeare was a connection I shared with my husband Quentin too. When we met and somehow got on to the subject of Shakespeare, he loved the way that I could recite long Shakespeare speeches.

When Quentin was a teenager he was buying Shakespeare books with his pocket money and reading them at night. He wanted to know why Shakespeare was a favourite author of Jim Morrison (the lead singer of The Doors).

We knew that the best way for anyone to hear Shakespeare was in performance with professional actors bringing the words to life. We had both experienced the dreadful 'read around the room' approach at secondary school. I knew that I was lucky having had actor parents and a father with a life-long passion for Shakespeare. If only every child could have that sort of introduction. Shakespeare did not write his words wanting them to go in books. His words were meant to be spoken by actors who love the words and know how to use those rhythms and give them life. Then it dawned on us. Maybe we could create Shakespeare software? Maybe we could create the perfect introduction to the Bard for *every* child?

Early Shakespeare

Teachers were constantly asking for a follow up to the Fairy Tales. Shakespeare is the only compulsory author on the National Curriculum and is taught in so many countries. We decided that together we could make Shakespeare more accessible.

Creating Shakespeare software

Using the familiar SEN Assist format we found a way to introduce the stories and language of Shakespeare so that *every* child could access and enjoy it.

We began by breaking down the story with repetitive use of the first 100 high frequency words. We included an option to have symbols above the words as so many children are visual learners. As the words are read aloud by our animated Shakespeare character they are highlighted, which attracts the child's focus (the objective being to draw the eye towards those words so that in time the child will learn to read them).

Figure 18.1 *Screenshots from Early Shakespeare*

There are all sorts of clever, inbuilt ways which allow a teacher to differentiate for a mixed-ability group. SEN Assist is all about inclusion. A mainstream class can use the software together, and each child can show how much they *can* do. It's all about getting the approach right.

Children with SEN often find it easier and quicker to learn through the computer than by listening to a teacher talk because, to quote one of my past students with autism, teacher talk can be 'too complicatey'. These children often prefer to feel they are learning *with* the teacher than being taught. Using the Early Shakespeare software, the teacher and child can discover and learn together.

Shakespeare's language is often lost in simplified versions of the plays, but the rhythm of those words is so crucial. The child's first introduction to the sound of Shakespeare should be as he intended – through actors. Shakespeare's plays were written to be performed, not taught. Too many adults recall enduring hearing a teacher read or having to take turns reading. The Early Shakespeare voiceover artists are professional actors, who have trodden the boards at the RSC and the National Theatre.

Shakespeare Day

On 23 April 2014 our school held a great big 450th birthday celebration for Shakespeare. I wanted the day to be memorable and school budgets are always stretched so I applied to Surrey Heath Arts Council and got a grant. We had a huge cake and every child made a birthday card. Primary children performed *A Midsummer Night's Dream* and the secondary students acted out scenes from *Romeo and Juliet*. It was magical seeing our primary children dressed up as Titania, Puck and Bottom.

We played the Early Shakespeare software to give the performance a visual structure. The children had masks, which were the same as those on the software, which gave them a visual connection, allowing them and the audience to know which character they were portraying.

It was lovely to watch some of the comical moments. At one stage Oberon decided he wanted to go to sleep on the 'bank where the wild thyme blows' and our assertive Titania was having none of it. She knew that she was supposed to sleep on the bank, so she picked it up and moved it.

It was fantastic to see our secondary students acting out the balcony scene in *Romeo and Juliet*. All of the children taking part had severe learning difficulties, but they loved our Shakespeare Day. Our Shakespeare Day will stay in many of our children's memories. We can talk about them playing Romeo or Oberon and see them glow with pride. We love creating opportunities to see the children at our school feel proud. We know how important it is to raise their self esteem and self belief. Days like this should be built into every school year – different experiences that stand out when the staff all go that extra mile.

Figure 18.2 A Midsummer Night's Dream

Figure 18.3 Romeo and Juliet

Looking back over photos of our Shakespeare Day it is clear that *every* child was involved and enjoying Shakespeare. There was not a script in sight. There was no pressure. Just a lot of fun! Our school caters for children with severe learning difficulties and none of them felt intimidated by Shakespeare. Say the name and they will probably associate it with that celebration day, with dressing up, performing and with that great big cake.

Figure 18.4 *Shakespeare Day cake created by Maxine Elliott*

In the summer term our topic was planets. Towards the end of term I was reading a book about planets with a nine-year-old boy with autism. We discovered together that the planet Uranus has 27 moons named after Shakespeare characters. He asked if there was a moon named 'Hermia' and I was amazed. Not only had he made the Shakespeare connection, but remembered a character name from *A Midsummer Night's Dream.*

I've taught the most challenging groups of young people, and the Early Shakespeare software can keep the whole group completely focused for an entire literacy session. It really does make teaching Shakespeare easy!

One day I had to phone a parent and knew I would be out of class for a bit. I returned to my SEN class to find them all sitting beautifully. What were they doing? Shakespeare!

Figure 18.5 *Children create their own* A Midsummer Night's Dream *using puppets and a box theatre*

Shakespeare as 'autism therapy'

Shakespeare is now being recognized as having therapeutic benefits, with research currently being carried out at Ohio State University.

The rhythm of Shakespeare creates the sound of a heartbeat, which is repetitive, predictable and soothing to the ear. The actors often have exaggerated voices and facial expressions which can help children with communication difficulties link meaning with the words.

Clinical psychologist Marc Tassé, Director of the Ohio State University Wexner Medical Center's Nisonger Center, is leading a study that's evaluating the effectiveness of a unique autism therapy developed by Kelly Hunter, an award-winning RSC actress and author of *Shakespeare's Heartbeat: Drama Games for Children with Autism*.

> It's quite amazing to see how a Shakespeare play can be transformed into a therapeutic intervention that encourages students to communicate. (Tassé, quoted in Ohio State University n.d.)

Hunter and Tassé completed a successful pilot programme with 14 children with autism. The researchers reported significant improvement in communication, social relationships and language skills: 'Things like eye contact, emotion expression, emotion recognition, and expressive communication also improved dramatically', Tassé says (Ohio State University n.d.). They are now expanding the programme to 42 weeks with 20 students.

Hunter explains on her website:

> Two major themes underpin the work: the rhythm of the Iambic Pentameter, which creates the sound of a heartbeat, within which the children feel safe to communicate. Second is an exploration of the Mind's Eye, allowing children to explore imaginative worlds, which may otherwise be locked away. (Hunter n.d.)

CASE STUDY: Nicola

This case study was written by Kelly Hunter for the magazine Teaching Shakespeare.

I worked with a teenage boy with autism, back in Bromley. Nicola made very little eye contact, was obsessed with bus routes and had minimal verbal skills, compounded by English not being his first language. He displayed little empathy and aside from detailing the bus routes of south London he made little conversation. Towards the end of my time there, after nearly three years of developing these Shakespeare-based games with the group, I cautiously introduced the idea of acting out our own mind's eye images. I had no idea if the children would access anything. Without prompting Nicola vividly and carefully acted out a funeral service, from his distant childhood back in Romania, with physical accuracy, delicacy and emotion. It lasted a good fifteen minutes and everyone was spellbound. I've experienced many breakthroughs with children as they become more confident, make more eye contact, even speak a word for the first time, but Nicola's engagement with his own mind's eye was for me a revelation of the power of Shakespeare. The key to this work is to employ the great hum concepts of Shakespeare (and especially the ways in which these are embodied, at once intellectual and physical) to their best use – waking us up to ourselves. (Hunter 2013, p.10)

There is more information about Hunter's 'Heartbeat' method and also links to videos and articles on her website.[1]

Hold back the set texts

There is no excuse for introducing Shakespeare in black and white and reading it around a classroom:

Keep that pile of plays in the resource cupboard until you have your students so enthused that they will cheer when you produce them. Shakespeare did not set out to write set texts. His intention was to engage an audience – to entertain. (Devine 2014b)

When a secondary school teacher says the class are going to be doing Shakespeare, the students should all be thinking, 'Great! We know Shakespeare already.' We want them to think, 'That's easy. We did that in primary school.' We want to remove the mental block our teenagers get by introducing them to Shakespeare early.

There's a moment I love in the film *Dead Poets Society*. Robin Williams played an inspirational, unconventional English teacher. He gets up on the desk amidst his astonished class of private school boys and says:

Why do I stand up here? I stand upon my desk to remind myself that we must constantly look at things in a different way. You see the world looks very different up here... Just when you think you know something, you have to look at it in another way. Even though it may seem silly or wrong, you must try. (John Keating, played by Robin Williams, *Dead Poets Society*, 1989)

That is exactly what we want our young people to get from education. Never mind learning sets of facts or footnotes. We want them to learn to see things differently. We want them to look from that different angle and have the confidence and curiosity to investigate further. We want them to believe they could be right. That is how invention is born. That is how we evolve. We do not want to create

1   See www.kellyhunter.co.uk/sa.php.

followers, who learn rote facts, tap along with our tune and keep their heads down. We want to inspire leaders – the ones who question and explore. Often these same leaders were the students who didn't do 'good handwriting' or read well, when under pressure. We must nurture and protect children, raise their self esteem and inspire them to want to be in class because it's exciting. Keep them wondering about what will come next

Ideas for teaching Shakespeare

In a bid to inspire more schools to celebrate Shakespeare's 450th birthday in 2014, I wrote a guest article for *Innovate my school* (Devine 2014b):

Theatre in the classroom

Below are some of my notes and suggestions about how to introduce some of the most popular Shakespeare plays in your classroom. They are intended as a starting point – the sky's the limit!

Macbeth

Spark imaginations with some witchy props – a cauldron, pointy hats, long black cloaks. Set the scene by changing the lighting. Lights out – prime opportunity to talk about not having electricity and writing by candlelight with quill and ink. Get them making spells – adding whatever they like. Use some of the language, but not by reading text.

> 'Double, double toil and trouble;
> Fire burn and cauldron bubble.'

Get them acting mad. What does madness look like? Have a 'mad' competition where they get in pairs, talk about it and then act out 'madness'. Make them laugh so loud that the headteacher pops their head through the door to check what's going on.

Romeo and Juliet

Create the balcony scene with a ladder: 'O Romeo, Romeo! Wherefore art thou Romeo?' What age was Juliet? How old are people when they marry now? What if parents could still choose them a husband or wife? Look at some pictures of people parents might choose. Make them laugh and get them relating Shakespeare's stories to their own lives.

Bring in some foam swords and get them fencing. Have teams of Capulets and Montagues. Talk about the types of things that make young people fight. What can affect their moods at school – heat, hunger, home life? What makes them angry? Who are their friends? Act out Tybalt killing Mercutio, and then Romeo killing Tybalt. Have a court scene. Talk about justice. Talk about how people react quickly in the heat of the moment. Link this with relevant events – television, pop groups. Anything that gets them talking.

A Midsummer Night's Dream

Get the boys being fairies. Then see if the girls can do any better. Join in. Make it silly. Get them laughing. Use this prime time to introduce the idea that in Shakespeare's day all the actors were men and that the girls' parts were usually played by boys.

Show them how Shakespeare sent himself up in the play scene from *A Midsummer Night's Dream* (Act V, Sc.i) with Bottom's exaggerated and ridiculous use of 'O'.

'Oooooooh grim-looked night! Oooooooh night with hue so black!'

Act out the funny play with a big sweeping move on every Oooooooh! Then be still for the line. Try it with different children being 'Wall' and 'Bottom'.

Shakespeare for everyone

Get them up acting out the play with masks as the cartoon actors show them what to do step by step. Or get them to create their own box theatres and scenery and become directors of their own plays. Shakespeare Schools Festival offers an inclusive approach.[2] They provide students with the experience of performing shortened versions of the plays in real theatres. These are open to all schools. Usually they will have three or four schools including a primary, secondary and special educational needs (SEN) school, and they also offer continued professional development (CPD) to teachers and ongoing support.

Shakespeare Week

The Shakespeare Birthplace Trust have partnered with numerous organizations to create an all-new celebration – Shakespeare Week. Each child involved gets a free passport to a Shakespeare full of offers and opportunities.

---

2   See www.ssf.uk.com for more information.

Closing the curtains

When introducing Shakespeare, leave that pile of dusty old books in the cupboard. Arrange a fencing lesson, visit a theatre… Surprise them by breathing life into those words. Giving children the right introduction to Shakespeare means they will be less afraid of meeting other classic authors. Learning to love language will also improve their ability to express themselves, scaffolding future success.

Now sits expectation in the air.

Henry V (c.1599)

Chapter 19

Look Here! They Can!

Believing in Futures

The sum of things to be known is inexhaustible, and however long we read, we shall never come to the end of our story-book.

A.E. Housman (1859–1936)

Sometimes professionals will assume they know outcomes based on their past experience or training. They may give a bleak prognosis including a lot of 'can't and probably won't'. So I'd like to share some real stories of young people who should make professionals think twice before predicting negatives and make other professionals and parents believe in their instinctive 'can do' beliefs.

The young people in this chapter have learning differences – they've been let down by some and supported by others, but they share something which ups the odds greatly of achieving personal success and happiness. They have people believing in them, focusing on their 'cans', pushing for them, fighting for them and, most importantly, loving them without conditions.

I've asked some brilliant parents, carers and young people to share their stories and they have kindly agreed.

CASE STUDY: Oliver's story

Diagnosis: Down's Syndrome

Oliver Hellowell is an 18-year-old with an incredible talent for landscape and wildlife photography. His ambition is to be a professional photographer and he is well on his way to achieving this. He already has his own website and a huge worldwide following of people who love his photographs.[1] Oliver was diagnosed with Down's Syndrome at birth.

Figure 19.1 *Oliver Hellowell zooms in on the detail when photographing swans*

---

1   www.oliverhellowell.com.

His mum Wendy O'Carroll reflects on his early years and experiences with health professionals and schools.

At three months old Oliver had open heart surgery for three heart defects – it had been thought he would not survive to even reach the surgery.

At 18 months old we were told by a physiotherapist that Oliver had severe hypotonia (poor muscle tone) and that, although we would have to try and encourage a little physical activity, he would 'never be sporty'.

At two years old it was noted that Oliver laughed and cried without sound and at three years old I was told that he suffered from verbal dyspraxia as well as Down's Syndrome and that it was unlikely he would ever be able to manage speech which would be clear enough to be understood by an unfamiliar listener.

At mainstream primary school he was informally excluded on several occasions due to his 'impulsive and challenging behaviour' and was formally diagnosed with hyperactivity at 10 years old after his move to mainstream secondary failed. He was let down badly by a headteacher and SENCO who didn't want him in their school, and so after much heartache I moved him to a special school for children with moderate learning difficulties – where he learned even more bad behaviour!

But Oliver has a wonderful mum, who did not let any of these things stand in his way. She saw a beautiful little boy who, despite a Down's Syndrome diagnosis and a pile of professional 'can'ts', should still have a bright future. Filled with love and determination she supported Oliver towards aspiring and achieving.

As a little boy my son was the cutest little blue-eyed, blonde-haired boy you could wish for!

He couldn't speak so we learned to sign; my daughter Anna (eight years old when Oliver was born) and I taught Oliver to sign, and by the time he started school at four years and two months old he used over 350 signs! (He knew what he wanted to say, he just needed another way to say it!!)

I taught him to read using the methods recommended by Down Educational Syndrome International[2] and when he started mainstream primary school at the age of four years and two months he had a 'sight vocabulary' of over 70 words and in reception class was in the top reading group!! He now owns and enjoys over 300 books.

We did *loads* of physical activity with my little hyperactive boy, and when Anna's friend left his skateboard for Oliver to play with, I never dreamed as he kept sitting on it and wobbling on it that it was the perfect tool to learn coordination and balance (only the living room carpet to start with!) and that my boy was actually going to be a *skateboarder* – so much for never being 'sporty'. He is also good at and loves football, basketball and snooker.

---

2   www.dseinternational.org/en-gb.

We worked on his speech all the time at every opportunity, and the boy who would apparently 'never be understood by an unfamiliar listener' has been interviewed on the radio on four occasions over the past three years and in 2012 was the best man at our wedding, standing up and giving his best man's speech before all the assembled guests – not many dry eyes in the house that day. When Oliver was nine years old I was fortunate enough to meet up again with my now husband – Mike O'Carroll – who has been a best mate and father all rolled into one for Oliver. Mike is a photographer and all-round good guy who shares so many 'loves' and 'interests' with Oliver. They both love wildlife, the countryside, fishing, all things marine, bird watching and Oliver started to want to take photos 'like Mike'. Mike's patience and targeted tuition and guidance has enabled Oliver to enjoy and utilize the world of photography as both a tool for him to record what he sees in the way he sees it, and also as something which brings him a sense of achievement and self esteem.

Life with Oliver is all about 'enjoying the madness', as my husband describes it – and although life can be challenging it is certainly never dull!! Oliver is a funny, amazing, random kinda guy who brings a smile to my face several times every day – provides his own unique perspective on the world – and we are all the richer for his being here.

Oliver now attends a mainstream college in Taunton, Somerset, and hopes to be able to further his photography to a point where it can be his form of income. He wants to be 'a professional'.

And after everything else he has achieved against all the odds…

Who out there dares to say…

He can't?

CASE STUDY: Genevieve

Diagnosis: Dyslexia

When Genevieve was diagnosed with dyslexia, her mother Karen Hope was told that she needed to lower her expectations for her daughter. This is her story of how she and Genevieve proved those professionals wrong.

Twenty-five years ago when my daughter, Genevieve, was in grade two, I was called in for a meeting with her teacher. He told me he suspected she had a reading problem and he thought it might be dyslexia.

He wanted me to talk to the teacher in charge of the programme for slow readers. She did some tests on Gen and told me she was setting

Figure 19.2 *Genevieve with her mother Karen Hope*

up an appointment with a specialist for learning disabilities. More tests followed and I was told that Gen was very bright and most likely dyslexic. She also said there was no assistance or tutoring help in the Northern California school system for her problem. I have since found this resistance to acknowledge dyslexia and lack of funding is prevalent with school systems in North America. It was also difficult finding individuals in our education system who believed it existed.

When a child is assessed to decide whether they need special testing to determine learning problems and then what programme they should be enrolled in the school system, their school holds an IEP (Individualized Education Programme) meeting. This is made up of teachers, principals, special education instructors, school psychologists, parents of the child and other family members or representatives for the parents. I was told at one of these meetings for my daughter my expectations were too high for my child.

My expectations were too high!!!

I said if she couldn't read, write, handle money or do basic math, where would she be able to get a job? My expectations were too high – can you imagine? I even had one school psychologist tell me about a girl with dyslexia she knew in middle school who was a cheerleader, an artist and very popular. She told me the girl seemed very happy and wasn't concerned about her spelling and reading problems. I asked her how being a cheerleader, an artist and being popular was going to help in the *real* world.

Realizing the schools would be of no help I started to look for tutors or specialists in the phone book. I found a couple of experts who assessed Gen and confirmed she was dyslexic. It was explained to me she needed to have everything taught to her in whole and real images, not abstract. Also a dyslexic sees the complete picture of something first and then the parts. Think of the expression 'forest before the trees'. People who are dyslexic would need to understand what a forest is in its entirety before they could identify, see or visualize the individual trees. This is the key to their thinking and learning style, which is also what we call right-brain processing.

So I started to explain everything to her with real life concepts, and when I taught her a new piece of information I gave her the whole idea first. I'll give you an example. One day Gen was working on an arithmetic sheet in grade three. The exercise listed specific amounts of money like $1.00, 75 cents, $1.50, etc. The directions asked what six coins (pennies, nickels, dimes, quarters, etc.) you would need to add up to those amounts. This was too abstract for her. She couldn't begin to imagine what those coins would be. I got her a jar of change and poured the coins out in front of her. She knew what coins were because they were real, and she knew what to use them for and how much they were worth because she had bought items from stores with me. I then said count up the different coins until they added up to the amounts on her sheet. So a $1.00 could be three quarters, two dimes and one nickel.

She understood immediately and went through the exercise sheet in minutes!

Suddenly after years of confusion she could be taught! This was the start of *finally* understanding my daughter and how she thinks and how she learns.

From there I found some help from tutors who worked with dyslexics, any books on the subject and anyone else who had some ideas. I started to come up with ways around how she was being taught at school so she could actually follow the teacher by knowing what questions she needed to ask to understand and comprehend what was being taught and what was expected of her.

I also developed methods to teach her spelling, reading, arithmetic, telling time, measurements, etc., that helped her stay caught up with the class.

We had terrific progress!

Gen successfully graduated high school with good grades and the ability to go on to college successfully.

We also had the rest of my kids, my husband and me tested for dyslexia. We all have varying degrees of it. Turns out my father, my sister, one of my brothers and many of my husband's family are also dyslexic. We are all coping with it, and many of us are using our 'right-brain dyslexia gifts' very effectively! I have discovered that being right-brained and dyslexic can be an incredible asset.

Today my three dyslexic children are adults starting their own families. They are all doing very well in their fields of work and have overcome the stigma of dyslexia. They all can spell, read and write.

CASE STUDY: Dani Bowman

Diagnosis: Autism

Figure 19.3 *Dani Bowman speaking*

I have followed Dani's progress since we started creating our SEN Assist software in 2010. I could see she was a shining example of what can be achieved with drive, determination and family support.

Dani introduces herself on her website:

> I am a 19-year-old college student with autism. I love animation, illustration, and creating fun entertainment for children of all ages. I founded Power Light Animation Studios at age 11. I believe that many with autism can lead fulfilling and successful lives doing what they love. For me, that's animation![3]

When Dani Bowman was 11 she went to live with her aunt and uncle. Here's what they have to say about their experience nurturing her and believing in her.

Dani's uncle Patrick Eidemiller wrote:

> At 11, when she came to us, Dani was determined, motivated, and driven; yet missing the support and nurturing that she really craved, and she really didn't know how to ask for it.
>
> She dealt with the world on her terms, ignoring social interaction with humans, yet creating complex multiple character stories, dialog, and plot lines with her rapidly growing cast of characters and worlds.
>
> How could one who couldn't read our facial expressions draw wonderfully expressive characters? How could someone who had difficulty putting two sentences together tell a story for 20 minutes non-stop with no speech challenges at all? How could this girl struggle with reading a short essay in English, yet read her entire ninth grade biology book cover to cover before the school semester even started, and not pick it up again during the class year?
>
> All of these contradictions still baffle me today, but we've learned to leverage her strengths and interests in order to address her weaknesses.
>
> Mentoring others has made a huge difference to her own communication skills and confidence, while building on her love of helping others. Sometimes she's frustrated by her speech challenges, occasionally expects the world and society to bend to her issues, but as parents, we can't cut her any slack, she is nearly an adult now, and she must be a functioning, accountable member of society.
>
> It's not where you start in this world, it's where you finish.

Dani's aunt Sandra Vielma wrote:

> From the moment I realized Dani was different I knew I was going to have to tighten up my belt and just figure out what was that one 'thing' we needed to do to help her. Not a good thing or a bad thing, just a different thing. I did not realize there was going to be many many 'things'.
>
> We had never heard the 'A' word before, so we went to conferences; after conferences we found books, research, and so on and so forth. Like I'm sure most new parents of kids on the

---

3   See www.powerlight-studios.com.

spectrum do. Soon I realized that autism is not a bad word, it's just a different way of thinking, and I had to learn to listen in a different way.

It was a surprise and a blessing when Dani came to live with us. From the very start, I always believed in her, listened to what she was trying to say, even if her words were not very clear. I listened and saw her with my heart.

I'm in a perpetual teaching mode with her, a role I never expected, but am happy to do. I realize that by now she probably hears me like Charlie Brown hears his teachers 'mua, mua, mua'. I still keep on looking for ways to teach her.

When she wants something, I always find a way to make it happen, or at least I try (within reason of course). And in return she shines like a star.

I wanted the world to see what I saw when I looked at her, to see how amazing she is.

CASE STUDY: Jake Borrett

Diagnosis: Crohn's Disease and dyspraxia

Figure 19.4 Jake Borrett honing his writing skills

Jake Borrett is currently studying English Literature and Creative Writing at the University of Hertfordshire, and aspires to be a professional writer. He was diagnosed with Crohn's Disease at the age of 13 and dyspraxia at 18. In this blog post he reflects upon his time at school and the positive difference a comment from another child made to him.

'Dyspraxic, but also fantastic'

It is hard to admit but like many others I was bullied at school. This was mainly due to the 'differences' which dyspraxia often presents. I was often laughed at when I played sport or when my handwriting looked like barbed wire. Despite these times I will never forget what one of my friends told me. They said, 'Jake, you are the most courageous person I've ever known.' I thanked them, not truly knowing what they meant by this. Over the last few years, as I have understood my conditions more, I realize that perhaps what they were trying to say is that in spite of the suffering I faced I was not going to let those few negative people destroy my life. Instead I tried very hard to focus on those who made a positive difference. Of course this took time, but I still built up the courage to walk away from all those bad influences.

Stories like this are surprisingly common with those living with dyspraxia. It takes real courage to live with any learning condition, especially if it is one where you are prone to be attacked by horrible people. Ignoring them and their mean comments does take a lot of bravery.

No matter who you may be, just remember this. Every single individual who is fighting against a condition like dyspraxia is a real person. Just like many others, life throws them difficult challenges which they have to face. Overcoming these obstacles takes real guts, persistence and dedication. They are also fantastic individuals who have demonstrated and will continue to demonstrate how courageous and inspirational they can be to all those who are willing to listen.

Jake's school friend showed amazing empathy and insight, commenting that he was 'courageous'. That stayed with Jake and helped reinforce his belief in himself. What a wonderful friend! If you are teaching or supporting a child who finds things more challenging, please hold this story in mind. Remember the impact a positive observation can have.

Predictions

Our spoken observations and predictions make such a huge difference to the child. If we believe big and instil this, then the child will want to go out and show the world they *can*. If we think small and talk of stumbling blocks and can'ts then we are not only forecasting, but helping paint a duller future.

Children absorb our words and reflect on them.

Picasso's mother

Picasso recalled, 'When I was a child my mother said to me, "If you become a soldier, you'll be a general. If you become a monk, you'll be the Pope." Instead I became a painter and wound up as Picasso.' I love that quote. Picasso's mother didn't know what her son would be or try to influence his direction, but saw that whatever he chose to do he would be a leader. What else did she say that has been washed away with time? But that insightful, exciting prediction her son remembered. Now those words have outlived him and go on inspiring others.

Richard Branson's headteacher

In our more recent history the entrepreneur Richard Branson, who has been open about his struggles with dyslexia, recalls his headteacher predicting what his future might hold: 'On one of my last days at school, the headmaster told me that I would either end up in prison or become a millionaire. That was quite a startling prediction, but in some respects he was right on both counts!' (Branson 2012). I wonder if the young Branson took those words to heart and thought, 'Well I don't want to be in prison, so I'd better be a millionaire.' Maybe that headteacher was very perceptive and knew just how to make the right comment that would motivate and shape a positive future for that non-conformist youngster.

Responsibilities

The adults surrounding a child have a huge responsibility. Predictions not only stick with a child, but can shape their future. We must inject positive after positive. Get children thinking about what they *could* achieve. Teach them that obstacles are challenges and that they can overcome any obstacle by using their amazing problem solving skills. Set things up so that they have to practise thinking and problem solving. Hone these skills. Recognize them. Ensure that other children see them too.

Inspiring futures

If you are teaching a child who does not seem to be achieving their potential and may need a different teaching style, it is up to you to investigate. Look to their future and be that teacher they recall as believing in them, supporting them and changing their direction.

Your visual learner might not do perfect cursive handwriting, but they may have an original mind and a unique way of looking at things.

Embrace these learners; encourage them. Never, ever put them down or allow anyone else to. You never know what these children might achieve. Imagine being that parent or teacher recorded in the memoirs of a future Disney or Einstein or even Mark Zuckerberg (founder of Facebook).

Our visual learners are not *all* on a path to historic greatness, but it is our responsibility to ensure that whatever path they choose they have their self esteem intact and the potential to be happy.

Chapter 20

Happy Endings

Nothing great was ever achieved without enthusiasm.

Ralph Waldo Emerson (1803–1882)

We never know where the ripples of a single positive interaction will lead a child. People so often hold on to the negatives. Most people can recall one negative comment about themselves quite quickly. It is harder to recall the positives. This is why we must build on those positives all the time. Most children will love to hear they are doing great and never assume that a child who is not yet speaking does not understand. These children may be able to understand your every word and also pick up on your feelings.

Provide a platform for hope, promoting feelings of security and enjoyment introduce a sense of wonder, creativity and self belief.

A child does not need to be 'the best', but we must strive to help them achieve 'their *personal* best'.

Teachers may be aware of a million boxes to tick, but the good teacher begins by zooming in on sparking children's curiosity and raising the self esteem of *every* individual child. The good teacher will always teach to a child's strengths.

Best lesson feedback

We were getting towards the end of the summer term and it was sports day. To try to keep things a bit normal for my class I decided to stick to the timetable as much as possible. I'd taught this very special class for the whole academic year, so we had done the groundwork – building trust, creating routines and getting to know each other so well.

We were doing numeracy (3D shapes). Over the term the lesson structure had become familiar. We would begin with a 3D shapes song on the interactive white board, which got their attention. The students would have a fun time dancing together while the song explained the attributes of 3D shapes and they had learnt it. They had even developed their own little routine with actions. Not all the students joined the throng – some stood back and danced at a safer distance. That was fine. This was routine – they knew the expectation.

Next they would complete a set of tasks and then build a 3D shape using a cardboard net, while staff quietly modelled for any children who got a bit 'stuck'. At the end of the lesson I held up the 'finished' symbol and gestured for the students to line up. They were a great little class and had learnt to follow a visual structure, each standing on a 3D shape in the order displayed on the door. (This would change each day for fairness.) As the children went to line up, one of them (a boy with autism) unexpectedly ran up and gave me a little hug, then looked up at me and gave me a fleeting smile.

'What was that for?' I asked (surprised and delighted at this unusual display of affection).

The boy said, 'For getting it right.' It was a wonderful moment. I thought I'd done a mediocre lesson, but for him I'd ticked all the boxes. So what had I got right? He was off and lining up before I could ask him why.

I thought about it a lot and even now I'm not completely certain, but I believe that it was the fact that there was a clear structure, some fun, the chance to move on in his own terms, respect, very little language and something 'normal' on what would be a different, and therefore difficult, day. Perhaps that bit of normal helped him brace himself for all the changes associated with sports day?

Hands up, Ofsted – I did not stretch that class as I could have, but sometimes lessons are not about stretching. They are more to do with supporting, loving and understanding.

I learned something, though – it showed me that what our students believe is 'getting it right' may not be what we imagine. Sometimes we over-complicate and try to tick too many boxes. If I'd been teaching a lesson that I knew would be observed, I may have spoken more. I may have placed more demands on my students. I may have taught less… I would not have got it right for *that* boy on *that* day.

Who are we really teaching for?

That fleeting hug was a little gift – a moment that made me feel better than any post-observation feedback ever has or ever will.

That little boy's beautiful, honest reaction taught me so much.

Priorities

My priority will always be that a child leaves my class as confident as they can be with their self esteem intact. I want them to believe in themselves, believe in possibilities and not fear making mistakes.

Focus on the relationship

The teacher–student relationship must be built on mutual respect and trust. From the moment you introduce yourself to students as their teacher, they begin assessing this relationship. They are deciding whether you are good enough to teach them and whether you are interesting or worth watching. You must be all these things and more, but you must be quiet and subtle too. The student must know that you love them for who they are, get who they are and care deeply about who they are and who they might become. They must know that you believe in them and plan to learn from them as well as teach them.

In a recent interview Sir Ken Robinson said:

> Schools should be there to help people learn, and at the heart of this is the relationship between the teacher and a learner. The conceit of teaching is that we can help people learn; and we have to focus on the relationship. Much of what has happened in education in recent years has distracted from this relationship and focused on testing, data-driven outcomes and so forth. The consequence has been that the relationship between teachers and learners has become impoverished; this has disaffected teachers and students alike. (Quoted in Thought Economics n.d.)

When I read that article I thought, 'How absolutely spot on you are.' These tick boxes could get in the way. I've heard of teachers teaching to the tick boxes because then the students make the progress they should. Teaching to tick boxes breaks the trust and shows students no respect or love. Students taught in this way might show raised standards and be statistically pleasing, but they do not make the progress they *should*.

When I was at school

I was the child who did not have 'good' handwriting, but loved creative writing. I was the child who had difficulty with handing homework in and general organization. I was the child who could not remember the alphabet because of a nursery visual that showed 'u' should always come after 'q'. I was the child who couldn't tie my shoe laces or ride a bike. I was the child who was outside the tennis court learning to throw and catch the ball. I was the child a sports teacher once mocked when we were learning to throw the javelin, saying that the others should stand well back because my javelin, would most likely go backwards. I was the child who aimed the javelin right at the sports teacher so that *she* jumped backwards.

I was the child who asked for a typewriter *every* birthday until I got one. I was the child who wrote reams of poetry and could learn long Shakespeare speeches with ease because I so loved those words.

I was the teen who was questioned by an English teacher – What was I doing in an A Level English lesson when I couldn't do joined-up writing? I was the teen who felt so frustrated by all the red pen corrections because I knew my essay was good. I was the teen who spoke up about injustice. I was the teen who sat in my A Level lessons doing intricate cross stitch embroideries. While the teacher talked (a lot), I would be there stitching, stitching, stitching. I was the teen who even took my cross stitch into my A Level exams.

I was a lucky child. I attended schools where the put-down teachers were few and you did not fear speaking up. I had amazing actor parents who believed that imagination and creativity were more important than ticking academic boxes. I understood early that the path less travelled would be more interesting.

And now I'm the teacher, the author and the 'expert', who will do anything I can to ensure that today's children who learn differently discover *their* abilities and believe in themselves as they journey towards fulfilment.

CASE STUDY: Malachy's yearbook

Our son Malachy was coming towards the end of his time at infant school. He was asked to do a picture of something he loved about school for the yearbook. I was surprised when he chose a handwriting lesson and wrote 'I love handwriting' in a thought bubble. His teacher, Mrs Stocchetti, was in the picture too, with a big smile on her face saying, 'That's great!'

The bottom half of the picture was taken up with what looked like grass, each bit drawn individually. When I enquired he told me that it was the carpet (obviously). This showed me a lot about how our son perceives the world. It also revealed that his teacher was as inspirational as I'd believed during the two years she had taught him. She had got his attention, and made him love what (if taught badly) could become a chore. She had also planted a permanent, positive comment in his head. What a brilliant teacher!

CASE STUDY: My husband Quentin (the blaggard)

My husband Quentin went to school in Northern Ireland. He told me about a conversation he had had with his physics teacher after he had just chosen his A Level options (Physics, Maths and Art):

Teacher: 'What do you want to do art for, Devine? It's a waster's subject.'

Quentin: 'Art is all around us. Who designed that physics book on the table? Who designed your clothes? Who designed your nice bag?'

Teacher: 'Ahh – Devine, you blaggard!'

A week later that physics teacher asked Quentin if he would design a poster for Physics Week. Quentin replied: 'I thought art was a waster's subject, sir?'

I'm thankful that Quentin did not listen to that teacher. He now has an incredibly interesting, 'no two days are the same' career as an artist and multimedia designer and comes up with some amazing ideas, which require a combination of art, physics and maths.

CASE STUDY: Donovan's 'Hopes and Dreams' assembly

When our son Donovan was six his class were asked during circle time to think about their futures. What would they like to do when they grew up? The teacher noted down what the children said as she was planning an assembly based on 'Hopes and Dreams'.

All the children had to take costumes to school relating to what they wanted to be. I asked Donovan what he needed to take in to wear for the assembly as the other parents were talking about getting costumes. Donovan said that the teacher had told him he could wear 'whatever he wanted'. Donovan has always said he'd like to be an animator (like his Daddy), and animators generally wear what they want. They don't do uniforms or suits. Jeans, T shirts and hoodies will generally do. So Donovan picked out his clothes – jeans, a T shirt and his favourite SpiderMan hoodie.

We watched the assembly – there were ballet dancers, gymnasts, doctors and teachers. They each did their little bit. 'When I grow up I want to be a footballer', and so on…

And then out came Donovan with his T shirt on back to front, looking all dishevelled and cute. 'When I grow up I want to be happy,' he said with twinkling eyes and a great big smile. Lots of 'Ahhs' followed from all the parents. Donovan had stolen the show, but had also made the audience think. It also influenced the headteacher's speech to the parents.

What do we want most for our children? What's most important in the grand scheme of things? We want them to grow up and be happy.

Conclusions

Children with learning differences are our best teachers, and my aim is to share the structures, motivators and resources that I have seen work for them so that other parents and professionals can simplify and get creative.

Our priority must be to create an atmosphere where *all* children can achieve their best while providing motivating opportunities for them to enjoy, explore and discover.

Thank you

If only we could have more hours dedicated to reflecting, improving and developing ideas. Thank you for giving some of that time. Thank you for being someone who puts a child's learning journey first.

We sometimes forget how much influence we can have on children's futures. Layer on the compliments and build their self esteem whenever you get the chance. Show them that you believe in them. You may just give them wings.

And finally...

As your little learners grow up and take flight.
Do not stop, but pay it forward.
Share your journey so that other parents and teachers may also learn.
We *can* change things (one child at a time).
One life at a time...

Don't judge each day by the harvest you reap but by the seeds that you plant.

Robert Louis Stevenson (1850–1894)

References

Adler, R., Rosenfeld, L. and Proctor, R. (2001) *Interplay: The Process of Interpersonal Communicating (Eighth Edition)*. Fort Worth, TX: Harcourt.

Amen, D. G. (2014) 'Five facts that crush ADD/ADHD stigma.' Available at www.amenclinics.com/blog/5-facts-crush-addadhd-stigma, accessed on 20 May 2015.

BabyCenter (n.d.) 'Developmental milestones: Understanding words, behavior and concepts.' Available at www.babycenter.com/0_developmental-milestones-understanding-words-behavior-and-co_6575.bc, accessed on 2 June 2015.

Barnett, K. (2013) *The Spark: A Mother's Story of Nurturing Genius*. New York, NY: Penguin Group.

Bauman, H-D. L. (2008) *Open Your Eyes: Deaf Studies Talking*. Minneapolis, MN: University of Minnesota Press.

BBC (2014) 'Should teachers use Minecraft in our classrooms?' Available at www.bbc.co.uk/news/education-27936946, accessed on 20 May 2015.

BBC Radio 4 (2015) 'One to One: John Harris talks to Penny Andrews about autism.' Available at www.bbc.co.uk/programmes/b0537492, accessed on 29 July 2015.

Bohdanowicz, K. (2014) 'Mr Glen by Jeremy Irons.' *TES Magazine*, 23 May. Available at www.tes.co.uk/article.aspx?storycode=6430100, accessed on 3 June 2015.

Borrett, J. (2014) 'Diving into dyspraxia.' Available at www.jakeborrett.blogspot.co.uk/2014/07/diving-into-dyspraxia.html, accessed on 18 May 2015.

Branson, R. (2012) 'Turning a disadvantage to your advantage.' Available at www.entrepreneur.com/article/224172, accessed on 18 May 2015.

British Association for Music Therapy (2012) 'What is music therapy?' Available at www.bamt.org/music-therapy.html, accessed on 3 June 2014.

Carbo, M., Dunn, R. and Dunn, K. (1986) *Teaching Students to Read through Their Individual Learning Styles*. Upper Saddle River, NJ: Prentice-Hall.

The Earl of Chesterfield (2007) *Chesterfield's Letters to His Son 1746–1771*. Gloucestershire: Echo Library.

Churcher, S. (2008) 'Harry Potter: The brain disorder which means I can't tie my shoelaces.' *Mail on Sunday*, 16 August.

Cowley, S. (2015) 'You cannot be serious.' Available at www.suecowley.wordpress.com/2015/02/12/you-cannot-be-serious, accessed on 20 May 2015.

Davies, G. (2011) 'Inspiring attention and communication.' Available at www.youtube.com/watch?v=mbsKmMH0XjI, accessed on 29 July 2015.

Davies, G. (2014) 'Attention Autism.' Available at www.youtube.com/watch?v=nFYnc4xcZ6k#t=136, accessed on 29 July 2015.

Devine, A. (2012) 'Motivation for learning.' *Special Magazine*, published by Education Solutions on behalf of NASEN, UK. September, 49–51.

Devine, A. (2014a) *Colour Coding for Learners with Autism: A Resource Book for Creating Meaning through Colour at Home and School*. London: Jessica Kingsley Publishers.

Devine, A. (2014b) 'Teaching Shakespeare is a piece of cake.' *Innovate my School*. Available at www.innovatemyschool.com/industry-expert-articles/item/868-teaching-shakespeare-is-a-piece-of-cake.html, accessed on 29 July 2015.

Devine, A. (2015) 'Reasons to be hopeful.' *Teach Nursery Magazine 5*, 1.

Di Cintio, M. (2015) 'For gifted children, being intelligent can have dark implications.' *Calgary Herald*, 30 January. Available at www.calgaryherald.com/life/swerve/gifted-children-are-frequently-misunderstood, accessed on 20 May 2015.

Down Syndrome Association of Orange County (n.d.) 'Down syndrome myths and truths.' Available at www.dsaoc.org/aboutdown_myths.html, accessed on 29 July 2015.

Down Syndrome Education International (n.d.) 'Development and learning.' Available at www.dseinternational.org/en-gb/about-down-syndrome/development, accessed on 2 June 2015.

Down's Syndrome Association (n.d.) 'What is Down's syndrome?' Available at www.downs-syndrome.org.uk/about-downs-syndrome/what-is-downs-syndrome, accessed on 2 June 2015.

Dyslexia Help (2015a) 'Morphological awareness.' Available at www.dyslexiahelp.umich.edu/professionals/dyslexia-school/morphological-awareness, accessed on 2 June 2015.

Dyslexia Help (2015b) 'More on teaching spelling.' Available at www.dyslexiahelp.umich.edu/professionals/dyslexia-school/spelling/how-should-spelling-be-taught/more-on-spelling, accessed on 2 June 2015.

Edelson, S. (n.d.) 'Learning styles and autism.' Available at www.autism.com/understanding_learning, accessed on 2 June 2015.

Endow, J. (2013) *Painted Words: Aspects of Autism Translated.* Cambridge, WI: Cambridge Book Review Press.

Farmer, D. (2007) 'What is a gifted child?' Available at www.nswagtc.org.au/information/general-reference/112-what-is-a-gifted-child.html, accessed on 20 May 2015.

Formby, S. (2014) *Children's Early Literacy Practices at Home and in Early Years Settings: Second Annual Survey of Parents and Practitioners.* London: National Literacy Trust.

Garwa, D. (2014) 'Why and how I taught reading to my daughter with down syndrome.' Available at www.twominuteparenting.com/how-i-taught-reading-to-my-daughter-with-down-syndrome, accessed on 3 June 2015.

Geiser, T. (2013) 'How to practice preschool letter and name writing.' Available at www.education.com/magazine/article/preschool-letter-writing, accessed on 29 July 2015.

Gifford, A. (2015) 'SnapType for occupational therapy has more updates and features now.' Available at www.assistivetechnologyblog.com/2015/01/snaptype-for-occupational-therapy-has.html, accessed on 29 July 2015.

Gioia, V. (n.d.) 'Successful individuals with disabilities and disability awareness for all of us.' Available at www.educatornetwork.com/HotTopics/accessibility/disabilityawareness, accessed on 2 June 2015.

Goleniowska, H. (n.d.) 'Focus on Oliver Hellowell: Photographer with Down's syndrome.' Available at www.downssideup.com/2014/02/focus-on-oliver-hellowell-photographer.html, accessed on 2 June 2015.

Goodman, K. (2013) 'Richard Branson on dyslexia.' Available at www.virgin.com/news/richard-branson-on-dyslexia, accessed on 29 July 2015.

Grace, J. (2013) 'Reading with the five senses.' Available at www.theguardian.com/teacher-network/teacher-blog/2013/nov/06/sensory-stories-reading-five-senses, accessed on 29 July 2015.

Grandin, T. (2006a) *Thinking in Pictures.* London: Bloomsbury Publishing.

Grandin, T. (2006b) 'Q&A: Temple Grandin on autism and language.' Available at www.npr.org/templates/story/story.php?storyId=5488844, accessed on 29 July 2015.

Greene, N. (2015a) 'The Lotto numbers are easier to predict than someone with ADHD.' Available at https://niallsadhdnotes.wordpress.com/2015/02/15/41, accessed on 29 July 2015.

Greene, N. (2015b) 'Defiance and ADHD.' Available at https://niallsadhdnotes.wordpress.com/2015/02/15/defiance-and-adhd, accessed on 29 July 2015.

Greene, N. (2015c) 'We with ADHD are descendants of hunters ACHOO.' Available at https://niallsadhdnotes.wordpress.com/2015/02/15/we-with-adhd-are-descendants-of-hunters-achoo, accessed on 29 July 2015.

Greene, N. (2015d) 'An ADHD perspective on life without organisational skills.' Available at www.niallsadhdnotes.wordpress.com/2015/02/24/an-adhd-perspective-on-life-without-organisational-skills, accessed on 3 June 2015.

Griffin, M. (n.d.) 'What's the difference between dysgraphia and dyslexia?' Available at www.understood.org/en/learning-attention-issues/child-learning-disabilities/dysgraphia/difference-between-dysgraphia-dyslexia, accessed on 2 June 2015.

Hakim, J. (2007) *Reconstructing America: 1865–1890 (History of US).* New York, NY: Oxford University Press.

Halifax, J. (2015) 'Dyslexia dictionary: Lichfield doctor father and son lead way in helping young sufferer.' *Birmingham Mail,* 4 January. Available at www.birminghammail.co.uk/news/health/dyslexia-dictionary-lichfield-doctor-father-8372918, accessed on 26th August 2015.

Hodgson, J., Buttle, H., Conridge, B., Gibbons, D. and Robinson, J. (2013) *Phonics Instruction and Early Reading: Professional Views from the Classroom.* Sheffield: NATE.

Hunter, K. (n.d.) 'Shakespeare & autism.' Available at www.kellyhunter.co.uk/sa.php, accessed on 29 July 2015.

Hunter, K. (2013) 'Shakespeare and autism.' *Teaching Shakespeare, 3.*

Intensive Interaction (2015) 'What is Intensive Interaction?' Available at www.intensiveinteraction.co.uk/about, accessed on 3 June 2015.

Isaacson, W. (2007) *Einstein: His Life and Universe.* New York, NY: Simon & Schuster.

Jackson, J. (2012) 'Why phonics tests spell trouble.' *The Independent*, 28 November.

Jasper, K. (2014) 'Shaming students one wall at a time.' ConversationED.

Johann Heinrich Pestalozzi website (n.d.) www.jhpestalozzi.org, accessed on 2 June 2015.

Jolly Learning (n.d.) 'Teaching literacy with Jolly Phonics.' Available at http://jollylearning.co.uk/overview-about-jolly-phonics, accessed on 29 July 2015.

Kennedy, R. (n.d.) 'Maria Montessori.' Available at http://privateschool.about.com/od/montessoriindex/p/Montessori.htm, accessed on 29 July 2015.

Kirkpatrick, J. (2008) *Montessori, Dewey, and Capitalism: Educational Theory for a Free Market in Education.* Claremont, CA: TLJ Books.

LaJeunesse, S. (2014) 'Helping kids with autism read, write and communicate.' Available at www.news.psu.edu/story/336801/2014/12/03/research/helping-kids-autism-read-write-and-communicate, accessed on 18 May 2015.

Le Roux, T. (n.d.) 'Pencil grasp development.' Available at www.ot-mom-learning-activities.com/pencil-grasp-development.html, accessed on 2 June 2015.

Lego Education (2015) 'StoryStarter.' Available at www.education.lego.com/en-gb/lesi/elementary/storystarter, accessed on 20 May 2015.

Madda, M. J. (2015) 'Why your students forgot everything on your PowerPoint slides.' Available at www.edsurge.com/n/2015-01-19-why-your-students-forgot-everything-on-your-powerpoint-slides, accessed on 20 May 2015.

The Makaton Charity, (2015) 'About Makaton.' Available at www.makaton.org/aboutMakaton, accessed on 3 June 2015.

Massara, G. H. (2015) 'Off the beat: Alternative wiring, or living with Asperger's.' *The Daily Californian*, 11 January. Available at www.dailycal.org/2015/01/11/alternative-wiring-living-aspergers, accessed on 3 June 2015.

Masters, A. (2013) 'Crossing the Midline.' Available at www.therapyworkstulsa.blogspot.co.uk/2013/07/crossing-midline.html, accessed on 2 June 2015.

Maytham, D. (n.d.) 'Talking matters.' Available at www.senmagazine.co.uk/articles/articles/senarticles/talking-matters, accessed on 2 June 2015.

McLaughlin, T. (2015) 'A dyslexic author's writing tips for dyslexic kids.' *The Guardian*, 22 January. Available at www.theguardian.com/childrens-books-site/2015/jan/22/a-dyslexic-authors-writing-tips-for-dyslexic-kids?CMP=share_btn_fb, accessed on 20 May 2015.

Miller, S. (2013) *Why Use Symbols?* [video file]. Available at www.youtube.com/watch?v=mw-7-N0WGEA, accessed on 3 June 2015.

Montessori, M. (1966) *The Secret of Childhood.* New York, NY: Fides Publishers.

Montessori, M. (2009) *The Absorbent Mind.* Thousand Oaks, CA: BN Publishing.

Nicholls, J. (2014) 'Campaigners stress AAC users' right to speak.' Available at www.senmagazine.co.uk/senjoom3/index.php/story/campaigners-stress-aac-users-right-to-speak, accessed on 2 June 2015.

Nind, M. and Hewett, D. (2005) *Access to Communication: Developing Basic Communication with People who have Severe Learning Difficulties (Second Edition).* Oxford: David Fulton Publishers.

Ofcom (2014) *Children and Parents: Media Use and Attitude Report.* Available at http://blogs.lse.ac.uk/media-policy-planner/2014/10/09/ofcom-releases-2014-report-on-media-use-and-attitudes-of-children-and-parents/, accessed on 26 August 2015. London: Ofcom.

Ofsted (2011) *Removing Barriers to Literacy.* London: Ofsted.

Ohio State University (n.d.) 'Shakespeare takes center stage in autism therapy.' Available at http://osuwmc.multimedianewsroom.tv/story.php?id=552&enter=2, accessed on 29 July 2015.

Ossola, A. (2015) 'Teaching in the age of Minecraft.' Available at www.theatlantic.com/education/archive/2015/02/teaching-in-the-age-of-minecraft/385231, accessed on 20 May 2015.

Oxford Owl (2014) 'The Year 1 phonics screening check.' Available at www.oxfordowl.co.uk/home/reading-owl/expert-help/the-year-1-phonics-screening-check, accessed on 2 June 2015.

Patino, E. (n.d.) 'Understanding dysgraphia.' Available at www.understood.org/en/learning-attention-issues/child-learning-disabilities/dysgraphia/understanding-dysgraphia, accessed on 2 June 2015.

PECS (n.d.) 'What is PECS?' Available at www.pecs-unitedkingdom.com/pecs.php, accessed on 2 June 2015.

Piirto, J. (2011) *Creativity for 21st Century Skills: How to Embed Creativity into the Curriculum.* Rotterdam: Sense Publishers.

Pistorius, M. (2011) *Ghost Boy.* London: Simon & Schuster.

Robinson, K. (2006) 'Do schools kill creativity?' Available at www.ted.com/talks/ken_robinson_says_schools_kill_creativity/transcript?language=en, accessed on 29 July 2015.

Royal Shakespeare Company (n.d.) *A Manifesto for Shakespeare in Schools: Stand Up for Shakespeare.* London: Royal Shakespeare Company.

Sandison, R. (2014) '10 things every teacher should know about autism.' Available at www.autism-society.org/living-with-autism/blog/10-things-every-teacher-know-autism, accessed on 18 May 2015.

Sawer, P. (2015) 'Emma Thompson and husband decide to educate daughter Gaia at home.' *The Telegraph*, 7 February. Available at www.telegraph.co.uk/education/educationnews/11397662/Emma-Thompson-and-husband-decide-to-educate-daughter-Gaia-at-home.html, accessed on 3 June 2015.

Schleicher, A. (2010) 'The case for 21st century learning.' Available at www.oecd.org/general/thecasefor21st-centurylearning.htm, accessed on 3 June 2014.

Seaberg, M. (2013) 'The spark and synesthesia: Savant Jacob Barnett calculates using coloured shapes.' Available at www.psychologytoday.com/blog/sensorium/201305/the-spark-and-synesthesia, accessed on 20 May 2015.

Siegel, L. S. (1998) 'Agatha Christie's learning disability.' *Canadian Psychology/Psychologie Canadienne 29*, 2, 213–216.

Silverman, L. K. (2002) *Upside-down Brilliance: The Visual-spatial Learner.* Denver, CO: DeLeon.

Standards and Testing Agency (2014) 'Phonics screening check: Scoring guidance.' Available from www.gov.uk/government/publications/phonics-screening-check-2014-materials, accessed on 29 May 2015.

Story Massage website (n.d.) www.storymassage.co.uk, accessed on 2 June 2015.

Tanz, J. (2015) 'The techies who are hacking education by homeschooling their kids.' Available at www.wired.com/2015/02/silicon-valley-home-schooling, accessed on 18 May 2015.

TEACCH (2015) 'What is TEACCH?' Available at www.teacch.com/about-us/what-is-teacch, accessed on 3 June 2015.

Thought Economics (n.d.) 'Learning to be who we are.' Available at http://thoughteconomics.com/learning-to-be-who-we-are, accessed on 29 July 2015.

Tobii (2015) 'Learning to write with literAACy.' Available at www.tobii.com/en/assistive-technology/global/user-stories/cerebral-palsy/learning-to-write-with-literaacy, accessed on 2 June 2015.

Tolan, S. S. (1996) 'Is it a cheetah?' Available at www.stephanietolan.com/is_it_a_cheetah.htm, accessed on 20 May 2015.

Wainwright, T. (2008) *Fun with Phonics: Letters and Sounds Pack.* London: BBC Active/Educational Publishers.

'waterbendercarorain' (n.d.) 'My life with dysgraphia.' Available at www.teenink.com/nonfiction/personal_experience/article/409433/my-life-with-dysgraphia, accessed on 2 June 2015.

Weaver Dunne, D. (2007) 'How can teachers help students with ADHD?' Available at www.educationworld.com/a_issues/issues148c.shtml, accessed on 2 June 2015.

Webb, J., Amend, E. R., Webb, N. E., Goerss, J., Belan, P., Olenchak, F. R. and Rosso, J. (2005) *Misdiagnosis and Dual Diagnoses of Gifted Children and Adults: ADHD, Bipolar, OCD, Asperger's, Depression, and Other Disorders.* Tucson, AZ: Great Potential Press.

Whittle, L. A. (2015) 'Creative confidence builds a strong future.' Available at www.edudemic.com/creative-confidence-builds-strong-future/?utm_content=buffer2c266, accessed on 20 May 2015.

Williams, R. (1989) *The Dead Poet's Society.* Peter Weir (dir.). Buena Vista Pictures.

Wright, M. (2014) 'The story so far…' *SEN Magazine*, November/December, 43.

List of Useful Websites

Attention Autism

ginadavies.co.uk

Handwriting Without Tears

www.hwtears.com/hwt

Intensive Interaction

www.intensiveinteraction.co.uk

The Makaton Charity

www.makaton.org

PECS

www.pecs.com

See and Learn

www.seeandlearn.org/en-gb

SEN Assist

www.senassist.com

Sensory Stories

www.sensorystories.com

Sign2Sing

www.sign2sing.org.uk

Social Stories

www.thegraycenter.org

Story Massage

www.storymassage.co.uk

TEACCH

www.teacch.com

Index